About the editors

Ineke Buskens is a cultural anthropologist with a passion
for research methodology and women's empowerment, and
a deep appreciation for cultural diversity and individual
human uniqueness. She graduated in Leiden, the Netherlands, and has lived in Ghana, India and Brazil. In 1990
she arrived in South Africa and in 1996 she founded her
company Research for the Future. She has worked since as
an independent international research, gender and process facilitation consultant. In her research she focuses on
emancipatory approaches that envision a sustainable, just
and loving world, in her research training on bringing out
the genius in every participant, in her facilitation work on
gender awareness and authentic collaboration. Ineke is currently leading the GRACE Network, which has twenty-eight
research teams, located in nineteen countries in Africa and
the Middle East, involved in gender research in information
and communication technology for women's empowerment.
Ineke is a student of Ramtha's School of Enlightenment in
Yelm, Washington, USA and this learning journey inspires
her to embrace the unknown in all aspects of her life.

Anne Webb is the GRACE research coordinator. Her commitment to feminist qualitive research is rooted in participatory
action research approaches. She has worked with communities and research teams for the past fifteen years pursuing
the reduction of inequalities. Trained in sociology, adult
education and gender studies in Toronto (Ontario Institute
for Studies in Education) and The Hague (Institute for Social
Studies), her education has involved people from all walks
of life and locations, formally and informally, in Canada,
Europe and Africa, and is a continually enriching process.
Anne currently resides in Quebec, Canada.

AFRICAN WOMEN AND ICTS

investigating technology, gender and empowerment

edited by Ineke Buskens
and Anne Webb

Zed Books
LONDON | NEW YORK

International Development Research Centre
OTTAWA | CAIRO | DAKAR | MONTEVIDEO | NAIROBI
NEW DELHI | SINGAPORE

Unisa Press
PRETORIA

African women and ICTs: investigating technology, gender and empowerment was first published in 2009 by

in southern Africa: Unisa Press, PO Box 392, Pretoria 0003, South Africa

www.unisa.ac.za/press

ISBN 978 1 86888 561 9

in the rest of the world: Zed Books Ltd, 7 Cynthia Street, London N1 9JF, UK and Room 400, 175 Fifth Avenue, New York, NY 10010, USA

www.zedbooks.co.uk

ISBN 978 1 84813 191 0 hb
ISBN 978 1 84813 192 7 pb

International Development Research Centre, PO Box 8500, Ottawa, ON, Canada K1G 3H9

info@idrc.ca / www.idrc.ca

eISBN 978 1 55250 399 7

Set in OurType Arnhem and Futura Bold by Ewan Smith, London
Index: ed.emery@thefreeuniversity.net
Cover designed by Andrew Corbett
Printed in the UK by the MPG Books Group

Distributed in the USA exclusively by Palgrave Macmillan, a division of St Martin's Press, LLC, 175 Fifth Avenue, New York, NY 10010, USA

A catalogue record for this book is available from the British Library
Library of Congress Cataloging in Publication Data available

Contents

Acknowledgements

We want to thank, in the first place, Heloise Emdon, International Development Research Centre (IDRC) Acacia Programme Manager, who had the vision to have African women's information and communication technology (ICT) stories told. We also want to thank Jenny Radloff, Chat Garcia Ramilo and Anriette Esterhuysen, of the Association for Progressive Communications, for conceptualizing the idea of an African ICT gender research network, together with Heloise. We want to thank IDRC for funding us and believing in us. Ramata Thioune and Edith Adera especially have been a source of inspiration and strength.

It has been a privilege to work with the women respondents who have contributed to our understandings of women's journeys towards empowerment, and what roles ICTs are playing and could play in these. We have been greatly enriched by our research encounters with you. We are thankful to those organizations that created pathways for us to reach the women we needed to speak with.

It is impossible to mention all those who have been assisting us and nurturing us as individuals and as a network. We want to particularly thank Helena Bailey, Leverne Gething, Lois Gibbs, Richard Grant, Nancy Hafkin, Grant Marinus, Tamsine O'Riordan, Nidhi Tandon, Fatima Timjerdine and Tatjana Vukoja. We are grateful to our families and friends for your patience and for putting up with our absences. Your love was the hand on our back as we went forward.

We also want to thank each other for staying true to our passion and each other, taking in our stride the tensions and conflicts which such a diverse collection of people inevitably creates. Our alignment with the purpose we all stand for has been our strength and our convergence.

The GRACE Network

Foreword

Women in Africa are undeniably participating in the information and communication technology (ICT) revolution and they are doing so in many and varied ways; the changes that the use of these tools have brought about are visible everywhere. Furthermore, the prospects of ICTs for development and women's empowerment seem promising. Yet women's stories about their experiences and use of these tools are not heard: are their lives changing for the better because of these new technologies? If so, in what ways are they changing? Are there areas in which women could and should participate in this ICT revolution but are not, because they are women? How can women's perspectives, insights and realities in relation to the use and potentials of ICTs be integrated into ICT policies that are currently being developed and implemented across the continent?

These were the questions that led the Acacia Programme of the International Development Research Centre (IDRC), which supports research in Africa on information and communication technologies for development (ICT4D), and the Association for Progressive Communications (APC) to call together in 2004 in Johannesburg, South Africa, a collective of African academics and activists known for their passionate involvement with women's empowerment and ICTs. The perspectives of the women of Africa needed to be narrated and this knowledge needed to be brought to the world by African researchers. It was envisioned that a research network would emerge from this group of individuals that would operate as a virtual research team. The idea was accepted and GRACE (Gender Research in Africa into ICTs for Empowerment) was born. While the research teams were all encouraged to follow their individual research passions, design their own methodology and formulate their own research questions, there was a common ground and an alignment to a shared purpose.

The thinking in development studies has evolved: the idea that providing interventions in the form of infrastructure suffices in attracting the intended beneficiaries and brings about change is outdated. The trickle-down approach – which counts on the developed aspects of the economy uplifting the more disadvantaged

– actually leads to greater inequalities. Rights-based approaches to inequality, however, continue to draw attention and result in forward movement. The current focus on the 'agency' of the intended beneficiaries themselves for the purpose of development and empowerment also seems relevant and timely. Needed in any development thinking is a questioning of how to ensure women benefit from development.

The group of academics and activists called together in Johannesburg were aligned with the purpose of women's empowerment, and accepted that their knowledge quest needed to be grounded in efforts to understand women's agency. The focus on agency, however, necessitated that the researchers would be able to recognize this capacity in their respondents and make it visible in their reflections and their writings. This led to an emphasis on qualitative research methods; to a commitment to continuous research learning; and to the honouring of a culture of mutual respect, sharing and support.

Challenging though this brief may have been and probably still is, it has undoubtedly been this same brief which has led to the success of GRACE as a viable researcher network contributing not only to the debates on ICT4D from a gender perspective in Africa, in the South and wider afield, but also to the pool of solid and sustainable research capacity in the field of ICT4D and gender.

It is my hope that the book you are holding in your hands right now will enrich your thinking and encourage your questioning and reflection. The questions raised in this book, the perspectives examined and the realities revealed, reach farther than Africa, and farther than the field of ICTs. Anybody interested in questions of gender inequity and empowerment may find this book rich reading.

Heloise Emdon, Ottawa, October 2008

Introduction

INEKE BUSKENS AND ANNE WEBB

Now sit upright with your back straight.
Relaxed, hands on your knees, bum on the chair.
Take a deep breath and close your eyes.
Take another breath, inhale through your nose, exhale through your
  mouth.
And another one. Relax.

Observe your thoughts, your emotions, your body reactions, from the
  inside.
Do not judge, do not give meaning, just observe.
Whilst you are sitting in your egg, just observe.
Focus on what you need to focus on:
Go to your respondents, hear their voices, see their faces.
Take a deep breath, relax.
Be aware you are sitting here, in your egg.

What is the most important message they are giving you?
What do they say?
Take a deep breath, relax.
You have all the knowledge you need, you have done the work, now just
  allow them to speak to your writing.
Let the words come, do not censor them, just observe.

Ineke Buskens

Producing practical, functional knowledge for change

This type of reflection may not seem very technologically advanced,
but with the relationships between information and communication technologies (ICTs), women's empowerment, gender discrimination, access,
entrepreneurship, advocacy and so forth being so multidimensional, we
had to start with centring ourselves. We were undertaking a momentous
task in trying to better understand how and if women's empowerment
is being impacted by, and is impacting, their use of and contributions
to ICTs; we were setting out to explore the external, structural barriers
women experience, as well as the internal/conceptual factors which

prevent or enable them to use ICTs to their advantage, and the strategies they use to overcome impediments (Buskens et al. 2004).

The insights gained from this exploration form the content of this book. The authors bring together a questioning of the place of ICTs in the lives of women in Africa who are getting on with the daily struggle for greater autonomy and equality with the perceptions of the women themselves, and a context that predominantly focuses attention on the promises of ICTs for development rather than the ongoing divisive inequalities.

For three years fourteen research teams (involving about thirty women and men) in twelve countries pursued their research interests. Annual in-person research training and working sessions, and a steady flow of virtual discussion, questioning, feedback and resources, supported this process.[1] The researchers conducted their studies in their own geographical regions, in some cases in their communities, or at their workplaces, in local languages and, sometimes, with themselves included among the respondents. They delved into issues they were drawn to due to their own experiences, interests and commitment to women's equality and social justice, within the overarching theme of the GRACE (Gender Research in Africa into ICTs for Empowerment)[2] project.

The results, we think, are impressive for the depth of knowledge and understanding gained about women's realities and the meanings they give to those realities. They are also impressive in terms of revealing the potential, if there is the political will among decision-makers, to counter the current situation globally, which sees women benefiting less from the information society than men and also contributing less to it (Huyer et al. 2005). This situation is problematic if societies as a whole are to benefit from ICTs and use them to further their development, and if the vision of development pursued is to equitably reflect and fulfil the interests and needs of the population, not only of those in positions of power.

Unearthing the meanings during the research process, and then understanding their significance, also required centring ourselves. The ostrich-egg exercise was used more than once, as were other self-reflection practices. We primarily used qualitative research techniques, as these yield in-depth data and enable us to reveal various dimensions and aspects of phenomena. The research questions and methodologies and the research training, as well as the ongoing mentoring and support programme accompanying the research, were grounded in the principles of critical emancipatory research (Buskens 2002; Buskens and Earl 2008).

The methods used in each case were identified by the authors as the best suited to learning about the lives and the thinking of their respondents. The respondents were approached as active agents in determining their own reality, rather than as victims of their situation. This may seem to contradict the point that women's lives are not well understood and are not setting ICT development directions; however, we wanted to find out how women understood their current situations, we wanted them to think beyond their current realities and to consider what needed to be in place for them to pursue their visions. To do this sort of reflection and thinking women had to see themselves as having the capacity for action on their own behalf (Buskens 2002, 2006; Buskens and Earl 2008; Hannan 2004; Kabeer 2003). It is this sort of thinking which produces practical, functional knowledge that can lead to change.

But making sense of that knowledge also requires taking into account the norms and values of our societies that shape our consciousness and behaviour. It is not a simple matter to become aware of the factors shaping our perspectives and values, nor is it easy to visualize a reality that would transcend our own conscious knowing and imagining. But this is the challenge undertaken by the authors in this volume – to structure their research, and then their own analysis and interpretation, to try to make sense of the research participants' perceptions and pursuit of empowering change in the context of their current realities and their dreams. This required heightened reflexivity on the part of the authors as they worked within their own sociocultural milieu.

Working in familiar environments facilitated building rapport with research participants, and recognition of local specificities, but the orientation of recognizing in the research context and in oneself as a researcher the normalized social, cultural, gender, economic (and so forth) relations and assumptions is not simple. As empowered ICT users the authors also hoped that the benefits they were experiencing were shared by others. As would an 'outsider' be, the authors working as 'native anthropologists' (Rodriguez 2001) were confronted with the task of revealing and questioning their own assumptions and biases, becoming aware of their own lenses, and managing to 'make the normal anthropologically strange' (Buskens 2006, 2002). This condition of self-awareness or reflexivity is a key quality of the qualitative research approach engaged.

Particular self-reflection practices contributed to the authors revealing connections between words and actions, even when on the surface the two seemed at odds. As a centring and self-awareness process, and to increase their capacity to recognize the multiple layers of consciousness and the associated layers of meaning, the authors practised a process developed by Ineke called the Transformational Attitude Interview (Buskens 2008). It provides a process for in-depth interviewing that reveals experiences,

3

values and dreams, and the discrepancies between them. In exploring what it would take for the desired reality to become attainable, barriers (both within us and external) are recognized and the strengths and conditions needed to be coherent with the desired vision of the world identified.

Unsettling the hierarchy?

In the following chapters the authors see ICTs as tools that can help people transform their realities. As with earlier forms of information technologies, we do not see ICT products as changing inequitable systems and values. ICT is socially constructed, 'as an artifact of a particular environment, created by particular stakeholders for particular purposes' (Heeks 2002: 5). While those purposes may or may not be explicit, they are 'formulated within a broader discourse of modernization and development, which is based on the assumption that a deficiency in [Western] knowledge is partly responsible for underdevelopment' (Schech 2002: 13) in the developing world. This, however, is an assumption at once arrogant and naive, glossing, as it does, over the political-economic realities and relationships that hold the 'developed' and the 'developing world' captive to each other.

It is furthermore generally recognized that the nature and direction of the information society's development is not grounded in the realities of women, particularly women who experience poverty as well as gender discrimination, and who do not hold positions of power in the public realm (Hafkin and Huyer 2006; Huyer et al. 2005). Currently, the limited documentation of gender issues in relation to the impact of ICTs 'makes it difficult, if not impossible, to make the case to policymakers for the inclusion of gender issues in ICT policies, plans and strategies. As the UNDP puts it, "without data, there is no visibility; without visibility, there is no priority" (cited in Huyer and Westholm 2000)' (ibid.: 50). The investigations in GRACE demonstrate the complexity of gender inequalities perpetuated in ICT environments and currently only sparsely examined from the perspective of the women users (ibid.; Sciadas 2005).

While we recognize ICTs can be used to enhance our lives and contribute to our well-being, effective use of time, economic development and so forth, they can also exacerbate gendered life situations, relationships and images and thus play a conservative, reactionary role. As such the crux of the matter is not so much the issue of access and affordability, although these are significant factors; it is more a question of experiencing the right and having the space for self-determination.

ICTs create different time and space coordinates, but what comprises space for self-determination is not unequivocal; it holds different meanings and different descriptions in different contexts. Further, the use of ICTs to enhance one's life presupposes a measure of control over one's space and time.

The chapters

The authors in this volume raise a number of questions from their understandings of the perspectives and experiences of the women using ICTs who were involved in their research. The authors look at what is affecting the women's use of the ICTs available to them, and in some cases the effects of lack of availability. They discuss a complex web of factors.

The research respondents all had exposure to particular ICTs, such as cell phones, computers and the Internet, CD-ROMs, and radio. How the women engaged with the technology, and the possibilities they saw and/or pursued in terms of accessing, using and controlling (in terms of the object and the content) ICTs, the impact they experienced, and the implications of those impacts when considered in their broader socio-economic, cultural context, varied considerably, but also reveal certain overarching questions vital to understandings of an equation of ICTs for development, or for poverty reduction, or gender equality, or social justice.

We have made four groupings of the respondents' options and choices in relation to their use of ICTs, against the question of empowerment.

The women in the chapters in Part One are affected by ICTs in a 'passive' way. Their lives have been changed by the various technologies but they are not at all or only in a very limited way able to access and use these tools. These women's lack of access and use is related to lack of infrastructure (including electricity and hardware), poverty (their main priorities being involved with survival) and illiteracy. These factors are often partly and sometimes completely gender-related. For instance, in some contexts women were affected by ICTs as the technologies had entered their realm through family usage, community access and awareness of potential uses and benefits, even when the women did not actively seek to utilize them. Some technologies were found to be irrelevant, and some a 'mixed blessing'.

The women respondents in Part Two are benefiting from or would benefit from 'female-only' spaces they create for themselves or which could be created for them through and with ICTs. In these spaces they can find refuge, express themselves, learn, network and trade. It seems that in certain situations women's environments are so seriously gender imbalanced that they do not get the opportunities to enhance their lives and expand their contributions to their societies within existing physical public spaces. The virtual ICT-created spaces would enable women to enjoy and utilize new freedoms. By creating new forms of space – using a cell phone when violence is perpetuated in isolating physical spaces; creating supportive learning and work environments that do not require entering the patriarchal public sphere; enhancing existing advocacy networks – women are creating new options and liberties for themselves. What, however, does the desire for or pursuit of women-only spaces through the use of technologies indicate about women's choices and engagement with ICTs? How should we look at this desire to separate from rather than confront existing power structures, from a gender equality perspective? Is this an expression of empowerment for the women involved; are these empowering options that they are creating?

In Part Three, women use ICTs to increase control over their time and space in their personal and professional lives. Their use of ICTs, however, often challenges and upsets existing gender roles and the gendered 'norms' within existing public spaces. Women experience independence through the physical act of using ICTs, and create socio-economic gains. At the same time, because their use of these technologies enables them to handle their triple roles better, it can be argued that ICT use contributes to the maintenance and possibly even strengthening of the traditional gendered division of labour and thus to the general gender imbalance. Some women, however, have been able through their use of ICTs to not only enhance their lives, but also transform their realities. They have transformed gendered images and conditions in their personal relationships and their communities.

In Part Four the authors speak with women who use ICTs to enhance their lives according to their own designs. These women are creating new spaces for themselves and others to live in, think in and work in, and they are affecting public spaces in various ways at the household, local, national and international levels. By changing their own conditions and breaking 'glass ceilings', they are becoming sources of inspiration for others. These women vary from a CEO of a national ICT corporation, who has access to extensive resources, to a hairdresser who needed to save for two years to buy the cell phone that enabled her to start her business and is now able to buy her own house and even rent out a room.

These four groupings can be approached as scenarios, as stations or stages. In every stage, at every station or in every scenario, the question can be raised as to what level of empowerment would need to be in place for women to access and use a particular ICT or to participate in spaces created with and through ICTs. Our research indicates that there are certain 'empowerment thresholds' at every level, comprising supportive internal and external factors in various combinations. Yet at every level, even at the level at which women would have the fewest choices because of general deprivation of basic necessities (such as electricity), women would express their agency. Amartya Sen states: 'nothing, arguably, is as important today in the political economy of development as an adequate recognition of political, economic and social participation and leadership of women'. Yet at the same time, he admits that the 'extensive reach of women's agency is one of the more neglected areas of development studies, and most urgently in need of correction' (Sen 1999: 203).

In bringing more clarity to the way women exert their agency in relation to the use of ICTs, how gender issues hinder or enhance women's access to and use of ICTs, how women have accomplished their dreams in relation to ICT use, what they needed in order to get there, what obstacles they faced, and how they managed to overcome their internal and external barriers, the authors contribute to a better understanding of the potentials of ICT use. Being the powerful tools that they are, ICTs deserve serious attention. Not to grant them this attention could result in missed opportunities for women, and risk ICTs reinforcing, unintentionally, women's discrimination and disempowerment.

Notes

1 In addition to training in qualitative methodologies, IT training was provided during the first two annual GRACE workshops through an initial partnership with the Association for Progressive Communications (APC), specifically the APC Women's Programme.

2 This project was funded by the International Development Research Centre of Canada. The views expressed in this chapter and throughout the book are those of the authors and do not necessarily represent the opinions of the funder. For more information on the GRACE project, please see our website, www. GRACE-Network.net.

References

Buskens, I. (2002) 'Fine lines or strong cords? Who do we think we are and how can we become what we want to be in the Quest for Quality in Qualitative Research?', *Education as Change*, 6(1): 1–31.
— (2006) 'Gender research in Africa into ICTs for empowerment', *IICBA Newsletter*, 8(2), UNESCO.
— (2008) 'Transformational Attitude Interviewing', www.GRACE-Network.net.
Buskens, I. and S. Earl (2008) 'Research for change – Outcome Mapping's contribution to emancipatory research in Africa', *Action Research*, 6(2): 173–94.
Buskens, I., A. Esterhuysen and J. Radloff (2004) 'GRACE: Gender Research in Africa into ICTs for

Empowerment', Project proposal, www.GRACE-Network.net/publications/GRACE%20proposal.pdf.

Hafkin, N. J. and S. Huyer (2006) *Cinderella or Cyberella? Empowering Women in the Knowledge Society*, Bloomfield, CT: Kumarian.

Hannan, C. (2004) 'Women's rights and empowerment: gender equality in the new millennium', Presentation to the United Nations Day Banquet, Dallas chapter of the United Nations, 24 October.

Heeks, R. (2002) 'i-development not e-development: special issue on ICTs and development', *Journal of International Development*, 14(1).

Huyer, S., N. Hafkin, H. Ertl and H. Dryburgh (2005) 'Women in the information society', in G. Sciadas (ed.), *From the Digital Divide to Digital Opportunities: Measuring Infostates for Development*, Ottawa: Orbicom/ITU, pp. 134–94, www.orbicom.ca/media/projets/ddi2005/index_ict_opp.pdf.

Kabeer, N. (2003) *Gender Mainstreaming in Poverty Eradication and the Millennium Development Goals*, Ottawa: Commonwealth Secretariat/IDRC/CIDA.

Rodriguez, C. (2001) 'A homegirl goes home: black feminism and the lure of native anthropology', in I. McClaurin (ed.), *Black Feminist Anthropology: Theory, Politics, Praxis and Poetics*, London: Rutgers University Press.

Schech, S. (2002) 'Wired for change: the links between ICTs and development discourses', *Journal of International Development*, 14(1).

Sciadas, G. (ed.) (2005) *From the Digital Divide to Digital Opportunities: Measuring Infostates for Development*, Ottawa: Orbicom/ITU, www.orbicom.ca/media/projets/ddi2005/index_ict_opp.pdf.

Sen, A. (1999) *Development as Freedom*, New York and Toronto: Anchor Books.

UNEP/GRID-Arendal (2006) *Planet in Peril: Atlas of Current Threats to People and the Environment*, UNEP.

1 | Doing research with women for the purpose of transformation

INEKE BUSKENS

Qualitative research with women of the nature that the authors in this book have conducted poses certain challenges. Both researchers and research respondents have grown up in androcratic societies.[1] This means that both parties will look at themselves and each other through the filters formed by and within the prevalent sexist thinking. While there will undoubtedly be great variance between the filters within and between individuals, groups, communities and countries, which will remain unknown to varying degrees, the fact that everybody still does have a sexist filter of some sort is inescapable.

Women as research respondents

Women have internalized unexamined assumptions and biased conceptions about their being, capacities or the lack of them to such a degree that they often do not really know who they are and what they want. Women may believe that as persons they are less worthy, capable, competent and talented, etc., than they really are. Furthermore, the culturally accepted concepts in male-dominated societies do not always allow women to express their realities and experiences. The dominant androcratic ideology is also often judgemental and denigrating of women (Daly 1973; Belenky et al. 1986; Gilligan 1982).

In asking women to talk about their lives, qualitative researchers also implicitly ask them to choose the concepts with which to do that. As these concepts will be influenced by images serving an androcratic culture, they might be normative, denigrating or simply unsuitable to reflect women's realities. When the concepts women have internalized about themselves sabotage their human journey, they will experience tension and conflict between what they inherently know about themselves and what they believe they are capable of. They may not even know that the sociocultural concepts they hold about women in general speak to their personally constructed female self-image all the time. Asking women about their feelings is accessing the area of personal truth and experience while simultaneously opening up their relationship with this dominant culture. It is exactly in the mental space between culturally acceptable concepts and personal truth that women keep the tension between how they think they are/should be and how they really feel (Anderson and Jack 2006).

What can researchers expect in their conversations with women?

Women may be very sensitive to what they expect researchers want to hear, because they feel insecure when they have to express who they think they are and what they are feeling. Women often do not have concepts that 'feel really right' for them and which represent their experiences fully. Women may thus contradict themselves and speak between the lines. Women may measure themselves against the stereotype they hold of 'the good woman' and sometimes they do that in conjunction with sharing where 'they themselves are really at'. They may speak in 'stereo' at times, voicing the culturally accepted part of their female role as well as the muted sounds of their authentic personal experience (ibid.).

Women may share experiences while critiquing what they are saying simultaneously through meta-statements. The concepts women are using may be 'concepts in construction', and women may try out different concepts the next time. Sometimes they may use culturally accepted concepts to critique their own life; sometimes they will use their own personal experience to critique culturally accepted concepts. Many women have a lot of unfulfilled dreams as well as anxieties and doubts concerning the fulfilment of these dreams. In-depth research may bring all this up and cause distress. Counselling capacity is therefore an appropriate asset for researchers (ibid.).

Research with women: the Zimbabwe exemplar

In the following, the research project undertaken by the GRACE team from Zimbabwe is discussed to highlight the type of research decisions that typically characterize qualitative research with women and the opportunities for valid and useful knowledge construction such research offers. This research is fully presented in Chapter 6.

At the University of Zimbabwe, three researchers, university librarians at the time of the research, had noticed that male students were outnumbering the female students in the library computer lab by far. The library computers are accessible to all students from all faculties. The statistics they had gathered on the basis of the logbooks and the student enrolment ratios confirmed their observations. At the time of this research, the library had not acquired enough computers to accommodate all students who needed access. The rule of 'first come, first served' was therefore applied.

On the basis of their statistics and participant observation, the researchers designed an in-depth qualitative study to understand this situation. In their analysis of these female students' stories about their access to ICT labs on campus, the researchers found that there were various reasons that explained the female students' limited access. Only one reason will be discussed here – namely that the competition for access often resulted in physical shoving; in other words, the male students would push the female students away.

The researchers could have stopped at this point and would, with the data they had gathered, have been able to compose an insightful story about the relationship between women students, the use of ICTs and institutions for higher learning in Africa.

The researchers then turned their focus, however, to the two main 'anomalies' their research had yielded: the few female students who did access the computer labs, whom they started calling 'deviants' because they deviated from the norm, and the fact that quite a few of the 'normal' female students, when asked about how they felt about not being able to access the computer lab as they would have liked to, did not question the 'first come, first served' rule at all. In these respondents' minds, this was a perfectly acceptable rule and an improvement on what they were used to previously. At the same time, these very same students lamented the fact that they would have to turn to Internet cafés and colleges in order to gain computer access.

Turning to the 'deviants', the female students who did access the library computers, the researchers found that these students not only were younger, but also had more ICT experience. Furthermore, these students were very aware of the other female students staying away and the reasons why they did so. They were aware of the discrepancy between the apparent fairness of the rule and the unfairness that resulted from it.

Regarding the 'normal' women students, it would have been understandable at this point for the researchers to have become impatient and judgemental and assess these 'normal' respondents as contradicting themselves, being confused and not able to take an opportunity when it was provided. Fortunately they did not. The researchers understood the fact that their respondents had formed their opinions, their thinking, in a social setting where the 'first come, first served' rule is considered democratic and fair – in other words socially accepted. The researchers were aware of the fact that such a concept would be the dominant and maybe the only concept their respondents would have to give meaning to their experience of no access. They were sensitive to the fact that women often do not have the right concepts at their disposal to say what they really feel. They understood that this phenomenon does not reveal any individual intellectual or emotional shortcomings on the part of women, but speaks to the reality of having been born and grown up as women in androcratic societies. As researchers they also understood that this phenomenon of apparent contradiction, when analysed properly, would yield insight into deeper layers of meaning and experience.

The researchers could have concluded that the qualities the 'deviant' students had were the qualities necessary for all other female students to have in order to succeed in getting access to the lab computers. Fortunately they did not. Their analysis went a level deeper and includes the two respondent groups' processes of creating meaning for the experience of non-access and the rule of equal access. And in linking their understanding about the two groups, a new concept emerged: the confidence in self, able to challenge gender discrimination in an ICT context, may be grounded in ICT experience.

On the basis of this case study, it becomes clear that research with women can be done successfully by researchers who are willing to go beyond what seems obvious and are prepared to keep unveiling layers of meaning and experience until the moment a level of deeper insight is reached which can make sense of all the data on the basis of one coherent explanatory model. Undoubtedly, the researchers' drive to get practical knowledge that would be usable and able to generate sustainable change would have inspired and motivated them to keep the analysis process open and not close it prematurely.

Relating with women respondents

Research with women asks of researchers to listen well, to contextualize, to be able to fully accept and contest what they hear, and to be as methodologically innovative as needed and as possible. Research that aims to be receptive to and engage women's agency for the purpose of transformation requires of the researchers even more: it requires that researchers encourage women respondents to think beyond their current realities, and to consider what needs to be in place for them to pursue their visions.

Listening to women, really listening to women, means listening to what is said and how it is said, but also listening to what is not said and what cannot be said. It will be very important to listen carefully to what is said 'between the lines' and observe non-verbal communication. Researchers may have to hold a 'space of not-yet-understanding' for quite a while because it is important not to make sense 'too soon'.

Because the moments of contradiction and paradox point towards the places where the tension between women's acceptance of their socio-cultural values and their authentic experiences and dreams for themselves are held, researchers need to be able to recognize these and use them. Using such moments often involves challenge and confrontation, acting from deep knowledge of the contexts in which women are situated and without judgement of women's choices, thoughts and emotions. When focusing on the thoughts, emotions and choices women respondents express, the concept of 'adaptive preferences' has to be brought into the equation: women have internalized the myths of gender inequality that are prevalent in their society and have formed an attachment to identities informed by such myths and the practices that are coherent with them (Nussbaum 2000). Women may have accepted the 'unacceptable as natural' and may share 'their truth' from this perspective. If such truth were not to be examined, women could be made into 'informed' agents of their own disempowerment even in processes that were meant to be empowering and transformative. At the same time, however, it is important to be sensitive to women's boundaries and respect the unfolding of their emotions, thoughts and choices.

In order to understand women's dreams and desires beyond their female-accepted role, it is often necessary to create a mental space for them where they can experience that part of themselves and give it a voice. Research designs and methods will have to take into account that women's potential for sovereignty and change, as well as their socialization into limitation, exist in women simultaneously. Techniques that stimulate women's creativity and free expression could be combined with in-depth interviews and participant observation.

Relating to oneself when doing research with women

Researchers should listen to themselves while they are listening to women. Not only because their personal discomfort can alert them to discrepancies between what women say and what they actually feel (Anderson and Jack 2006), but also because it is important for researchers to get to know their own mind filters, to make themselves aware of any unconscious prejudice they may hold (Buskens 2006, 2002; Smaling 1990, 1995, 1998). Given the research focus of gender influence in the context of women's empowerment in the research encounter, both female and male researchers will be confronted with their own gendered self and the sexist filters they have. The more they are prepared to look into the mirror and own what they see, the richer their relationship with their respondents will be, the richer their research process and the richer their data. The confrontation with their own gendered self and the experience of the gender dynamics in the research relationship may mean something different for men to what it means for women. Where men could be unaware of many of the unobvious interpersonal communication dynamics, women could lose awareness because they could revert to unexamined judgement.

A long-time taboo subject, female sexism has now been openly discussed (Chesler 2001). Fear of identification and connection with other women seems to be the shadow force behind female sexism. Women's sexist attitudes towards other women are linked to a country's general sexism rate: the higher the general sexism rate is, the more prevalent female sexism will be. In their study of nineteen countries in five continents, Glick and Fiske found that of the four countries with the highest sexism score, three were in Africa: Botswana, Nigeria and South Africa (Glick and Fiske 1996, 1997; Glick et al. 2000; quoted in Chesler 2001).[2] Women's aggression towards other women expresses itself predominantly indirectly – in the form of shunning, shaming, judging and even stigmatizing (Chesler 2001). Even being feminist does not seem to guarantee a lack of hostility towards other women.[3]

To maintain a reflexive attitude is important in all qualitative research; in gender research with women it is absolutely crucial. In questioning research decisions, and the emotions and thoughts the research encounters bring up, researchers have the opportunity to get to know more about themselves. When researchers ask the questions 'What shall I do now?' and 'Why am I doing this?', they also ask themselves the questions 'What is the self I am bringing to this research moment now? What is the self that expresses itself in relation to the research focus and the research participant now?' This reflexive questioning brings researchers into direct relationship with the sexist filters they have, and possibly other prejudices. This can be very hard and painful. In order to support themselves in maintaining this reflexive attitude, researchers have to be gentle with themselves. It is important to keep striving to become the best one can be, make sure that the resources to do so (emotional, mental, social and financial) are in place and come to an understanding and acceptance of relapses. This attitude could be called self-love, and the discipline in which this attitude expresses itself could be called self-care. In that sense, self-care can thus be constructed as a methodological prerequisite (Buskens 2002), because without it reflexivity is not a sustainable attitude.

According to Chesler, female sexism can be overcome through a disciplined practice of sisterhood. This discipline has to be grounded in self-love (Chesler 2001). Women may find it particularly challenging to love themselves. One of the most devastating effects of oppression is the alienation of self, where people lose loyalty to themselves, to their profoundest feelings and to their love of self (Fanon 1967, quoted in Mageo 2002).

The challenges male researchers face in gender research with women, however, where they encounter their gendered selves and sexist filters, may be, although of a different nature, just as profound. This makes their commitment to a discipline of self-reflexivity and hence self-love just as imperative.

Research for change

In research for change, such as GRACE, the researchers' focus often speaks directly to their own work and life. In GRACE, the research question was: 'How do women in Africa use ICTs for empowerment?' None of the GRACE researchers would be able to do the work they do, empowering themselves, if it were not for their use of ICTs. In turning to their own communities for their research, sharing language, ethnicity, religion and sometimes even the village of birth or working in the same organization, the GRACE researchers operated as 'native anthropologists' (Rodriguez 2001). This has enabled them to establish close relationships with their respondents; it has also challenged their reflexivity, courage, perseverance and love for self. Furthermore, most of the researchers are women researching other women. The more directly the mirror is in front of one's face, the potentially richer one's insights into self and the other become, the more confrontational the research experience will be and the more important self-care becomes.

Looking in the mirror and becoming aware is a transforming act in itself. The act of self-reflection in itself brings about change (Reason and Bradbury 2001; Meulenberg-Buskens 1998; Van der Walt 2000). This can be challenging, even when the change is wanted, foreseen and embraced, because every change also carries loss in it. In research, which has the explicit purpose of constructing knowledge for empowerment and transformation, change is on the agenda for everyone. It is thus imperative that researchers learn how to work with the change process, not only in their respondents but also in themselves.

Maintaining a stance of critical questioning and alignment with a future of hope, while weathering the adverse conditions and emotional storms caused by direct confrontations with women's disempowerment in and through the research context, is a complex and all-absorbing endeavour. The challenge becomes even greater when researchers turn to their own communities and living environments in their research. No research quest, however, can go beyond the minds that conceptualize and fire it. It is thus imperative that the minds that are intimately familiar with and affected by the status quo are the minds that phrase the questions that will yield insight into the potential of women's empowerment.

Researchers who are not afraid of change in themselves and in their environments will not be afraid to witness and even evoke change in their respondents. It is the acceptance of the vulnerability that comes with such a commitment which ultimately gives researchers the credibility to engage in research with women for the purpose of transformation.

Notes

1 Androcracy refers to the domination by powerful men, which differs from male domination or patriarchy. See Eisler (1995).

2 In their study of nineteen countries in five continents, Glick and Fiske found that 'whereas women as a group scored lower than men on hostile sexism in every nation studied, their scores on benevolent sexism were often no different than or sometimes significantly higher than men's'. In the four countries with the highest sexism score (of which three were in Africa: Botswana, Nigeria and South Africa), women endorsed benevolent sexism significantly more than men did. Female benevolent sexism looks favourably upon the type of woman that adheres to traditional values and disapproves strongly of women who break the mould. This form of sexism serves to maintain the status quo. Women's sexist attitudes towards other women are linked to a country's general sexism rate, and southern Africa can be classified as very sexist. The more sexist the nation, the more that women, relative to men, will accept benevolent sexism.

3 In a 2000 study of 155 American college women, working- and middle-class, of varied ethnic groups, Cowan (quoted in Chesler 2001) found 'that women's hostility towards other women is unrelated to their self-labeling as feminist or to a feminism scale' (p. 150). Although a similar study has not been done in Africa, cross-cultural studies have found high rates of sexism in Africa (Glick and Fiske 1996, 1997; Glick et al. 2000, quoted in Chesler 2001), and given the fact that a country's general sexism rate correlates with its rate of female sexism, the possibility that a similar study would find similar results in Africa cannot be dismissed.

References

Anderson, K. and D. Jack (2006) 'Learning to listen: interview techniques and analyses', in R. Perks and A. Thomson (eds), *The Oral History Reader*, 2nd edn, London: Routledge.

Belenky, M. F., B. Clinchy, N. Goldberger and J. Tarule (1986) *Women's Ways of Knowing: The Development of Self, Voice and Mind*, New York: Basic Books.

Buskens, I. (2002) 'Fine lines or strong cords? Who do we think we are and how can we become what we want to be in the Quest for Quality in Qualitative Research?', *Education as Change*, 6(1): 1–31.

— (2006) 'Gender research in Africa into ICTs for empowerment', *IICBA Newsletter*, 8(2), UNESCO.

Chesler, P. (2001) *Woman's Inhumanity to Woman*, New York: Thunder's Mouth Press.

Cowan, G. (2000) 'Women's hostility towards women and rape and sexual harassment myths', *Violence Against Women*, 6(3): 238–46.

Daly, M. (1973) *Beyond God the Father – Toward a Philosophy of Women's Liberation*, Boston, MA: Beacon Press.

Eisler, R. (1995) *The Chalice and the Blade – Our History, Our Future*, San Francisco, CA: Harper.

Gilligan, C. (1982) *In a Different Voice. Psychological Theory and Women's Development*, Cambridge, MA: Harvard University Press.

Glick, P. and S. T. Fiske (1996) 'The ambivalent sexism inventory: differentiating hostile and benevolent sexism', *Journal of Personality and Social Psychology*, 70(3): 419–512.

— (1997) 'Hostile and benevolent sexism: measuring ambivalent sexist attitudes toward women', *Psychology of Women Quarterly*, 21: 119–35.

Glick, P. et al. (2000) 'Beyond prejudice as simple antipathy: hostile and benevolent sexism across cultures', *Journal of Personality and Social Psychology*, 70(5).

Mageo, J. M. (2002) *Power and the Self*, Cambridge: Cambridge University Press.

Meulenberg-Buskens, I. (1998) 'Reflections on research methodology and research capacity building in a participatory action research project in South Africa

1996–1998', in S. Fehrsen et al., *Coping Strategies Project Report South Africa*, Unpublished research report, Brussels: EU.

Nussbaum, M. C. (2000) *Women and Human Development: The Capabilities Approach*, Cambridge: Cambridge University Press.

Reason, P. and H. Bradbury (2001) *Handbook of Action Research: Participative Inquiry and Practice*, London: Sage.

Rodriguez, C. (2001) 'A homegirl goes home: black feminism and the lure of native anthropology', in I. McClaurin (ed.), *Black Feminist Anthropology: Theory, Politics, Praxis and Poetics*, London: Rutgers University Press.

Smaling, A. (1990) 'Role-taking as a methodological principle', Paper presented at the William James Congress, Amsterdam, August.

— (1995) 'Open-mindedness, open-heartedness and dialogical openness: the dialectics of openings and closures', in Maso, Atkinson, Delamont and Verhoeven (eds), *Openness in Research: The Tension between Self and Other*, Assen: Van Gorcum.

— (1998) 'Dialogical partnership: the relationship between the researcher and the researched in action research', in Boog, Coenen, Keene and Lammerts (eds), *The Complexity of Relationships in Action Research*, Tilburg University Press.

Van der Walt, H. (2000) 'Nurses and their work in the Tuberculosis Control Programme for the Western Cape: too close for comfort', Unpublished PhD thesis, UCT, Cape Town.

ONE | ICT tools: access and use

2 | Women's use of information and communication technologies in Mozambique: a tool for empowerment?

GERTRUDES MACUEVE, JUDITE MANDLATE, LUCIA
GINGER, POLLY GASTER AND ESSELINA MACOME

As professional women working in the field of information and communication technology (ICT), our assumption was that all women can benefit (as we have) from making use of ICT. A number of gender studies (Johnson 2003; Payton et al. 2007) have shown that the main users of ICT (especially computers, Internet and e-mail) are young males, and that women are marginal users, suggesting a gap between discourse and the reality of women's empowerment through ICT. Scholars like Sharma (2003) and Stephen (2006) suggest, however, that ICTs can empower women through enhancing participation in economic and social development and facilitating informed decision-taking. These authors argue that ICTs have the power to reach women who have been outside the ambit of other media and can facilitate communication among them and other dispersed networks, enabling them to mobilize, participate in debates and express themselves.

We therefore aimed to investigate whether women in Mozambique's rural areas, who have access to ICTs through telecentres and the expanding mobile phone networks, are becoming more empowered. Generally, farming is the basis for survival for rural women, accompanied by petty trading in the informal sector. Most of these women are illiterate (the national illiteracy rate is 53 per cent, but it is 66 per cent among women; UNDP 2006) and they do not speak the official language (Portuguese), let alone English, the language of so much of the information available on the Internet. Rural women play an extremely important role in society and in poverty reduction, and at the same time comprise the poorest and most marginalized group (Fórum Mulher/SARDC WIDSAA 2005).

In this context, we undertook to investigate the following questions:

- Do women in Manhiça and Sussundenga in rural Mozambique use the ICTs available in the districts? If so, what for? If not, why not?
- Does the use of the available ICTs empower the women? If so, how? If not, why not?

We hope that our findings will be useful to guide and adapt rural ICT interventions so that they may work in favour of women's empowerment rather than – perhaps unwittingly – increasing the gender gap.

Our understanding is that there is no single model of empowerment. The word 'empowerment' has been defined in a number of ways. For example, for Bush and Folger (1994) empowerment means restoring people's sense of their own worth and strengthening their ability to resolve their own problems, while for the Norwegian Agency for Development Cooperation (1999) it means increasing opportunities for both men and women to control their lives: empowerment equals power to make decisions, be heard, set agendas, negotiate and face difficulties on one's own. Empowerment is also defined as a group's or individual's capacity to make choices and then to transform those choices into desired actions and outcomes (Alsop et al. 2006).

For us empowerment can include many factors – economic, social and political (World Bank 2002; Alsop et al. 2006; United Nations 2005). For the purposes of this chapter and the particular context, we define women's empowerment through ICTs as meaning the role played by access to ICTs in expanding the assets and capabilities of women, specifically women in rural Mozambique. Assets include both physical and financial assets (World Bank 2002) and capabilities, the latter meaning the ability to carry out valuable acts and to achieve or reach valuable states of being, dependent on each individual and his/her context (Sen 1987, 1992, 1997; Sen and Nussbaum 1993).

When we refer to ICTs in this chapter we mean radios, computers, e-mail, Internet and telephones (mobile and landline). We discuss how each of them has been used in empowering rural women in Mozambique based on fieldwork conducted during December 2005 to February 2006.

Study context

Considering the size and heterogeneity of Mozambique, we decided to study two rural districts: Manhiça in Maputo Province in the south, and Sussundenga in Manica Province in the central region. These areas were chosen because both have benefited from the presence of ICTs in telecentres, including community radio stations, for several years, and therefore offered an opportunity to explore what has been happening in areas where (in technical terms) a minimum level of ICT access is available.

Mozambique's installation of the first district-level telecentres in 1999 marked the beginning of an effort to bring ICT within reach of rural areas and underprivileged groups, including women. The telecentres were conceived as development centres and are locally owned, providing access to computers, IT training, word-processing and graphic design, public phone (landline), fax and photocopiers, e-mail, Internet and information services. Community radio stations for local broadcasting were integrated into most telecentres in a later phase. The most recent communication tool to be installed in increasing numbers of districts is the mobile phone. Although the reach of mobile phones deep into the countryside is still extremely limited, mobile phone users in Mozambique already by far outnumber landline phone subscribers.

There are two mobile phone operators in Mozambique. Both operate in Manhiça, and one started up in Sussundenga at the end of our research period. The public telecommunications company still has a monopoly on the infrastructure and on landline voice services – a handful of phone booths are available in both districts studied, in addition to those in the telecentres, and key local government sectors, organizations and businesses. The lack of good and cheap access to a telephone connection (or often any connection at all) is a major constraint on e-mail and Internet use; another important factor is the shortage of ICT professionals countrywide.

Eighty per cent of Mozambique's total population (20 million, 52 per cent of whom are women) is rural, and 80 per cent of rural workers are women, of whom only 2 per cent are in the formal sector. Manhiça district, 80 kilometres north of Maputo, has a population of nearly 200,000, with a poverty rate estimated at 60 per cent in 2003. Sixty per cent of women and girls over five have never attended school and only 12 per cent have completed primary education, although 20 per cent speak Portuguese. Ninety per cent of the economically active female population work in agriculture, for the family or for themselves, and 15 per cent of the district's farmers are girls under ten years of age (MAE 2005a). Sussundenga, on the other hand, is three times the size of Manhiça, with half the population. Here only 9 per cent of women speak Portuguese and 83 per cent are illiterate (compared to 62 per cent of men). Ninety-six per cent of active women work in agriculture, although it is worth noting that 12 per cent of teachers and 52 per cent of health workers in the district are female (MAE 2005b).

Exploring the use of ICTs by rural women in Mozambique

Our field data are essentially qualitative, collected through semi-structured interviews, group discussions in various configurations, observation and life histories. The interviews were conducted in local languages with women visiting the telecentres during the period of fieldwork, local

23

female leaders and professionals, and women selected randomly in the area around the telecentres, including in schools, hospitals, markets and in the street. Seventy-four women were interviewed (forty-four in Manhiça and thirty in Sussundenga): teachers, nurses, homemakers, those who are unemployed, market and street sellers, and leaders of women's associations. We also analysed the telecentres' own usage statistics, which are organized by age group, sex and the services used.

Community radio – still an effective empowering tool in a rural context
The local community radio stations that broadcast from the telecentres are certainly the most used ICT for all the women interviewed. Radio broadcasts are free to the listener, and access does not depend on having mains electricity or individual radio ownership – people listen together in public places and at home. Running costs are generally low, making the radio the most affordable ICT in rural areas, particularly where wind-up radios are available.

There are, however, people who cannot afford to own a radio. For example, a head of household in Manhiça told us that she never used any technologies and she wouldn't like to have a radio or a telephone since they meant more costs: 'Radio batteries are expensive.' She wanted only to have something to eat every day. 'What would I use a phone for?' she asked. When we interviewed her she was at the telecentre to collect her lost identity card: someone had found it and taken it to the telecentre, and an announcement was made on the radio. The woman's neighbours heard it and told her. Without the radio to act as a trusted central point she would not have discovered where her card was.

Around 95 per cent of the interviewees confirmed that they listen to radio, and many in both districts told us that they know the programme schedules. The most popular programmes are the public information announcements, especially death notices; in these women's sociocultural context, participating in the mourning of community members and relatives is an essential part of the fabric of society, and the radio is the fastest and most economical way of reaching a large number of people. News programmes and special programmes for women were also popular. News programmes enable women to acquire information that reduces their isolation both within their communities and nationally and internationally, and the women's programmes cover a range of topics, such as the behaviour of adolescents within the family, precautions to be taken at home, HIV/AIDS, cooking, children's health and social behaviours. The educational radio programmes, especially those for women, help improve capabilities to operate as HIV/AIDS activists, for example, and to change the way they deal with healthcare, social and other problems within communities and families.

We believe that there is a process of hearing and learning from the radio and applying it within families and educating others. In general, the women said that radio programmes are very important to them, because it is through them that they find out what is happening in the world.

The radio also involves local women directly as volunteers to produce and present programmes. In this manner they learn new skills and gain confidence through occupying a public space. In turn, the fact that the programmes are being made by people they know (or even their own family members) inspires greater trust. The volunteers lamented, however, that although they enjoy the work, the lack of incentives leads to problems at home, as exemplified by a woman in a discussion meeting in Sussundenga: 'We feel apprehensive when leaving our homes and coming here to the telecentre ... because our husbands often question ... what are the economic gains from collaborating with the telecentre that help the family?'

How can access to a simple radio be empowering to rural women? The community radio provides information that rural women need and value because it is accessible, in their own language, and increases their capability to act, whether they receive the information directly or indirectly. Even today oral communication is the most powerful and affordable means of getting information for most Mozambicans.

Volunteering at the radio and telecentre is also seen as an opportunity for socialization in the rural communities. Some scholars, such as Carnoy (1975) and Sen (2003), have argued that going to school not only enhances literacy skills but also enables children to learn how to socialize, which is good for their future. Similarly, although they do not earn material assets, in addition to technical skills the telecentre provides its female volunteers with a learning experience of socializing with other women, playing a public role in the community, self-organization, and mobilizing assets and ideas to solve problems of common interest. For many of the young women volunteers this may be their first such experience outside school or leisure activities.

The role of the mobile phone in empowering rural women We found that awareness of mobile phones was high in both districts, and even though the network had not been fully installed in Sussundenga at the time of the fieldwork, the few mobile phone owners could use them by climbing a nearby tree or when they went to the provincial capital. After radio this was already the technology most commonly used by women in Manhiça.

With the use of landline phones declining owing to people's limited purchasing power, especially in the rural areas, and the rapid expansion of the mobile network (Muchanga and Mabila 2007), there seem to be two main reasons why even poor women find the mobile phone beneficial: its mobility, which means that they can save time, using it without having to abandon their workplaces; and the fact that their key contacts, clients or suppliers also have them – so they can interact directly rather than having to travel, leave messages or queue at a public phone at an agreed time to receive a call. The same is true regarding contact with family members in Mozambique and abroad.

At the time of our fieldwork the cost of inter-urban landline calls was still relatively high. Pre-paid mobile phone cards have no hidden costs, while owning a landline has a fixed monthly cost whether or not it is used, adding to the women's view that the cost of mobile phone use is compensated for by time, economic and social benefits, even though the landline phone booth was cheaper for local calls. Hence, the mobile phone is not simply replacing the landline, but is contributing to an exponential increase in the volume of voice communications. Although some of the activities described could be carried out through landlines, many could not, and most would be less efficient.

In Manhiça we found women whose husbands are working in South Africa communicating with them via mobile phone. The female sellers in the markets use mobile phones for business matters and to communicate with work colleagues. For example, market sellers of *xicadju* (fermented cashew juice) in Manhiça, who buy to resell, use mobile phones to tell their suppliers in Gaza Province that they need more stock, ending the need for long and sometimes fruitless journeys.

A representative of a women's organization in Manhiça told us that: 'For me, the cellular telephone is my feet, my work.' She uses the mobile phone to communicate with her members, wherever they are. We also found a woman who used her mobile phone to seek work – she could be contacted when a temporary job came up. Another Manhiça woman, who divides her time between the field and domestic work at home and has a family of ten, told us that when there is no food in the house, they use the mobile phone to contact relatives in South Africa to ask them to send food. Other women have opened small businesses selling pre-paid credit cards for mobile phone use. One interviewee makes a profit from her three phones, which helps to pay school fees and household expenses, while she also assists clients – mostly other women – by teaching them phone use or dialling for them.

Although most of the women we spoke with did not own mobile

phones, they shared the phones of family members and friends. For example, a *xicadju* seller in the market told us that sometimes her friends ask to make calls, send messages and *bips* (callback requests). Even though unable to send text messages, some illiterate women knew how to receive and make calls, and recognize a name on the phone contact list. Others did not even know how to dial a number, but used the phone by asking someone else to help. Those without mobile phones can ask their neighbours for help: 'I don't have a mobile and no one at home has one, but I keep the numbers of more distant relatives with me in case of emergency, when I will ask my neighbours to call them.' Interestingly, some who did not own mobile phones also mentioned the importance of being able to phone the police in the case of problems.

We (the researchers and women interviewed) find the use of mobile phones both socially and economically empowering. Socially, the mobility and flexibility of the mobile phone provides the capability to maintain regular contact with families regardless of distance; as a result, family links and support networks are strengthened. Also, through sharing phones women are reinforcing their unifying networks, while increased access to communication facilitates organization of collective activities and campaigns. In addition, the mobile phone is stimulating some women to learn minimal numeracy so that they can recognize and dial numbers, which could be a step towards literacy.

Mobile phones are also helping poor women to increase their incomes in various ways: cost-effective communications help their trading, while the emergence of a market in phone use has opened up a space for women to establish small businesses. Family contacts can also resolve economic problems, as when Manhiça women call South Africa to ask relatives for emergency food supplies.

Thus, through mobile phones women are enhancing their capacity to provide assets that help them resolve their major daily concerns, in a socio-economic process that increases their autonomy.

Promising tools – but less revolutionary in a rural context

ICT-related tools, namely computers, e-mail and the Internet, were essentially available in the telecentres or at a few workplaces (we did not find anyone among our interviewees who owned a computer); outside of the telecentres the only female users are a minority of educated women. It was surprising to find from the individual interviews, however, that even when women have access, they make little use of it at work because of 'lack of time'.

Around 31 per cent of the women we spoke to use computers, e-mail and the Internet. Users of these ICTs were mainly women who work in health, administrative services or non-governmental organizations, plus students, nuns and telecentre workers. This percentage is relatively high for a rural context, because we conducted our interviews mainly in the district capitals, where the public services and infrastructure are centred.

A prime example of use is by the women's organization representative in Manhiça: she uses the computer to prepare projects, and occasionally uses the Internet and e-mail, accessing all of these technologies through the telecentre. She recognizes that using the telecentre's services involves costs, but says that this is better than having no access to the technology. Her computer course took place in Maputo, where she travelled every day, but her children have learned at the telecentre since it was established.

Although we found women who had benefited from free computer training courses at the telecentres in each district, they were disappointed because the course had not helped them to get salaried work locally owing to the lack of jobs. Also, there had not been any follow-up enabling them to go on using the telecentres, which they could not afford from their own resources.

When we compared the telecentres' usage statistics with our own data, we found that the results coincided: on average at both centres two-thirds of visitors are male and one-third female. Moreover, the majority of clients (and particularly women) were there to get photocopies made or to use the public phone rather than to use the computers, Internet or e-mail. E-mail and Internet access has not yet won credibility due to its cost and unreliability.

Those who did not use these technologies at all gave many reasons, such as: 'they aren't for people like us'; in other words, a perception existed that uneducated or illiterate people, non-Portuguese speakers, women or poor people were automatically excluded from access to them. For others, while recognizing potential benefits such as learning new skills and access to information, they do not see the immediate material benefits. Therefore they would rather spend their time selling in the market. Among the reasons market sellers gave for non-use were 'no time', 'who will look after my stall?' or 'too expensive', but their essential argument was that they are absolutely obliged to focus on providing for their families' basic daily needs on a day-to-day basis and cannot think about anything that does not relate directly to that. They have not seen examples illustrating practical advantages for them of use of these technologies.

For most of the women in the districts visited, computers, e-mail and the Internet are not currently seen as increasing assets and abilities in the areas most valued, namely their survival and social issues. Computers do, however, help the relatively few women users to improve and professionalize aspects of their work.

Conclusion: lessons learned

When we began this research, we hoped to find that access to ICTs was contributing to the empowerment of rural women in Mozambique at some level, since we recognize that we ourselves have benefited from our opportunities to embrace the new technologies. Our findings confirm, however, that while the women involved in the study are making constructive use of the mobile phone and community radio, most rural women do not find computer-related ICTs (computers, e-mail and the Internet) particularly relevant or sufficiently useful to their immediate survival needs. In some cases these women are unaware of the possibilities of computer-related ICTs.

We respect the heavy responsibilities and never-ending workload faced by rural Mozambican women (and other poor women around the world), and have learned lessons from their rational methods for choosing priorities. We recognize that we cannot make generalized assumptions about needs and benefits based on our personal experience. It would also be wrong, however, to conclude that these women are unable or unwilling to make use of ICT owing to educational limitations, lack of vision or cultural constraints.

We find that women have already started appropriating the mobile phone, finding their own ways to overcome difficulties of literacy, language and costs, working together and using it as a tool for expanding their assets and capabilities with no need for technical training or back-up. Perhaps this is the best example of self-empowerment through utilizing new ICTs – which is not happening with computer-related ICTs, given the way they are presented to rural women. We are of the opinion that rural women cannot appropriate computer-related ICTs and consequently be empowered by them unless much more attention is given to making computer-related technologies and tools useful for them. These technologies are currently presented with limited content about issues relating to rural women's survival (e.g. information for small business and agriculture), and limited usability and mobility. If these factors were corrected, women might more easily use computer-related ICTs, within their constraints of time, money and skills. For rural women computer-related ICTs present limited communication facilities compared to mobile phones, which women can use to talk and exchange their daily worries concerning survival.

Changes need to be made in this society, where women are fighting for survival, otherwise the digital gender gap will grow. We said earlier that women are not being empowered by computer-related ICTs – not because they do not find the ICTs in the telecentres useful, but because they are fighting for socio-economic survival. Hence, improvement of their socio-economic conditions could help them to see technologies in other ways, and to become empowered. At this stage of development the women's absolute priority is tools that will increase their capabilities and their assets in the short term, by enabling them to work more efficiently, save time and costs, and achieve economic self-sufficiency for themselves and their households.

Our main conclusion is that when something responds to the actual needs of a group of people, it is appropriable by them. If computer-related ICTs were providing a real solution to rural women's immediate problems, they would have appropriated them and used them to strengthen their ability to solve problems, make decisions and choices, and take desired actions.

Recommendations: towards real ICT use and empowerment

Our conclusions are not new and our theory is ahead of our practice. We now understand better that in order for rural women to find computer-related ICTs empowering, it is not enough just to provide equipment. This means that the telecentre and other institutions involved in women's development and empowerment have to make great efforts to provide content in formats usable by rural women, by placing more emphasis on capabilities and socio-economic issues that rural women value. These issues include prices, agricultural production methods and family well-being. Creating other socio-economic conditions, such as the means for surviving, may help women to be able to give some of their time to making use of computer-related ICTs, and to be empowered by this use in a number of (not necessarily economic) ways.

We also recommend striving to put in place a reliable and efficient connectivity infrastructure to improve the performance of ICTs, and the integration of computer-related ICTs and other technologies to maximize the potential for each to facilitate women's pursuit of empowering conditions and realities. To increase accessibility relevant information and data provided through the Internet could be made available offline in the telecentres as well as via radio, in Portuguese and local languages; similarly, data communications via mobile phone can be promoted as the technology becomes available in the rural areas.

In addition, literacy is key – without literacy there can be no empowerment, particularly for women and girls (Sen 1999; Dighe and Reddi 2006). We therefore strongly recommend the improvement of women's literacy in rural areas. We believe that women's literacy, combined with increased relevance of content, could result in computer-related ICT tools becoming an asset to women's pursuit of the means for survival and for control of their lives.

References

Alsop, R., M. Bertelsen and J. Holland (2006) *Empowerment in Practice – from Analysis to Implementation*, Washington, DC: World Bank.

Bush, R. and J. Folger (1994) *The Promise of Mediation*, San Francisco, CA: Jossey-Bass.

Carnoy, M. (1975) 'The role of education in a strategy for social change', *Comparative Education Review*, 19(3).

Dighe, A. and U. Reddi (2006) *Women's Literacy and Information and Communication Technologies: Lessons that Experience Has Taught Us*, Commonwealth of Learning – Commonwealth Education Media Centre for Asia.

Fórum Mulher/SARDC WIDSAA (2005) *Beyond Inequalities 2005: Women in Mozambique*, Maputo and Harare: Fórum Mulher/SARDC.

Johnson, K. (2003) 'Telecentres and the gender dimension: an examination of how engendered telecentres are diffused in Africa', Unpublished MSc thesis, Georgetown University, Georgetown.

MAE (Ministério de Administração Estatal) (2005a) *Perfil do Distrito de Manhiça. Província de Maputo. Série Perfis Distritais*, Maputo: MAE.

— (2005b) *Perfil do Distrito de Sussundenga. Província de Manica. Série Perfis Distritais*, Maputo: MAE.

Muchanga, A. and F. Mabila (2007)

'2006 Mozambique telecommunications sector performance review', Unpublished report, Maputo: Universidade Eduardo Mondlane.

Norwegian Agency for Development Cooperation (1999) *Handbook in Gender and Empowerment Assessment*, www.norad.no/default. asp?V_ITEM_ID=967, accessed 29 March 2008.

Payton, F., L. Kvasny, V. Mbankn and A. Amadi (2007) 'Gendered perspectives on the digital divide IT education and workforce', Proceedings of the 9th International Conference on Social Implications of Computers in Developing Countries, São Paulo.

Sen, A. (1987) *On Ethics and Economics*, Oxford: Blackwell.

— (1992) *Inequality Re-examined*, Oxford: Oxford University Press.

— (1997) *On Economic Inequality*, Oxford: Oxford University Press.

— (1999) *Development as Freedom*, New York: Knopf.

— (2003) 'The importance of basic education', Full text of Amartya Sen's speech to the Commonwealth Education Conference, Edinburgh, available at: www. guardian.co.uk/education/2003/ oct/28/schools.uk4.

Sen, A. and M. Nussbaum (eds) (1993) *Capability and Well-being: The Quality of Life*, Oxford: Oxford University Press.

A tool for empowerment?

Sharma, U. (2003) *Women's Empowerment through Information Technology*, New Delhi: Authors' Press.

Stephen, A. (2006) *Communication Technologies and Women's Empowerment*, New Delhi: Rajat.

UNDP (2006) *Human Development Report 2006 – Beyond Scarcity: Power, Poverty and the Global Water Crisis*, New York: UNDP.

United Nations (2005) *Gender Equality and Empowerment of Women through ICT*, New York: Division for the Advancement of Women, Department of Economic and Social Affairs, United Nations.

World Bank (2002) *Empowerment and Poverty Reduction: A Sourcebook* (Draft), World Bank, siteresources. worldbank.org/intempowerment/ Resources/486312-1095094954594 /draft.pdf, accessed 31 March 2008.

3 | Considering ICT use when energy access is not secured: a case study from rural South Africa

JOCELYN MULLER

Background

There is growing interest in the role information and communication technologies (ICTs) can play in enhancing the effectiveness of poverty reduction programmes in the South and efforts to achieve the Millennium Development Goals. Literature often speaks of ICTs such as the Internet, for example, as the 'shining light' for developing countries (Gurumurthy 2004; World Bank 2004). Yet what is often overlooked is that an adequate energy supply is a prerequisite for the development potential of ICTs to be realized. The intention of this chapter is to explore what women in a small rural community in South Africa think are the limitations of and potential benefits that may be realized through the provision of energy services (using the mini-hybrid system) in relation to their access to and use of certain ICTs such as cell phones, radios and televisions.

Developing countries – and particularly rural people within these countries – suffer from a lack of investment in basic infrastructure and services, including energy provision. Power supply systems, which are essential for the use of most information technologies, rarely extend to rural areas; the trend over the last three decades has seen the number of people without electricity in rural areas in Africa doubling (and tripling in the urban areas) as a result of increasing urbanization (ITDG 2005). In fact, the International Energy Agency (IEA 2006) estimates that a total of US$200 billion worth of investments in electricity will be needed to help halve the number of people living on less than US$1 a day by 2015. Subsequently, in the rural hinterlands where poverty is still pervasive, people rarely benefit from the urban-based, technology-led ICT boom. Reaping the gains of the knowledge society is possible for some but close to impossible for the majority. The predicted 'trickle-down' effect remains elusive.

Women are the least likely to reap the gains of ICTs in sub-Saharan Africa, where the number of female-headed households varies between 50 per cent and 80 per cent of rural households as men migrate to urban centres seeking employment, leaving their wives behind (ITDG 2005). This is a double-edged sword in itself. The gendered division of labour means that a woman's domestic responsibilities, including caring for the sick, elderly and children, make it difficult for them to simply 'pick up and leave' for urban areas. This urban bias means that more men than women are likely to be exposed to ICTs (which are unavailable in rural areas); in addition, men have more purchasing power to buy or access the ICTs they wish to use. Women are therefore less likely to own ICTs such as TVs, cell phones and radios and instead use their income on meeting the household needs for food, clothing and other essentials.

An estimated 90 per cent of the rural population in Africa, of which most are women, remain without electricity. Women are therefore disproportionately affected by energy poverty, which renders them most vulnerable to subsequent impacts (Clancy and Khamati-Njema 2005). Hence, energy poverty and ICT poverty are genderized.

In the areas in Africa where people do have access to either conventional (e.g. coal-generated) or renewable energy sources, the quality of electricity supply from either conventional or renewable sources is often poor and unreliable owing to the failure of governments to invest in maintenance and servicing of the existing infrastructure (ITDG 2005). This limits the services and technologies that can be used. Linked to this factor is the fact that electricity is often unaffordable for poor households; this results in decisions to restrict the use of it to black-and-white TVs, radios and lighting instead of using electricity for energy-intensive thermal services like cooking and space heating. Illustrative of this is that per capita electricity consumption levels in Africa fell from 431 kWh to 112 kWh from 1980 to 2000, indicating unmet and suppressed demand which can mainly be attributed to increasing poverty levels (ibid.).

In response to global and regional concerns about the lack of modern energy services in most of Africa on the one hand, and the impact on the environment of the use of conventional energy sources (such as fossil fuels) on the other, renewable energy technologies have become increasingly recognized as an avenue to explore. None of the urgent gendered energy needs, however, such as fuel for cooking, space and water heating, can be solved by the renewable energy sources currently being deployed. Hence none of the problems related to the use of traditional energy sources – such as inefficient use of wood fuels, localized environmental emissions due to use of crop residues and animal waste as fuels and the adverse health effects of indoor smoke and time spent in collecting these fuels – are being addressed. Another factor hindering further deployment or penetration of renewable technologies is that the functional rate of renewable energy programmes is rarely assessed beyond the implementation and/or completion dates, and they often become white elephants (Villavicencio 2002).

Research context

This chapter arises from a participatory research journey in Lucingweni, a remote rural village in the Eastern Cape, South Africa. Local women took part in a process designed to capture their knowledge and values in relation to their energy and ICT priority needs and effect a shift in thinking, intended to reinforce the meaningful empowerment of women who are often relegated to subordinate positions in society (Hill 2003).

In Lucingweni a mini-grid hybrid system was commissioned in 2004 as a renewable energy rural electrification pilot project by the National Energy Regulator of South Africa (as mandated by the Department of Minerals and Energy) and installed by Shell Solar. The renewable energy system comprises a 50 kW array of Shell Solar 100W photovoltaic (PV) modules and 36 kW wind generators. Two hundred and twenty households in the village were connected to the system, allowing each the use of four lights, a radio, a television and a cell phone charger. The system was designed to provide a maximum of 1 amp with a daily limit of 1 kWh per twenty-four-hour period compared to approximately 6 kWh per month per household for the stand-alone solar home system. The average consumption of low-income households using conventional electricity is approximately 138 kWh per month. The mini-grid system was also intended to provide electricity for street lighting and water pumping. There is also a supply of 230V to two shops and a battery storage facility that was intended to support a community centre with communal ICT services.

The activities of the community centre would probably be extended to eventually become one of the government's Multi-Purpose Community Centres (MPCCs) as part of its integrated rural service delivery plan. MPCCs have been identified as the primary approach for the implementation of development through the provision of communication and information services to people to ensure that they have the resources required to support improved livelihoods. The mini-grid system was supposed to provide the electricity needed for an MPCC in Lucingweni.

In 2005 Lucingweni appeared to be the ideal site to investigate how the delivery of basic energy services from a renewable energy technology delivers access to ICTs in a remote rural setting. Upon my research team's initial site visit, however, it became apparent that the system has had a difficult history, which continues to this day. The community informed us that since the launch of the mini-grid in 2004 there had been a number of ongoing problems, including the unreliability of supply, inadequate maintenance and servicing support and a lack of local technological capability, as well as unavailability of components locally. Even during and after this research a number of problems have arisen, including the settling of ownership of the system among government departments, concerns of corruption and, to crown it all, in February 2007 extensive vandalism of the array of solar panels. It gradually became evident that the whole mini-grid experience in Lucingweni, launched with great expectations for development, had a very negative impact on the local community.

The research approach

It was within this complex context that our research into energy and ICTs for empowerment was conducted in South Africa. We adopted a people-centred development approach that hinged on the integration of energy, ICT and gender concepts in the research methodology (Eade 1997). We used participatory research methods, focus groups, free attitude interviews (FAI) (Buskens 2005a), the transformational attitude interview (TAI) (Buskens 2005b), as well as outcome mapping (OM) (Earl et al. 2001). All of these participatory methods were selected to create an empowering dialogue with and between the women who participated in the study. By following this approach we attempted to achieve a number of objectives:

- To introduce to the women participatory tools and techniques that explicitly build learning and reflection into their lives.
- To develop skills and confidence in the women to use certain qualitative and participatory methods and techniques.
- To offer a participatory methodology for the women to creatively integrate their vision for energy and ICTs, so that it reflects their values, needs and desires, individually and collectively.
- To develop the capacity of the women to use ICTs.

Initially the research team intended involving only women who had access to energy from the mini-grid system. Lucingweni consists, however, of six different villages, and the area that was electrified using the mini-grid constitutes only a fraction of the community. The community was insistent that the other villages should all be represented. The community then proceeded to elect one woman from each village to participate in our research project. The women participants selected were: Zanele Mangxa, Nontobeko Landule, Sindiswa Manipa, Sylvia Skwati, Nozamile Nkosini and Nothiswa Nkosini. This approach complemented the research as we were able to develop a broader understanding of the variations in perceptions of, access to and use of energy in the area and how this impacted on the use of ICTs in Lucingweni.

By telling their life stories and reflecting on their lived realities, the women involved expressed their perceptions of the effects that energy and certain ICTs have had on their lives (Mbilinyi 1992). The primary objective of the TAI process was for the women living in Lucingweni to communicate the ways in which they visualize energy and ICTs contributing towards an improvement in their livelihoods.

Defining key concepts and creating a vision

Before addressing the key issues relating to the development potential of energy and ICTs, it was important to spend time defining the concepts of energy and ICTs with the participants. This was an essential part of the empowerment process since drawing meaningful input from the participants was dependent upon them creating an understanding of the concepts and the related issues and options available before envisioning their energy and ICT development objectives.

Establishing the energy and ICT vision for development in Lucingweni

Following introductory discussions that focused on the concepts of energy and ICTs, a reflective process was introduced and repeated to enable the participants to define their individual and joint vision in relation to energy and ICT services in Lucingweni. They did this by reflecting on their lived realities of energy and ICT use and the perceived constraints to accomplishing the vision; further, they explored the potential strategies for overcoming the constraints. To determine the communities' energy priorities the participants were asked to imagine their 'energy dreams' as current reality – this process stimulated the women's creativity in imagining new possibilities, which inspired them to work towards a common vision. Each individual developed her own vision and then shared her ideas with her partners and the group. Individual visions became a shared vision. Their collective energy and ICT vision encapsulated the desire for a power supply that enables:

1. *Domestic activities*
- Cooking
- Boiling water
- Water pumping
- Lighting – including street lighting
- Charging cell phones
- Homework – lighting
- Radio
- Watching TV

2. *Community services*
- ICT centre with computers, faxing, e-mailing, printing, Internet access, typing, photocopying facilities
- Catering – school feeding scheme
- Invitations to community gatherings – using radio, writing letters, using SMS

3. *Small businesses*
- Spaza shops – public phones, lighting and refrigeration
- Hair salon
- Sewing group
- Farming fruit and vegetables – water pumping for irrigation
- Laundry facilities

Sylvia was able to reflect upon her core life-giving conditions and deliberate upon the aspects of her energy and ICT experiences that she most values and intends to enhance in the future. She expressed her desires saying that:

> If everything had to go my way I would like to have electricity so that I can play my radio, charge my phone and be able to cook. It would be easy for us to charge our phones if we had electricity.

In her photo journal Zanele reflected on her vision:

> When I was working on this dream I did not have a clear understanding of what was happening but now I can feel that I am about to succeed. I can see myself having an electricity and gas project and our schools having computers to teach our children. This is my dream and I am taking a photo standing next to it.

Creating a vision for the future is an exploratory experience, it involves exploring possibilities that are based on extraordinary moments founded on lived realities. Each woman who took part in the reflective processes of the research was challenged to envision a more valued future which was both practical, in that it was grounded in her own history, and generative, in that it recognized her existing capacities and then sought to expand her potential beyond the current perception.

What are the lived realities?

The women we worked with explored the inconsistencies between their dreams and their present living conditions by creating a map describing their current reality, and their internal and external constraints in relation to their dreams. Inner constraints are those factors that you can control or have influence over that prevent you from achieving your dreams, such as certain skills, behaviour and emotions. Outer constraints are those that you have very little or no control over, such as your socio-economic context, environment and gendered culture.

In Nozamile's photo journal she described her lived reality using cooking as an example, intermingling this with her gendered understanding of women as users and providers of energy, and wrote that:

> I took a photo of my neighbour cooking with black pots; when the food is ready she dishes out for her family. She is cooking with wood that she collected from the forest; the forest is very far but it is the way we live here at Lucingweni. We were born in this situation but we would like to improve the way we live if we can. We can see that the other areas are better than where we live. I wish that there could be light [electricity] here at Lucingweni.

Sindiswa was also able to make the distinction between the way that men and women used wood:

> Men can't make a fire using wood, they waste it by using more wood than what they need because they do not know that it takes long and it is difficult to collect wood.

The women's reflections supported the notion that the priority use of energy in households in developing countries is for cooking, followed by heating and lighting. Households in Lucingweni appear to follow this trend, and generally use a combination of energy sources for cooking broadly categorized as traditional (such as dung, agricultural residues and wood fuel), intermediate (such as kerosene) or modern (such as liquid petroleum, biogas, ethanol gel, plant oils, dimethyl ether and electricity). The service provided by the mini-grid in Lucingweni does not address these priority energy needs.

The women repeatedly interspersed their energy and ICT experiences with other basic priority needs:

> The water we have gets finished in the river in summer time even in the big rivers. We have taps and we thought that we would get water from this, but no progress has been made with the water project. We don't know what the problem is. The government has installed these water taps and pipes, but still we have no water.

This seasonality of water access leads to vulnerability and has caused many serious problems here in the past. During a feedback meeting this was emphasized:

Water is a problem. You find water that is not flowing, but we use it because there is no other alternative. We drink this water and cook with it. We have had a problem with cholera and it hit us hard here at Lucingweni. In the past two years people died from cholera and we had nurses coming with their tents as people were sick from drinking dirty water. We now boil water as the nurses have taught us that this is how we can stop cholera in the village. We boil this water using wood that we collect from the forest.

According to the women participants, the health crisis was exacerbated by the lack of accessible healthcare clinics, public transport and telephone services in the area. If development challenges are to be responded to in terms of urgency, energy (conventional or renewable) technologies in rural areas must be able to relieve these stresses.

The women consider the fact that the mini-grid supplies basic energy services to only 220 households discriminatory. While some women were said to complain of the problems with the mini-grid system, women like Nothiswa, who lived in other parts of the village, were upset because they had been excluded:

My village is not electrified and I hear people talking about this electricity [from the mini-grid system], saying that they do not like it. I wish that I had it in my village so that I can experience it myself and know what they are talking about.

Sylvia also said her part of the village did not have electricity and that:

We still have a difficult time when we want to charge our cell phones because you have to give [the phone] to someone that is going to town so that they can charge it for you and you have to pay them.

She also said, however, that households connected to the system hardly benefited anyway since the service was mainly used for lighting and the charging of cell phones only, and they were unable to use radios or televisions because they would need a special aerial, which most people could not afford:

A lot of people do have cell phones but the TVs are scarce. One needs an aerial to get a radio or TV connection.

Sindiswa complained about the unreliability of the energy supply. She said that on the occasions that the system was working, they were able to use it only for about two hours a day. According to the women these 'special' occasions hardly added up to more than six months of continuous use. When the community queried this with local staff employed by Shell Solar, who installed the system, or the local traditional leadership, they were told either that they were overusing the system and this had caused it to crash, or that certain components had failed and replacements were being imported.

On the occasions that the renewable energy system was working, Sindiswa acknowledged that many of the households connected to the system would use the electricity for cooking. One of the problems, according to her, is that

> this electricity is very weak. We were told that we could not cook with it but sometimes we were tempted, especially if one is tired of collecting wood. Some people bought hot-plate stoves and used them for cooking and this tripped the supply. We were not told if it was switched off because we used stoves or not.

This level of consumption exceeds the design capacity of the mini-grid. It seems the community has not been sufficiently informed about the system and the level of energy it supplies.

The mini-grid does provide opportunities for the use of certain ICTs. The women described how ICTs allow information to be disseminated more widely than before; cell phones, for instance, made it possible for them to talk to people sometimes thousands of kilometres away; television enabled them to see what was happening on the other side of the world (sometimes even almost as it happens), and the Internet, if they had access, would support immediate access to and exchange of information. Nothiswa expressed a keen sense of physical isolation, and felt that ICTs were key to accessing the public services and reducing her sense of isolation. This sense of isolation from services, markets, government institutions and information also led to the desire for roads to be built as a matter of urgency.

Through dialogue the women were able to recognize inequalities of ICT access and use. Nozamile explained how at first it was only men who had access to cell phones because they lived and worked in the urban centres (as her husband does). Historical, cultural and socio-economic disadvantages experienced by women result in their restricted access to resources that allow them to purchase items considered a 'luxury', such as cell phones. Their limited decision-making power is also a factor that requires consideration in terms of household purchases.

It was shown that, in spite of their difficulties, the women in Lucingweni did use ICTs such as cell phones to their benefit, and the renewable

41

energy programme there has promoted the uptake of cell phones and micro-enterprises for cell phone and battery charging. In fact Nozamile said that:

> My son charges cell phone batteries for people in the village, he does this by using energy from the [solar power, transferred to a car] battery and an inverter because we do not have electricity in this village.

The women proudly announced that they understood the cell phone technology better than men did – mainly because they did not have enough money to buy airtime so learnt how to send and receive text messages (SMS). Sindiswa remarked:

> The way I use my phone is different from the way the men use it. I like to SMS. Men do not like this and they do not know how to do it anyway. Men do not believe in this. They fear that the other person may not have money to respond to the message. Women become more knowledgeable in using the cell phone and they know most of the features because we don't have money to make calls.

One of the initial intentions for the renewable energy pilot project in Lucingweni was to establish a community centre as part of it. According to the women, the contractor promised to build an ICT centre. Nozamile said that:

> The village was promised by the contractor that he would build a structure which would have computers for the village, but this did not happen, instead a small structure in the form of a hall was built but there were no computers in sight.

The centre would have had communal ICT facilities, which Nontobeko was keen to access. She wanted to learn computer skills and was of the opinion that this would increase her chances of employment. She realized that access to ICTs could enhance and develop her capacity.

Conclusion

While energy itself is not considered a basic need, it is a precondition for basic needs to be met. Basic needs are understood as the minimal requirements to sustain life, such as food security, accessible health-care, availability of clean water, and adequate sanitation facilities. They also include the ability to access education and information that allow individuals and communities to make productive use of the available basic goods and services. It became evident that the renewable energy programme in Lucingweni has never really benefited the rural households in the manner described or anticipated, particularly not in relation to the basic needs expressed by the women we spoke with.

It has also become clearer that access to new ICTs is still a faraway reality for the vast majority of people, such as the women involved in the research. Lack of provision of basic infrastructure and services hampers deployment of ICTs. The lack of adequate, reliable and appropriate energy sources in particular impedes access to and use of ICTs. A computer needs electricity to operate, and so do televisions and the Internet. With the current electrification levels in Africa, the potential of ICTs to play a substantial developnent role will remain limited.

References

Buskens, I. (2005a) 'The free attitude interview manual', GRACE Methodology Workshop, 9–21 July, Khaya Lembali, Durban, www.GRACE-Network.net.

— (2005b) 'Transformational attitude interview', GRACE Methodology Workshop, 9–21 July, Khaya Lembali, Durban, www.GRACE-Network.net.

Clancy, J. and B. Khamati-Njenga (2005) 'Concepts and issues in gender and energy', Energia in cooperation with ETC Netherlands, pp. 1–78.

Eade, D. (1997) *Capacity Building: An Approach to People-centred Development*, Oxfam.

Earl, S., F. Carden and T. Smutylo (2001) *Outcome Mapping: Building Learning and Reflection into Development Programs*, Ottawa: International Development Research Centre.

Gurumurthy, A. (2004) 'Gender and ICTs: overview report', Brighton: IDS.

Hill, M. (2003) 'Development as empowerment', *Feminist Economics*, 9: 117–35.

IEA (International Energy Agency) (2006) 'World energy outlook 2006', Paris: IEA/OECD.

ITDG (2005) 'Energising poverty reduction in Africa: Europe's chance to help light up Africa', Practical Action.

Mbilinyi, M. (1992) 'Research methodologies in gender issues', in R. Meena (ed.), *Gender Theoretical Issues*, Harare: SAPES, pp. 31–70.

Villavicencio, A. (2002) 'Sustainable energy development: the case of photovoltaic home systems', Discussion paper, Roskilde: UNEP/Risoe.

World Bank (2004) 'Engendering information and communication technologies: challenges and opportunities for gender-equitable development', Washington, DC: Gender and Development Group and Global Information and Communication Technologies Departments, World Bank, www.worldbank.org/gender/digitaldivide/ict_brochure.pdf, accessed August 2008.

4 | Rural women's use of cell phones to meet their communication needs: a study from northern Nigeria

KAZANKA COMFORT AND JOHN DADA

This research is an attempt to understand how rural women in northern Nigeria use mobile phones to meet their communication needs. The global trend in mobile phone technology development presents a mixed blessing for women's empowerment, its use contributing to both integration and fragmentation of existing family structures. This research aimed to identify the challenges and benefits rural women in northern Nigeria face when they adopt the use of mobile phones. This focus helped us also to gain insight into how the lack of access affected the way in which the women met their communication needs.

Gender disparity is very easily observable in the ownership of, access to and use of mobile phones. This research is crucial at this point since it helps to identify how women in this part of Nigeria are involved in the much-publicized mobile phone 'explosion' in the country.

Women who live in rural areas are at a particular disadvantage in the digital world, facing multiple barriers relating to both gender and location. Their roles are found more at the consumer end of the information technology chain (Mulama 2007). The challenges of managing a rural household create a heavy daily workload for women, leaving them with hardly any spare time to become familiar with new technologies.

In Nigeria women represent the majority of the rural poor (up to 70 per cent), and they play a major role in the survival strategies of rural households. Nigeria ranks 139th out of 157 countries on the Human Poverty Index; out of 108 developing countries, Nigeria ranks 80th. It also ranked 139th out of 157 countries for the Gender-related Development Index (UNDP 2007). As subsistence farmers, Nigerian women are fully involved in agricultural production, harvesting, storage and marketing, yet their purchasing power parity remains at US$652, whereas in males it is US$1,592 (ibid.).

The catalytic role of information and communication technologies (ICTs) in facilitating development for the world's poor and marginalized people is widely recognized (SDC 2005). For example, women in the hand-woven textile sector in southern Nigeria felt that mobile phones facilitated their businesses (Jagun et al. 2007). In Bangladesh, women were the main beneficiaries of a Rural Information Helpline, both as service providers and as users (Raihan 2007). In rural Nigeria, however, ICT has acquired a social status that tends to emphasize existing gender inequalities. For example, for a long time the transistor radio has been a status symbol for the rural man, and he usually makes the purchase of batteries for his radio a priority above household necessities. The same attitude is seen in ownership and use of mobile phones by men in particular. Women's special responsibilities for children and the elderly mean that women typically cannot migrate to towns and cities as easily as men; this is where opportunities to learn about new technologies are more readily available.

ICT is therefore rapidly becoming one more signifier of the gender gap between men and women, with women having restricted access to ICT resources and opportunities (Wakunuma 2006; Mulama 2007).

Context of the study

Nigeria has witnessed massive growth in subscriber lines, from fewer than 25,000 analogue mobile lines in May 2000, to 45,536,231 in 2007. Nigeria had 8 million Internet users in September 2007, comprising 5.9 per cent of the population (Internet World Stats n.d.). These data, however, are not desegregated to reflect the slow progress in rural areas or women's access to these new facilities. This phenomenal growth has been in spite of the high cost of mobile phones; it costs the average user about US$600 per year, which is almost twice Nigeria's per capita GDP.

Of Nigeria's 140 million people, over 70 per cent live in rural communities where there are neither landline telephones nor electricity. Thanks to the low cost and long range of the cellular base stations, however, many rural areas receive some cell phone coverage. It is this fortuitous coverage which first brought some connectivity to a couple of rural villages in the Kafanchan area. By the end of 2005 two mobile phone service providers, Celtel and MTN, had set up base stations in Kafanchan, which led to an explosion in the number of users of mobile phones.

In contrast, efforts that started five years ago to reactivate landlines are yet to bear fruit. When the landlines were available, the cost of installation was such that they were largely used by government departments and in the homes of upper- and middle-class citizens, while public access was erratically available in selected locations. For some of the women who participated in this research, their only experience of a landline phone is that they have seen them – but they have never seen them work. The

Rural women's use of cell phones

absence of landlines in most parts of Nigeria has left a huge gap, which is now being filled by the mobile phone.

Part of the reason for the phenomenal growth in mobile phone use is the strong oral culture in Nigeria and the population's low literacy level, coupled with the absence of digitization of many Nigerian languages (Gardener 1994; UNICEF 2005). The Fantsuam Foundation is working on localization (Zitt Localization Project n.d.) of five of the minority languages of the Kafanchan area. Making these languages available in a digital format will also make them effective for text messaging (SMS).

The use of mobile phones to send text messages has been found to be 'easy, cheap and popular, and people can have access to information which is anonymous and discreet – particularly in rural areas of South Africa where stigma (HIV/AIDS) is still an obstacle to disclosure and openness' (Shackleton 2007: 6). When dealing with populations where there is low literacy and where the first language has not yet been digitized, however, this affordable facility becomes inaccessible.

Research methodology

The Fantsuam Foundation conducted this research in Kafanchan, Nigeria. Fantsuam has a thriving microfinance service for rural women farmers, and they were the partners for this project. The research team comprised microfinance field officers and ICT instructors from Fantsuam Academy.

Clients of the Fantsuam Foundation's microfinance programme were informed of the research, and those communities that were more easily accessible by road during the study period and which indicated interest were shortlisted for participation. There were thirteen participating communities: Zikpak, Ungwa Masara, Bayanloco, Garaje3, Fadan Kagoro, Kpunyai, Ungwa Rimi, Chenchuk, Zakwa, Yantuwo, Orire, Katsit and Zumunta. A total of 160 women participated.

This project used the following research methods: free call sessions, baseline information collection, focus group discussions, semi-structured interviews, self-reflection and questionnaires. These qualitative research methods were selected to ensure adequate coverage, recognition and documentation of the participants' experiences. The multiple-methods approach improved the reliability of the findings and provided opportunities for triangulation. The bulk of the research was conducted in the most widely spoken local language, Hausa. This made for rapid establishment of rapport and better appreciation of the group dynamics and non-verbal communications.

Findings: mobile phones bring mixed blessings

The lack of landlines in the research communities made the arrival of mobile phone services a desirable and welcome development. The various women's groups we met with pointed out the immediate advantages, especially how it helped them meet their communication needs. As the research went on, however, issues and observations were made which reduced the initially high rating of the positive value of mobile phones. It gradually became clear that mobile phones actually presented mixed blessings to our research participants.

Instant communication

In the rural communities studied there is high morbidity and mortality due to HIV/AIDS. Cell phones provide a reliable and quick means of informing distant relatives and ease some of the anxiety associated with funeral arrangements and related matters.

Mobile phones are expensive to run

The tariff system of the mobile phone network is highly exploitative. Owing to poor signal coverage in some areas, users can waste precious money trying to get connected. They get charged even when they do not succeed in getting connected. In addition, when the mobile phones were first introduced, top-up cards had a lifespan of only fifteen days; if not used within this period they lapsed, and more money had to be spent on a new top-up card. When a woman has to spend her last naira to make a call to distant relatives to request a remittance, and yet cannot get her message through because of poor GSM (Global System/Standard for Mobile) coverage, she feels cheated since she is forced to pay for the call.

Tariffs were a sore point for most of the women. For those who were able to pass on the cost of such tariffs to customers or distant relations, it was a necessary cost. The pricing regime of some service providers does not take account of the fact that some calls do not get to their destinations. This means that 'Hajo', one of our project participants, has to pay the full cost of an unsuccessful call, even when she had to borrow money to make that call. This makes the cost of meeting her communication needs higher than she anticipated: 'When I borrow money to pay for a phone call to my son, so that he can send me some money, and the phone call does not go through, and I am still charged for the call, that cannot be right, can it?'

Poor quality of mobile phone services sometimes makes their use frustrating. On occasion the service providers may offer no service at all, or very poor reception for days, and no explanation or apologies are given to the users. During periods of poor service (poor GSM signal reception leading to low voice quality) the units on the call cards are still debited, making it a double loss for the user.

These phones are also expensive to own

Affordability was a key concern for many of the women in this research project. Attempts by the women to get self-selected groups of six or seven women to share one phone ran into hitches. There were other communities, however, such as Kwoi, Kagoro and Zonkwa, where each woman could afford the cost of a mobile phone on her own – but they had no GSM signal coverage. The major mobile phone providers had not extended their services to these communities at the time of the research. This again illustrates that Nigeria is a fast-growing mobile phone market: at the moment demand far outstrips supply.

The women in places like Zikpak, Ungwa Rimi, Orire and Chenchuk had access and could afford the tariffs, and for them the mobile phone has become an indispensable tool in meeting their daily communication needs for family and business purposes.

We observed that the women's groups that had ready access to networks and could afford to use the mobile phones to meet their communication needs were typically located in semi-urban communities where there were more income-generating opportunities. These women therefore had a higher level of disposable income.

The issue of affordability has to be understood in the context of the women's household budgets. Although this study did not explore household budget allocation patterns, Banerjee and Duflo's (2006) study of the consumption patterns of the poor in sixteen countries revealed that a significant amount was spent on non-food items such as alcohol and festivals. Ceremonies are a regular feature in the lives of the communities in our study, and some of the communication needs identified were requests for remittance in order to host or participate in such ceremonies.

The interactive sessions during the focus group discussions afforded the women participants opportunities to access information that could be beneficial to their livelihoods. Invariably their requests for clarification started with 'Is it true that ...?', and were usually about issues that the women had heard about fleetingly as their husbands discussed them, or from other sources. An interesting request was on the issue of climate change; one woman wanted to know whether it was true that the recent late arrival and early departure of the rains had anything to do with the loss of forests to illegal mining activities. This question illustrates the impact of a global phenomenon on the livelihood of this female farmer. It also indicates that while the mobile phones may have been meeting some of the women's communication needs, they were not meeting their information needs.

Household budget versus phone top-ups

Some women complained to the research team that their husbands would rather spend money to buy top-up credits for their mobile phones than give such money for household expenses. The meagre family income now has stiff competition from the need to buy top-ups for phone credits.

Current tariffs are rather stiff, and this expense plays a mixed role in exacerbating the economic and power differentials within a household. Accusations of a spouse using meagre family income to pay for phone calls were made by both sexes, although we heard more from women since our research dealt with women. There were, however, women who mentioned that some of their friends also had spending priorities comparable to those of some men when it came to this use of limited family finances.

In a circumscribed space mobile phones can enhance sense of control

The local interpretation of the religious requirement of purdah places constraints on the 'acceptable space' for a woman; for example, it is necessary for some Muslim women who wish to engage in certain business transactions to have the services of a third party. Access to a mobile phone now makes it possible for these women to have direct links with their business partners without compromising their purdah status: 'With this handset, I am less dependent on third parties for my business as I can now talk directly to my customers.'

Face-to-face communication preferred

Mobile phones provide a cheaper way to stay in touch with distant relatives than travelling to see them. In closely knit communities, however, where a premium is placed on face-to-face communication, the mobile phone is seen as a threat to cohesion. One participant expressed it this way: 'I can hear his voice all right, but I need to see his face to be sure he understands what I said. This mobile thing seems to increase his distance from home.'

This 'distance' and sense of isolation is felt more keenly when voice quality is poor (as is often the case) or when calls do not go through.

'Each time after talking to my son, who lives in the UK, on a mobile phone, I feel as if something is missing in our conversation.' The initial relief this participant feels at the first sound of the voice of a relative who is far away is soon cut short 'because talking with someone you do not see is not a good conversation'.

The substitution of phone calls for the usual face-to-face communication can be disadvantageous for a culture that believes that 'speech is in the face'. This Nigerian proverb gives precedence to face-to-face communication over the voice-only communication that mobile phones provide. The gradual loosening of the traditional close family ties, however, as members seek economic pastures far from home, makes the mobile phone a 'better than nothing' option.

The groups of women who participated in the study generally acknowledged the economic value of faster contacts for business transactions through the use of mobile phones and remittances. The shrinkage of time and space brought about by this technology, however, as well as its replacement of face-to-face contacts within the extended family system, was a cause of worry for the group of women in Chenchuk. The concern was that the close bonds of the extended family that serve as a safety net and source of mutual assistance may be adversely affected by the constant use of mobile phones.

While it is relatively cheaper to stay in touch by phone, a phone conversation (especially when it has to be done with an eye on the tariff) is emotionally unsatisfactory. One woman said that she is unable to engage in meaningful conversation for the amount of money she can afford for such calls. For people who have such a strong oral culture, a good conversation necessarily takes longer. The resultant feeling of isolation was disempowering for these women.

Hence, a technology that has such great potential for economic empowerment, as in the case of the Muslim women partners in this research, also has a potentially emotionally destabilizing effect. The isolating impact of such a technology can be significant in closely knit communities where mutual dependence is the means of communal survival. With women as the bond that keeps many rural communities intact, the impact of this technology on their sense of self-worth and well-being must be taken into consideration.

Phone top-ups used as remittances

Mobile phones are increasingly being used to send small amounts of money to friends and relations. Some of the participants use them to send pocket and travel money to their children who attend schools far from home. They buy airtime and send a code that can be redeemed for cash at a roadside mobile phone kiosk.

The potential of using the mobile phone remittance system to make larger purchases is already being explored by second-hand car dealers, who try to avoid carrying large sums of money with them. The cashless society seems to be coming to rural Nigeria as an unplanned and unforeseen consequence of this technology.

Roadside phone kiosks bring in extra earnings

For some participants who provide a phone service for a fee, this is a useful source of income. They also charge a commission for remittances sent through their service.

Assas is an example of a woman who has increased her earnings by starting a phone service and deciding which type of phone to use for her call business. Assas's entrepreneurial initiative can be traced to the free phone calls the women participants were offered at the beginning of this research. Giving the women a phone to use in this way meant giving them a phone connection. It is important to emphasize that it is not the mobile aspect of the phone which was being tested, but rather the impact of access to any phone. This was demonstrated when Assas heard that her competitor had signed up for a newly proposed landline. She came to the Fantsuam Foundation to negotiate a new loan so that she could also register for this new service. She has already lost a number of her customers to her competitor, who is promising to provide cheaper calls through the new franchise agreement.

Assas is the breadwinner for her family and has five children and her parents to look after. Her call centre business is in addition to her day job as an ICT instructor teaching basic computer literacy. Safiya, on the other hand, as a user of phone services, has to undertake a long and difficult 15-kilometre journey by motorcycle taxi from her village to a highway phone kiosk, where she can make and receive calls. She needs to make these calls as part of a part-time job that supplements her income from manual farm work. The cost and travel time and possibility of poor voice signal reception at the roadside kiosk all add to Safiya's costs in meeting her communication needs.

It is cheap, but not accessible: text messaging

The SMS feature that makes mobile phones affordable was hardly used by participants, owing largely to low literacy capacities and a cultural preference for verbal communication. The number of languages used by these communities further compounded the issue of low literacy.

While the most commonly used language for economic and everyday external transactions was Hausa, most of the women would use their own languages, such as Jju, Atyap, Gworok or Fantsuam, when having discussions with family members and friends. Mobile phones therefore presented opportunities for them to speak in their first languages, whereas text messaging required that they should be literate, whether in Hausa or their own language.

Mere ownership of mobile phones without the ability or opportunity to use the SMS option in their own languages makes this technology still largely inaccessible and expensive for the illiterate rural women of northern Nigeria.

Conclusion

The research questions focused on the way in which rural women in northern Nigeria make use of the phone to meet their communication needs. The global trend in mobile phone technology development presents a mixed blessing for women's empowerment, having both integrating and fragmenting effects on existing family structures.

The research established that:

- Mobile phones provide coverage for these communities, which do not have landlines.
- Ownership and use of mobile phones entail high costs that make accessibility difficult.
- A cheap feature of the mobile phone, text messaging, was not readily accessible to most of the participants.
- The technology can cause conflict in families when a spouse spends money on their cell phone even when there are other urgent household needs.
- Access to mobile phones can be economically empowering for women.
- It can also weaken the bonds in traditionally closely knit communities when a phone call replaces face-to-face communication.

The qualitative nature of the research – the in-depth interviews, reflections on the transcribed responses and recollection of the women's emotional responses – was important in opening our (the research team's) eyes to the various issues, and showing things in a new light. The daily struggle just to provide the necessities of life is taken for granted; everybody just gets on with the struggle because that is the way they have always lived. The additional challenge caused by access/non-access to mobile phones has blended into the daily routine of various struggles.

The qualitative research processes enabled the research team members to step back a little and tease out this additional layer in the daily struggle that arrived in the form of a device called a mobile phone.

How and why should a device that could make life easier end up in some situations becoming almost an additional burden? The mobile phone, which should make remittance from friends and families in urban centres easier, is not readily accessible, or is only available at a steep cost – and not all its effects are positive.

In terms of cost, some service providers do not take into account the cost of calls that do not get to their destinations. This situation may have been caused by a software configuration that does not distinguish between successful and unsuccessful calls, and will require the service providers to review their billing systems.

There is no strong in-country lobby to counter the exploitative practices of service providers in relation to reception and tariffs. A recent court directive telling the providers to make a cash refund to customers was yet to be implemented four months after the ruling. As the Consumer Affairs Movement of Nigeria (CAMON) stated: 'what is happening in Nigeria at present regarding GSM services is exploitation of vulnerable consumers by GSM service providers' (2004: 2).

Our research supports the opinion of Mulama (2007: 5) from Nairobi, Kenya, when she observed that 'the benefits of ICTs are largely restricted to towns and cities, as most rural areas lack the infrastructure, equipment and skills needed for communities to take full advantage of these technologies'. The phones raised expectations in terms of meeting needs, but lack of affordable access made the realization of these expectations very difficult.

The 2006 Global Gender Gap Index, which assessed 115 countries, ranked Nigeria at number 94 (Hausmann et al. 2006: 17). Although the ranking was based on only four broad areas (economic participation and opportunity, educational attainment, health and survival, and political empowerment), the findings support the experiences of most of the women in this research. For these rural women gender-defined roles and responsibilities constitute significant constraints on their access to the resources and opportunities available through cell phone use. This is not underestimating the impact of other cultural factors that may not be directly gender related, such as preferential allocation of scarce household budgets to festivals rather than to meeting communication needs.

This exploration of how women in rural Nigeria use mobile phones to meet their communication needs has, among other things, revealed how global trends and technologies can have an immediate and significant impact at a local level. The research also found that women would give preference to their family roles and needs over and above their use of ICT: when the family needs time or money, and these are resources they can provide, women will drop their cell phone use.

Although mobile phones can be used for income generation and thus contribute to the economic empowerment of women, their use can also weaken the bonds in traditionally close-knit communities when users replace opportunities for face-to-face communication with a phone call. The SMS feature that makes mobile phone use affordable was hardly used by the research participants, owing largely to low literacy capacities and a cultural preference for verbal communication.

Thus, our investigation showed that ICTs do not automatically serve the communication needs of women – especially rural women. Mere ownership of mobile phones without the ability or opportunity to make use of an affordable technique such as SMS keeps this technology largely inaccessible and overly expensive for the rural women of northern Nigeria. The mobile phone therefore presents a mixed bag of positive and negative values and impacts. It is clearly not a panacea for all communication needs, although it has become an avenue to upward social and economic mobility for some women.

The sequel to this research will therefore be the provision of training for various women's groups on how to send and receive SMS, in their preferred languages, keeping the messages as simple as possible. This training will aim to empower even those women with low literacy abilities, so that they can begin to use SMS to meet some of their communication needs.

The emotionally destabilizing effect of mobile phones on close-knit communities requires more investigation.

References

Banerjee, A. V. and E. Duflo (2006) *The Economic Lives of the Poor*, Cambridge, MA: Abdul Latif Jameel Poverty Action Lab, Massachusetts Institute of Technology.

CAMON (2004) *Consumer Link*, Monthly bulletin of the Consumer Affairs Movement of Nigeria (CAMON) Centre for Consumer Protection, Competition, Trade, Environment and Sustainable Development, 1(1) July.

Fantsuam Foundation (n.d.) www.fantsuam.org, accessed 20 August 2008.

Gardener, L. C. (1994) *Nigerian Literature: Oral and Written Traditions*, www.usp.nus.edu.sg/post/nigeria/orality.html, accessed 3 October 2007.

Hausmann, R., L. D. Tyson and S. Zahidi (2006) *The Global Gender Gap Report*, Geneva: World Economic Forum.

Hopetun, S. D. and L. Dunn (2006) 'Mobile opportunities: poverty and telephony access in Latin America and the Caribbean', *Genderstanding Mobile Telephony. Women, Men and Their Use of the Cellular Phones in the Caribbean*, Background paper, Mona: International Development Research Centre.

Internet World Stats (n.d.) *Usage and Population Statistics*, www.internetworldstats.com/africa.htm#ng, accessed 19 August 2008.

Jagun, A., R. Heeks and J. Whalley (2007) *Mobile Telephony and Developing Country Micro-Enterprise*, Development Informatics Working Papers, IDPM, University of Manchester, www.sed.manchester.ac.uk/idpm/research/publications/wp/di/index.htm#wp, accessed 9 January 2008.

Mangha, E. T. (2005) *ICT and the Education of the Girl Child*, Paper presented at the African Regional Preparatory Meeting, Abuja, 3–7 July.

Mulama, J. (2007) *A Rural–Urban Digital Divide Challenges Women*, Inter Press Service, 15 February, www.ipsnews.net/, accessed 29 December 2008.

Raihan, A. (2007) *Livelihood Case Studies*, Development Research Network, www.pallitathya.org/en/case_studies/index.html, accessed 27 December 2007.

SDC (Swiss Agency for Development and Cooperation) (2005) *SDC ICT4D Strategy*.

Shackleton, S.-J. (2007) *Women'snet. Rapid Assessment of Cell Phones for Development*, Commissioned by UNICEF, Johannesburg: Newton.

UNICEF (2005) *At a Glance, Nigeria Statistics*, www.unicef.org/infoby country/nigeria_statistics.html, accessed 12 July 2007.

UNDP (United Nations Development Programmme) (2007) *Human Development Report 2007/2008*, Basingstoke: Palgrave Macmillan.

Wakunuma, K. J. (2006) *The Internet and Mobile Telephony: Implications for Women's Development and Empowerment in Zambia, Gender, ICTs and Development*, www.womenictenterprise.org/manworkshop.htm, accessed 23 January 2008.

Zitt Localization Project (n.d.) zitt.sourceforge.net/zitt.php?su=eng&ibe=2&PHPSESSID=c8e5d7d2f5d0d083f930e7a9962fe383, accessed 20 August 2008.

5 | Egyptian women artisans facing the demands of modern markets: caught between a rock and a hard place

LEILA HASSANIN

Many of Egypt's female artisans only produce crafts and are not involved in the selling process; they receive only a slim slice of the profits made in the sale of their wares. ArabDev (see www.arabdev.com), an information and communication technologies for development (ICT4D) organization working in Egypt, has been promoting the use of the Internet among low-income groups throughout Egypt, with a special focus on women. Several women in the training courses began asking whether ArabDev could assist them in selling their goods online. The women and various supporting non-governmental organizations (NGOs) wanted to explore this option as a way to improve their earnings.

Donors and development agencies supporting income-generating activities have been focusing on micro- and small enterprises as a tool for poverty alleviation in Egypt for years. According to this trend, development specialists believe that women benefit from becoming entrepreneurs – but are the conditions for this entrepreneur-oriented model realistic? Is 'entrepreneurship' a learnable skill for most women? Or are some key factors that are needed to make this entrepreneurship model a reality missing? To be effective, do entrepreneurship, self-sufficiency and a 'can make it' attitude need certain contextual circumstances that recognize the constraints that lower-income and lower-educated women face (Mueller 2006; Ofreneo 2006)?

Further, is globalization an economic opportunity for Egyptian women involved in handicrafts? Are global markets a realistic vending place for the crafts that Egyptian women produce – or are they in fact a barrier, increasing the socio-economic inequalities that these women face?

My examination of the potential use of the Internet to market women's handicrafts is in anticipation of the institutionalization of e-commerce in Egypt in the coming years, although an exact date for this has not yet been set by government. Currently the Information Technology Industry Development Agency (ITIDA) is responsible for setting up electronic systems needed for buying and selling online. Electronic-signature systems were established in 2005, paving the way for e-commerce. The electronic authentication of signatures is essential for e-financial transactions.

Despite the interest of artisan women in online marketing, I found that those I interviewed did not make substantial use of ICT. In fact, it became obvious that ICT constituted a new set of limitations, inequities and barriers that craftswomen are facing. It also became apparent that ICT is only a small part of the handicraft marketing cycle, and that there are other fundamentals in the production and marketing process that are hindering export of Egyptian handicrafts. The female artisans' main barrier to success in their micro-businesses is the low level of demand for Egyptian crafts in the domestic market. An Egyptian market for their crafts would make it more realistic for craftswomen to establish independent businesses. Local markets would make the use of ICT for marketing viable for some of the artisan women.

Methodology

Analysis in this chapter is based on the situations of artisan women and organizations working in the crafts sector. To gain an overall understanding of the requirements for online commerce, I also reviewed the regulatory and transport issues involved in crafts export, and made a quick market analysis of the national and international craft business as far as this relates to the female handicraft sector in Egypt. The central question is whether Egyptian crafts – in this case crafts produced and marketed by females – are marketable and competitive globally, and can therefore bring in sufficient income to cover expenses and generate profits. Further, could use of the Internet remove some of the existing trade barriers and the monopoly of intermediaries who are currently taking a sizeable portion of the craft trade profits away from the producers?

I did not plan to extend the study beyond Egypt, but to comprehend the conditions necessary for successful e-commerce for Egyptian craftswomen, it became essential to understand the overarching dynamics of the international crafts market. I visited the New York Gift Fair, a major global crafts exhibit, as an example of the global artisan market.

The female artisans

Ten women from different regions of Egypt were interviewed during 2005/06. Varying geographical locations were chosen to encompass some of the multiple cultures in the society. The research includes interviewees from Cairo, the community of Coptic solid waste collectors ('Zabaleen') in Old Cairo, Siwa, Aswan and Helwan, an industrial district south of Cairo. In addition to the craftswomen, some of the related NGOs' staff were interviewed, the major NGOs being El Bashayer, COSPE-supported women cooperatives (COSPE is part of the Italian Cooperation Agency in Egypt), the Association for the Protection of the Environment, and crafts associations supported by ArabDev.

Egyptian society is predominantly Muslim, with a Coptic minority. Muslim and Coptic craftswomen were included; women from both religions did not differ with regard to the focus of this chapter, and in both communities women are subject to the same traditional, patriarchal norms. Nubian and Siwan women were also included, since they have distinct traditional crafts and historical backgrounds.

The women's education attainments ranged from university degrees to diplomas gained by those who, through adult education programmes, had moved themselves beyond their initial illiteracy. The interviewees' ages ranged from eighteen to fifty-three. They ranged from single women to those who were married, married with children, and separated. Financially some of the women co-financed their households, and one woman was the main provider for herself and her two children.

Findings

The combination of crafts and ICT skill and use is rare There are few examples where craftswomen are directly involved in marketing their wares through the Internet in Egypt. Even mobile phones are not a tool commonly used by women in the marketing cycle. There are also very few cases where artisan women have experience with both handicrafts and information technology. Those who do are the exception rather than the rule.

One woman doing crochet at El Bashayer said that she had tried the Internet for new design ideas. A candle-maker in Helwan said she goes online to explore ideas for her products. In Siwa, a computer trainer from a local development organization who works at the local school continues to do traditional Siwan stitching in the evenings for additional income. Yet she does not combine her artisan work with her IT skills. Overall, examples of craftswomen using ICT were few, and certainly not the norm.

Craft production abandoned for ICT office jobs I began with the premise that ICT could offer access to wider markets and higher profit retention for Egyptian craftswomen. The research revealed, however, gaps in design, production and quality, which determine the competitiveness (or lack of it) of Egyptian handicrafts – and these have a greater impact on sales than the use of ICT for marketing.

The Internet has none the less been a resource for some of the women I spoke to. Among those women interviewed who did utilize ICT, several were formerly craftspeople who furthered their education, including computer and Internet skills, and subsequently changed their income-earning source to a clerical job. Craft production is often abandoned once a woman has marketable ICT skills; more income can be earned through clerical work than through handicrafts. Some craftswomen who made it 'up the ladder' through additional education became supervisors for other craftswomen, but stopped their direct production of crafts.

Exporting Egyptian crafts The difficulties facing women artisans and women involved in the crafts trade in terms of exporting Egyptian crafts competitively to global markets involve, among the many requirements for a successful export trade: literacy, language skills, technical know-how, knowledge of how to navigate the regulatory and legal aspects of the export trade, quality control, transport requirements, and availability of e-commerce.

Poor quality of craft products Most products bought from the craftswomen are not immediately sellable owing to their poor finish. The merchants are finishing many of the products themselves and reaping wide margins of profit by doing this. For example, they will take an exquisite but frayed piece of stitching, line it and sew the edges, and the piece will sell at a much higher price.

COSPE-trained Siwan women artisans in quality improvements, such as finishing techniques, without success. Most women claimed not to be able to clean up their embroidery because of their many household duties.

Low demand for craft and craft themes in the Egyptian market In Egypt there is not much daily demand for locally made crafts, other than for the simple, inexpensive crafts used by lower-income Egyptians (such as pottery urns for water, palm-reed baskets and ironwork used in rural areas). These types of crafts are not covered in this chapter since they fall into the category of objects used daily by the average Egyptian which have a slim profit margin, and are not marketable in their present form to other market niches. Most women interviewed are involved in crafts that are more sophisticated in their production and aesthetics, yet have lost their traditional use due to Western-style modernization, and have been relegated to the 'souvenir' category.

Selling crafts online What are the issues and challenges facing a woman who wants to establish an online crafts-selling business? Are there other

ICT tools beside the Internet that could help women to market crafts? There are some examples where e-commerce did work, and I present two such cases:

The Moroccan women weavers. Davis (2004) led a carpet-selling project: Women Weavers Online. The project sold carpets traditionally made by Moroccan women through a website without the women having to leave their villages, some of which were in remote and isolated areas. Davis showed that it was possible to market and sell rugs through the Internet. The article also illustrates, however, that establishing the website and marketing the rugs were only possible through the author, a well-educated American who used her social relations, language and technological skills to enable this commercial online outlet. Davis does not account for her expenses in the financial spreadsheet, which shows a marginal profit for the women weavers through international sale of their rugs; this gives an unrealistic picture of the financial and technical viability of this initiative, which could not have existed without her. The author herself is not optimistic about the possibility of training and recruiting a local person to take over from her to enable sustainability of this initiative.

Suzanne, the online crafts entrepreneur To understand the context, possibilities and limitations facing Egyptian women who want to pursue the dual focus of ICT tools and crafts, an in-depth study was made of a young Cairean woman who is arranging overseas exports of handicrafts through her website. Suzanne is a young, middle-class, single woman who (as is the custom in Egypt) lives with her parents. She attended a private, foreign-language school and has a BA in Finance. After holding odd jobs for several years, she decided to establish her own business marketing Egyptian souvenirs at fairs, and by establishing a website to sell internationally.

Suzanne is an avid Internet user, and is online for hours researching potential wholesale traders and even trying to peddle her wares through chat rooms. She has had good and bad experiences with her methods, but knows that keeping at it brings results in the end: in this way she identified a merchant in California who was willing to try some of the products she markets, with the promise that if they sold well he would be ordering more.

Her parents have been chiding her because she has been running up the phone bill. Suzanne has been discouraged by her sister and her parents in her commercial enterprise. They think it is taking more effort and upfront money (especially for the IT services) than it brings in, but Suzanne is persistent.

She has a website which she continually upgrades. Suzanne has excelled in finding back-office solutions for her e-business. One of the main challenges that faced her was the lack of e-commerce in Egypt, making it impossible to charge customers' credit cards through an online transaction. Suzanne had to find a creative solution, since having a credit card payment option is a necessity to be competitive in today's online craft business. Her site has a selling link to a US company, which provides e-commerce options to her customers.

In addition to finding alternative solutions to be able to sell her wares, finding reliable and cost-effective shipping for her micro-business was a major challenge for Suzanne. She researched all shipping and air companies to find economical shipping rates from a dependable company that she could trust to handle the goods with care.

Suzanne had also dealt with customs before in order to export her goods. The systems proved to be quite complex, and she had to hire someone who knew how to navigate them. She now uses an international company to manage shipping and related logistics since this company offered the most convenient solution for her micro-business.

Customs are a major issue for most import-exporters. At the New York Gift Fair an American merchant told me that the US customs regulations change each year, and that this is a problem for every exporter and importer; they never know what is going to be allowed to be imported next year. For example, someone may make a deal to import a load of textiles, only to find out that the US import regulations have changed, preventing them from importing them. Sometimes they circumvent this by giving the import lot a different name, and may get away with that – but this is not guaranteed. Therefore, most merchants have contact points at the customs offices to get to know about new regulations as soon as possible. Problems regarding these changes still often come up, however.

Suzanne is the epitome of persistence and the creator of inventive solutions which have enabled her, through trial and error, to establish a successful online crafts-selling business. The setting up of such a website, however, requires a highly enterprising attitude combined with education and technical skills or the money to afford outside technical assistance. Suzanne's command of English is excellent too – for most of the artisan women interviewed the absence of language skills is a major obstacle to use of the Internet for international trading. Suzanne was also aided by her family's financial support; as a single, middle-class woman in Egypt she is expected to be, if not fully supported financially by her parents, then at least substantially so. This freed Suzanne from worrying about living expenses such as shelter and food, which could have affected the input she has given (and still is giving) to her entrepreneurial project. Suzanne has a computer at home and had been an active Internet user for years before starting her enterprise. Her IT skills are quite sophisticated, making it possible for her to use the Internet as a marketing resource.

Conclusion

Although the Internet can be used for business-to-consumer marketing (as Suzanne's case demonstrates), in most cases it is not a cost-effective or competitive enterprise on this scale. ICT such as mobile phones can be used as a communication tool in the production and marketing process to bring women artisans closer to the information that would make their wares more marketable. The latter is a solution for cooperatives and development organizations geared to the empowerment of craftspeople. Online marketing could be a possibility if an organization is pooling a considerable number of producers together, thereby creating a portal for the wares. In the case of crafts, however, existence of a market first needs to be established for such a marketing portal to be effective.

The global crafts market is a highly competitive sphere, both in price and quality, and exporting is not a straightforward answer to craft marketing in the Egyptian case. The stiff competition facing Egyptian crafts in the international market has been an issue for every donor, merchant and NGO interviewed in this research. This is a fundamental concern that precedes the question of using ICT, especially IT, as a global marketing and selling channel for many of these goods.

ICT can be a vehicle for marketing crafts for entrepreneurially inclined women, as shown by the example in this chapter. Yet the same is not true for the larger numbers of low-income women. The formula whereby a collective enterprise handles the various stages of product design, quality control and marketing could be explored.

The examples from this research show that a global market is not a realistic possibility for Egyptian craftswomen. In fact, the most promising market for them would be a domestic one: for example, if Egypt could establish a widely based local demand for an Egyptian style in interior design, many of the traditional crafts now on the brink of extinction could be incorporated into products that are part of this revived design style. The establishment of such a market depends on creating demand and making crafts available to Egyptian consumers at various price ranges.

Government decision-makers and social leaders are well situated to promote greater demand for Egyptian crafts in interior design and fashion. This in turn would make it easier for craftswomen to market their crafts individually, collectively or through an intermediary, and ICT would be a promising tool to help them in this endeavour.

The common trend of looking for international market outlets for female Egyptian crafts producers through the Internet, other ICT-related tools or traditional marketing has not proved successful. To continue offering foreign markets as financially viable for these women is not ethical. Furthermore, to add new technologies such as ICT to the mix as a possible solution to their obstacles in reaching global markets is only an obfuscation of a widening trading gap, and the diminished options that these women have under the present circumstances.

References

Davis, S. S. (2004) 'Women Weavers Online: rural Moroccan women on the Internet', *Gender, Technology and Development*, 8(1): 53–75.

Mueller, S. D. (2006) 'Rural development, environmental sustainability, and poverty alleviation: a critique of current paradigms', DESA Working Paper no. 11, January, available online at www.un.org/esa/desa/papers/2006/wp11_2006.pdf.

Ofreneo, R. P. (2006) 'Problematizing microfinance as an empowerment strategy for women living in poverty: some policy directions', *Gender, Development and Technology*, journal of the Asian Institute of Technology (AIT), Bangkok, available online at www.upd.edu.ph/~cswcd/webpages/DOCUMENTS/faculty publications/PUBLICATIONS_Ofreneo2.pdf.

TWO | Female-only ICT spaces: perceptions and practices

6 | When a gender-blind access policy results in discrimination: realities and perceptions of female students at the University of Zimbabwe

BUHLE MBAMBO-THATA, ELIZABETH MLAMBO
AND PRECIOUS MWATSIYA

In Zimbabwe women's experiences of information and communication technologies (ICTs) are not divorced from their social contexts. 'But you are only a woman!' was a response a female teacher, and a respondent in our research, received when she volunteered to take charge of the computer laboratory in a school at which she was a senior teacher.

This chapter focuses on the experiences and reflections of women students regarding online learning at the University of Zimbabwe (UZ). It attempts to uncover inequity in female students' everyday learning experiences at the university and the social construction of gender within the context of their access to and use of the computer labs.

Recent research has indicated that in institutions of higher learning such as the community of the University of Zimbabwe, males continue to safeguard their privileged positions. Female students struggle, sometimes unsuccessfully, to have access to facilities such as the cafeterias, the sports facilities, the library and other common services on a basis equal to that of male students (Ndlovu 2001). The same research by Ndlovu confirms that one's sense of self is inevitably gendered by socialization. Men and women structure their masculinities and femininities according to their contexts, their class, their age and their ethnic and religious backgrounds. It is these gender considerations which shape the learning experiences of these students.

Gaidzanwa highlights her concerns on the issues of democracy in institutions: 'women have generally been underrepresented in universities and society in general' (1996). At the University of Zimbabwe until 1997 no female occupied any of the top three posts in the Student Representative Council (SRC). When the council got its first female secretary-general, her time in office was short lived as she resigned from the post in April 1998 owing to harassment by male students and lack of support from female students (Mashingaidze 2006).

The chapter is informed by the findings of research that was conducted at the University of Zimbabwe in 2005/06. The research examined the extent to which online learning empowered women graduate students. Prior to the research, the researchers had observed that the majority of the students at work at the computers in the library and in computer laboratories were male. This study was undertaken to gain an understanding of why this was the case.

Findings from this research will hopefully help influence those policy decision-making processes that would benefit from recognizing and reducing the effects of gender-blind policies, and which would be committed to supporting the capacity building of female students such that they can take full advantage of ICTs for academic purposes.

Research methods

In-depth qualitative research was done over a period of one year at the University of Zimbabwe. Those interviewed were female post-graduate students from the faculties of Education, Law, Social Studies and Agriculture. These post-graduate students had done their first degrees and were undertaking master's degrees. They were exposed to online learning more than the undergraduates. Some had a chance to write final-year dissertations in which they had to defend their line of thinking and were more comfortable talking about their experiences. Twenty-seven postgraduates participated. Some were full-time students while some were studying part time. At the time of the research, the researchers were full-time librarians at the university.

The University of Zimbabwe has several computer rooms referred to as laboratories set aside for student usage. The library's computers are in the lobby and therefore provide an ideal observation spot as one comes in or leaves the library. Most students do not have personal computers and depend on computer access provided by the university. Without the computer laboratories provided by the university, most students have no alternative facility to access computers and learning resources.

The researchers had observed that the majority of students at work at the computers in the library and in computer laboratories were male. For the purposes of this study, we also observed computer usage patterns in the laboratories located elsewhere on campus. The data also comprised informal interview notes and formal interview transcriptions. Furthermore, booking sheets were analysed as they are provided to the students every morning on a 'first come, first served' basis.

Focus group discussions were held, in the recognition that they induce social interactions akin to those that occur in everyday life but in greater focus (Denzin and Lincoln 2000: 15). The focus group discussions were essential in order to create a shared understanding of the objectives of the research, create a transparent atmosphere that reduced suspicion, and gather data on women's experiences with access to and use of computers for online learning. Participants were given the opportunity to explore their dreams about ICTs and their expectations of what ICTs in general, and computers in particular, could do for them.

Free attitude interviews (Buskens 2005) were also conducted, as these provided an opportunity for the researchers and respondents to assess and negotiate, and explore their thinking about their experiences, without interruption.

A few female students were found using labs in the male-dominated library lab environment, and they were purposefully sampled as 'deviant cases'. We use the term 'deviant case' as used in qualitative research, meaning that that which differs from the norm is deviant. Female students who used computer laboratories when the majority of female students did not were, according to us as researchers, 'deviant'. What benefits did they accrue from the use of the labs? And what was the driving force behind their usage of these ICTs when the majority of female students were absent?

Results

Female–male ratio of computer lab use Below is a table showing the bookings made by male and female students between October 2005 and March 2006.

Month	Male	%	Female	%	Total
October 2005	8,293	93	577	7	8,870
November 2005	6,772	92	571	8	7,343
December 2005	260	85	45	15	305
January 2006	360	81	86	19	446
February 2006	781	88	108	12	889
March 2006	4,721	84	897	16	5,618

In all months males outnumbered female students. Female students comprised 13 per cent of users while male students comprised 87 per cent of those who booked computer time. The percentage of female to male students enrolled at the university is 51 per cent female and 49 per cent male. The analysis of booking sheets corroborated our observation that male students predominate in use of the PCs in the computer labs. Even though female students are on campus less, it would be expected that booking statistics would mirror the enrolment ratio.

The 'normal students'

Appreciating learning new skills The UZ five-year strategic plan for 2003–07 was strongly committed to the implementation of ICTs in all areas of academic activities. ICT training was made compulsory for all students. Students have some knowledge and appreciation of ICTs and what they can do for them. They know and appreciate the benefits of online learning. 'I am empowered by ICTs because I have learnt new skills,' a female post-graduate student from the Faculty of Education asserted.

The women students did not lack confidence in their capacities, even in comparison with male students. 'There was no difference between me and my male counterparts; at times I could prove I could beat them – even at a higher level I could do the same,' a post-graduate student from Rural and Urban Planning stated.

Gendered expectations The majority of the female students expressed their appreciation of ICTs. One respondent noted that:

> It is really empowering because long [ago] I am sure in our African culture women were segregated, they were not supposed to learn, they were not supposed to touch some of these electronic gadgets because they [...] belonged to men. But now we are able to access the computer easily so I would say it is really helpful and it is really efficient and so we have been empowered as we can use the Internet.

Their opportunity for access was, however, inhibited by sociocultural demands on their time. They were expected to be home in time to attend to household duties. They could not have access to the computers after hours, even though the laboratories were open late. One respondent had this to say: 'Maybe a man can continue working in the computer lab till eight p.m. but as a woman I cannot. I have to rush home.'

Women's gendered roles prevented them from staying in the labs, much as they would have liked to spend more time working on the computers. They had no time to spend on campus beyond lectures because they were part-time students and had other responsibilities. The majority studied, were in full-time employment and had family responsibilities. This triple burden created competing priorities for time and responsibility. As stated in one of the responses above, family responsibility took pre-eminence over staying on campus to access the computers for learning. 'If I stay in the evening I will be accused of having affairs and so I must go home and do other things,' said a female student from the Faculty of Education.

Turning to male students for help 'When working with male students they make you feel like you do not know what you are doing,' according to a female respondent from the Faculty of Education.

Some female students strongly felt that they had to rely on the male students for assistance. They believed that ICTs were a preserve of their male counterparts. 'I sacrificed my own dignity to ask a male colleague to teach me – i could only learn from male students,' a female respondent from the Faculty of Social Studies contended.

First come, first served: the promise of equal access? At the time of this research, the library had not acquired enough computers to accommodate all students who needed access. Library computers are accessible to all students from all faculties and some departments do not have their own computer labs. Although access to all computer labs, the library computer lab included, was on a 'first come, first served' basis, fewer female students accessed the computer labs than male students. Some respondents felt the 'first come, first served' rule was fair in that whoever got there first would be entitled to access. For some of them this rule seemed like an improvement on having no access at all. Speaking about the situation at her department, one respondent stated, 'It's on [an] equal basis because if I get there, there are seventeen computers in our group [and] we are just fifteen so [you] can just go and get a computer [whether] you are a man or a woman. We are at par.'

First come, first served: creating a reality of inequality? Female students reported, however, that in most instances there is pushing and shoving when it comes to accessing the computers. 'When the pressure is on, the male students push and shove to get to PCs,' reported a female respondent from Rural and Urban Planning, speaking of the situation at her department. 'There is male domination in the computer labs – it is survival of the fittest,' noted a female respondent from the Faculty of Social Studies. This physical behaviour scared female students off as they did not want to be embroiled with the male students.

The respondents felt that the limited number of computers was a major concern for them. They claimed that one computer lab with twenty-five computers was inadequate for the three hundred or so graduate students in the social sciences; as a result there was pushing and shoving for access. The physically stronger male students would then prevail over the physically weaker female students.

Coping with 'first come, first served': students' alternative solutions As an alternative, some respondents opted to go to Internet cafés, although they said the practice was not sustainable as they are expensive. Others sought out different educational access points. 'I enrolled for a course [on] Introduction to Computers in a college in town,' one respondent in a focus group indicated. 'I enrolled in a course at Africa Virtual University,' said a female respondent from the Faculty of Education.

Suggestions for the future Some respondents thought that a more systematic reservation scheme would ensure access for those students who had other roles outside the university. They suggested that if a female lab could be set aside for them, then they would be able to juggle their other roles and at the same time have access to the lab for study purposes. As it stands, even if they juggle their timetables and come to the library they cannot find available computers as they are continuously used by male students. Furthermore, a women's lab would be free from jostling male students, making it more accessible for female students.

The deviant cases: female students who did access the computer labs A limited number of female students had been able to benefit from their access to and use of the computer labs at the university library.

In probing we discovered that most of these women students had been exposed to ICTs prior to joining the university and were comfortable in making use of the computers. They could write their assignments online; they could also communicate online and they could network easily. These 'deviant' students were undergraduates, campus residents, and younger than women post-graduate students.

They did not feel challenged by the majority of male students and strongly felt that the ICT arena should be shared equally by male and female students. They were aware that other female students were staying away. In a sense these deviant cases 'are storming the tower'. They are going into the labs that are male dominated, and continuing to work. While they are not changing the rules of play, they are pioneering. Perhaps if more women participated, a critical mass would be reached and female usage of computer labs would become normal.

Discussion

Does the 'first come, first served' practice really guarantee gender equality in accessing computer labs? Is the policy really fair?

To the 'normal' female students interviewed, 'first come, first served' was an acceptable idea. For many, in comparison to their previous experiences of no access, this rule was a definite improvement towards gender equity and even empowerment. Yet, while they could observe male students making more use of the labs, they could not make the connection between the application of this rule and the ensuing practical reality that disadvantaged them as women. The female students experienced gender inequalities in this, but overruled their interpretation of the reality in the labs by adhering to and supporting the policy of 'first come, first served'.

The female students felt no discrimination on the basis of their sex in terms of access, even though they were aware of the fact that the male students dominated the labs. What stood out foremost in their minds was the way their other, 'typically female' responsibilities and constraints prevented them from accessing the labs within the time limits available for students.

Discrepancy between the intent and the reality of the access policy: a gender analysis The UZ strategic plan (2003–07) placed emphasis on ICT competence: 'every student who goes through the UZ is to pass at least one compulsory course in Information and Communication Technology, irrespective of discipline' (University of Zimbabwe 2003). Graduates from the UZ were expected to have the necessary competitive edge resulting from the ICT programmes. Our research revealed, however, that the strategic direction may be impeded by gendered and unequal access to ICTs. As in all higher education institutions, learning resources, including ICT resources, were not allocated on the basis of gender. The university mainstreamed access without consideration for gender inequalities. The practical application of 'first come, first served' disregards the fact that women students may not be able to be there first, owing to other demands on their time. A second related point is that with limited ICT resources, competition for access often included physical shoving, in which case the physically stronger students prevailed.

This study thus provides an argument for a gender analysis of resource allocation, especially as regards ICTs. Such an analysis would provide insights into the creation of a gender-sensitive resource allocation model. In light of the exclusion resulting from a gender-blind policy position on access, it would seem that a gender-sensitive access policy would be a logical and fair demand.

Furthermore, we note with concern the 'gratitude' of women students for their limited and constrained access to computers. Grateful for the 'privilege' of apparently being included in the access policy, the 'normal' women students do not challenge the limited improvement they experience in the context of the male domination of the labs. The notion of equal access seems to take precedence over their experience of unequal access. To see their experience as contradicting the intent of an accepted equal-access policy is counter-intuitive, when one's thinking is aligned with societal values and meanings that one is familiar with. To see their experience differently, to reflect on it without adherence to existing ways of seeing things, would require creating new meanings. For such meanings to reflect the women's experiences, the thinking would have to transcend current concepts and imagery that have been formed in the context of a male-dominated society.

We all work with the familiar and draw upon concepts that make sense to us. This is one way in which patriarchy perpetuates itself. Women and men internalize values of male dominance and privilege, defend them and reproduce them. From this perspective, it is not unusual that the majority of women respondents accept as fair the 'first come, first served' policy. If all students could, in theory, approach accessing the labs on an equal footing, the policy should be equitable.

But why is it that there is discrepancy between how the 'normal' and 'deviant' women students perceive their experiences of a theoretically empowering access policy and the resulting reality? If this variation is due to the students' perceptions of what is happening and their reflections as to its meaning (for them) is being mediated by their consciousness, the way they have internalized certain ideas, how have their consciousnesses become different? Has the previous exposure to computers, and the confidence the 'deviant' women have in their use, enabled them to disregard dominant concepts? This would explain why the latter group apparently had more of an understanding of the discrepancy between the theory and practice of the access policy, and maybe more of an understanding that they experienced discrimination as women.

Recommendations

The study reveals the significance of recognizing the understandable gap and variance between what women experience and how they understand their experience. It also foregrounds the societal reality of gendered access to resources, its causes and its consequences.

It is evident from this study that mainstreaming access to ICTs and learning resources may not address women's needs. Is it perhaps time for higher education in general, and the University of Zimbabwe in particular, to open its practices to a gender analysis? This would provide information for interventions that could offer equitable access in practice, not simply in theory derived from dominant concepts such as 'first come, first served'.

It would furthermore be an empowering experience for the women students who gave meaning to their experiences, using the socially accepted concept 'first come, first served', to realize how this process of constructing meaning has actually estranged them from the reality of their own actual experiences. Learning to question dominant social norms and concepts, in relation to their own actual experiences and their feelings about these, will equip them to learn to critique other current unfair and discriminatory practices. A programme of education for empowerment aimed at stimulating such reflexive awareness among female post-graduate students would provide them with a valuable life skill that could help them to protect and further their career in a patriarchal context and society.

The student respondents stated that a computer laboratory exclusively for women would enhance their access to ICTs for learning. Such a lab would respond to the needs of women students in terms of being open at hours that are convenient to women and providing support that is tailored to enable them to effectively use ICTs. It is important for women students to build their self-confidence and self-esteem by providing the necessary training to make maximum use of ICTs, enabling them to make their own decisions and control their resources (Rowlands 2003). These female students should be given encouragement so that they have their hands on something real and physical. That way, they can discover, explore, learn and share.

In order for ICTs to be empowering to women, hurdles to limited access need to be realized, confronted and removed. As it was obvious that there was a link between confident use of ICTs and an awareness that the rule 'first come, first served' did not in itself guarantee equitable access, such a 'women-only' computer lab could be an important first step towards a real empowered use of ICTs for online learning for the students at the University of Zimbabwe.

References

Bahi, A. (2004) 'Internet use in Abidjan cybercafés', *CODESRIA Bulletin*, 1/2: 67–71.

Batezat, E. and M. Mwalo (1989) *Women in Zimbabwe*, Harare: Sapes Trust: Harare.

Buskens, I. (2005) *Free Attitude Interview Manual*, available at www.GRACE-Network.net.

Chagonda, T. (2001) 'Masculinities and resident male students at the University of Zimbabwe: gender and democracy issues', in R. B. Gaidzanwa (ed.), *Speaking for Ourselves: Masculinities and Femininities amongst Students at the University of Zimbabwe*, Harare: University of Zimbabwe.

Cottes, J. (2003) 'Young women's participation in international conferences in the new information society', *Women in Action*, 2: 14–16.

Daly, M. (2003) *Beyond God the Father: Toward a Philosophy of*

Women's Liberation, Boston, MA: Beacon.

Denzin, N. K. and Y. S. Lincoln (eds) (2000) *The Sage Handbook of Qualitative Research*, 3rd edn, London: Sage.

Gaidzanwa, R. (1996) *Speaking for Ourselves: Masculinities and Femininities amongst Students at the University of Zimbabwe*, Harare: University of Zimbabwe.

— (1999) 'The politics of the body and the politics of control: an analysis of class, gender and cultural issues in student politics at the University of Zimbabwe', *Zambezia*, 20(1): 15–34.

Maboreke, M. (1997) *Who is the Employee of the Labour Relations Act? Exploring the Gender Dimensions of the Labour Relations Legislative Framework*, Harare: Faculty of Law, University of Zimbabwe.

Mashingaidze, T. M. (2006) 'Gender and higher education in postcolonial Zimbabwe: tentative reflections on policy issues', *OSSREA Bulletin*, 3(1): 33–9.

Mason, J. (2004) *Qualitative Researching*, 2nd edn, London: Sage.

Ndlovu, S. (2001) 'Femininities amongst resident female students at the University of Zimbabwe', in R. B. Gaidzanwa, *Speaking for Ourselves: Masculinities and Femininities amongst Students at the University of Zimbabwe*, Harare: University of Zimbabwe.

Rowlands, J. (2003) *Questioning Empowerment: Working with Women in Honduras*, Oxford: Oxfam.

Runhare, T. (2003) 'Women perceptions of masculine technical careers: a comparative study of women in feminine and masculine employment occupations in the city of Gweru, Zimbabwe', *Zimbabwe Journal of Educational Research*, 15(3).

Sen, A. (1999) *Development as Freedom*, New York: Anchor Books.

University of Zimbabwe (2003) *University of Zimbabwe Five-year Strategic Plan, 2003–2007*, Harare: University of Zimbabwe.

7 | An alternative public space for women: the potential of ICT

LEILA HASSANIN

Throughout history and across cultures, spatial arrangements have reinforced status differences between women and men. The issue of space and how it is experienced through the lenses of gender is the subject of this inquiry. Women and men are spatially segregated in ways that reduce women's access to knowledge and income sources, thereby reinforcing women's lower status relative to men's. 'Gendered spaces' separate women from knowledge used by men to produce and reproduce power and privilege (Spain 1992: 3; Folbre 2001).

In Egypt females are officially encouraged to join traditionally male-dominated public spaces such as educational institutions and work environments to be able to learn and earn an income like their male counterparts. Joining public spaces in Egypt is, however, still hard for many girls and women. Even if they are able to gain an education and work for a while, in many cases this is temporary and reversed once a woman has a family of her own.

Public space here means what we define as the 'commons' – a geographic and social area where people are supposed to go about their daily lives. This definition is different from Habermas's 'public sphere' (Habermas 1989 [1962]), which holds a more political and bourgeois connotation. This chapter upholds the critique that Habermas's public sphere does not give adequate reference to gender, but here public space is used at a much more basic level – in fact it refers to what Habermas defined as the 'private sphere', the economic realm where people exchange goods and labour.

The spatial issues were an unexpected aspect of a study that looked at the role that information and communication technologies (ICTs) are playing in marketing handicrafts produced by women. In Chapter 5 in this volume, I discuss the limited capacity that Egyptian women artisans have to use ICT. The women's life stories also highlighted, however, the importance of having access to flexible learning and working options as a means to female empowerment.

In *A Room of One's Own* (1929) Virginia Woolf declares that 'a woman must have money and a room of her own if she is to write fiction'. It seems that this is true not only for fiction writers – the same applies to the average Egyptian woman, who needs an income and a supportive place in order to develop her own potential.

The research respondents emphasized the importance of having a 'place of learning' – in this case, a non-governmental organization (NGO) – where they are taught income-generating skills, can get advice and help, and are exposed to an awareness that helps them to reshape their lives. This space is a fusion between the domestic and the public sphere where women are exposed to education and paid work and their awareness of being able to shape their lives according to their aspirations is raised, while circumventing what would be deemed outright challenges to societal conventions (e.g. in some circumstances opting for higher education or working outside the house).

Different women reached their goals of self-actualization when they were allowed to gain education and skills within these blended spaces that combined the societal requirement for privacy with the educational and exposure benefits that public spaces offer. Frequenting these spaces made it possible for the respondents to become more empowered both privately and publicly. Some women even became advocates for female rights issues – and all of them are financially independent and have achieved higher educational levels than the average woman in their immediate environment.

Based on the findings, this research maintains that creating, supporting and increasing female-friendly domestic/public areas could assist girls and women to achieve socio-economic, educational and skills development goals that are elusive at present. Making these female learning and earning spaces more accessible would benefit society as a whole and unburden many women from severe barriers to their self-actualization.

Because of its nature, ICT is highly suitable for the creation, support and increase of such spaces. Judging from its present use in Egypt, ICT is underused in achieving much-needed educational and work frameworks that are space-flexible and could be of productive and social benefit to women, men and their families. This chapter gives some examples drawn from interviews with and observations of Egyptian women working in the crafts sector.

Siwa: blending traditionalism and IT

The Italian Cooperation for Development of Emerging Countries (COSPE) facilitated my contact with research participants in Siwa, an oasis close to the Egyptian–Libyan border where the organization has several projects with the Community Development and Environmental

Protection Association, a local NGO. Siwan society is quite different from the rest of Egypt. Siwans identify themselves more closely with Libyans in origin, being Berbers (*Amazegh* in the local language).

It is hard for an outsider to contact Siwan women directly. Siwan women and girls are secluded and appear in public fully covered. COSPE has been working with local NGOs and through them with Siwan females. One of these is Lamia (names have been changed to protect the privacy of interviewees), who is eighteen years old, has a visual arts diploma, and is the IT trainer at the secondary school in Siwa. Lamia had IT training through the NGO with other girls from Siwa, and then was selected as the female school trainer. Lamia's only contact with outsiders had been a female Italian officer from COSPE. The director of this association encouraged her meeting with me as a way for Lamia to gain further outside contact.

I met her at the school, where she was working with a class in the computer lab. Following local tradition, Lamia is in a black robe and niqab, showing only her eyes, while she is handling the latest Internet applications. Lamia has also completed a Cisco network training course and is a qualified IT trainer for local women.

In addition to her IT work, Lamia excels in traditional Siwan stitching, like most women from the oasis: 'Though I now hardly have time to stitch, I have been working on a neighbour's wedding dress.' Lamia shows me her exquisite stitching wrapped in layers of white cotton gauze.

After the class we go to the literacy class that Lamia's sister Iman gives at a private residence. We arrive at the house of an upper-middle-income family where a room is set aside for the PC with four terminals on a *tableya*, a round, low table traditionally used for eating in rural areas in Egypt. Iman is leading the class of four women. One of the trainees shows me the government's literacy software 'Fahima', which is user-friendly with visuals and audio. The Tableya IT Literacy Centre is mobile and circulates around the town to welcoming family houses so that local women do not need to walk long distances to go to the literacy class. It offers the classes in well-respected houses in the community. Women would not attend the classes if they were held in a public space such as a school.

It will be hard for Lamia, Iman and the other working girls (customarily in Egypt a woman is a married woman, hence the distinction here) from Siwa to work outside the house after they marry. Under Siwan tradition a woman lives with her husband's family after marriage and is not allowed to work outside the home. Many women have earned an income through stitching in the last decades, since the oasis opened up to the outside world.[1]

Lamia has a married sister who lives with her husband in Libya, where he works. She is able to work there because she is outside Siwa. 'I would like to marry and go to Libya too, this way I can continue my IT work. If I should stay in Siwa after marriage I will not be able to continue teaching at the school,' says Lamia. I ask whether she might be able to set up a house group like the literacy class, only for more advanced IT training. She said that could be a workable idea.

Abeer – career woman, single mother and university student

Abeer, who is thirty-five years old, is a single parent with two children whom she supports by being the head of the inventory department at an NGO, El Bashayer. To further her career she is completing her BA in Finance in the evenings. Abeer's family lives close by and her mother takes care of her children after school.

Abeer's children went to El Bashayer's nursery school when they were small, which helped her to continue her work at the NGO. She has been working at Bashayer for fourteen years and began at the nursery school, which she headed after several years of work: 'The teaching experience gave me a pedagogic background that I'm using to bring up my children. For a while I worked in the NGO's accounting section as I had a financial diploma and then I became responsible for the inventory department.'

Abeer began using a computer about ten years ago. She was trained at work so that she could use digital bookkeeping for the inventory system. Bashayer had hired a programmer to establish a tailored database for its inventory, but the programme gave faulty results and Bashayer soon stopped using it. Abeer wants to get Excel training in order to digitize her spreadsheets. This would cover the inventory needs for the time being. IT applications do not necessarily need to be sophisticated in many instances, but they do need to be realistic and useful to enhance productivity.

Says Abeer:

I used to have a computer at home, which allowed me to get more famil-iar with IT. My husband and I have been living apart for two years, and when he moved out he took the PC with him. Right now I do not have the money to buy one for myself, but I hope to be able to afford one in the future.

Her husband's beatings were the main reason for the separation. Her family tried to persuade her that the beatings 'will pass and things will be fine again between the two of you', but Abeer refused to accept the beatings. She had been her family's main income earner even during the marriage, and she saw this as an even greater reason not to tolerate her husband's physical abuse. Despite her earning power, Abeer does not like being the main breadwinner; she does not mind bringing in an income to bolster family status, but would have preferred to have a more financially responsible husband:

> Men these days are comfortable with their wives being the main income earners, it makes life easier [for men] – they are upholding their old rights and taking new ones. I don't mind being married on paper, it is easier for me to face society as a legally married woman than a divorcee, it is also better for the children. The only reason for me to divorce would be if he remarries; I would never allow a second wife.

Her income gives her indispensable freedom; without her education and her job she would not have been able to leave her husband. The NGO has been supportive with childcare and with educational development, both of which were important for Abeer to continue being able to be financially self-supportive.

Dreams lead to changed lives

Vivian and Salma are from the marginalized community of garbage collectors and recyclers, the Zabaleen. The Zabaleen are a distinct social group that mostly intermarries and maintains the strict, traditional Upper Egyptian habits of the area where they originate. The work tradition is passed from parents to children, with girls working with their fathers and brothers until they reach puberty.[2] Salma and Vivian spent their working childhood helping to collect garbage and sorting it. Because they were an income-generating part of the family they were not allowed to go to school lest this interfere with their work.

Vivian talks sadly about her childhood:

> Since I was six years old I have been working in garbage recycling as this is my father's job and the whole family participated in it. I never went to school, though I wanted so much to go. I would enviously watch the schoolchildren, looking at their clean clothes, resenting how they saunter to school when I had to accompany my father going off to work on a garbage cart.
>
> I always wanted more from life. I was strong willed and difficult to handle. When I heard about the literacy course at our local church, I kept asking my family to let me attend. They finally relented but I had to have the recycling and housework done for the day to be able to go. I took the course for three months and excelled in it. I was not going to stop here.

In the late 1980s the Association for the Protection of the Environment (APE) began offering weaving courses, literacy classes and income from the finished weaving products to Zabaleen girls. Salma and Vivian wanted to join the weaving training, but their parents disapproved. After long arguments with her mother, Vivian brokered a deal that she would contribute her income from weaving to household expenses.

After the training the girls were given looms to take home to weave the rugs. Upon finishing a rug they would deliver it to the APE to get paid. Without being able to use the loom at home most of these girls would not have been able to weave, since they would not have been allowed to work in a public space on a continual basis.

Encouraged by the training and the income, Vivian and Salma took their personal development a step farther by attending literacy classes, and then enrolled in a high school diploma programme over a span of seven to ten years. Today they are senior staff at APE: Vivian is the executive secretary and Salma heads the inventory system.

Salma's life has changed dramatically in the process:

> Through my work with an NGO I visited Paris in 1993 and China in 1995. Travelling to other countries made me more self-assured and broadened my perspective and understanding of life. Before my travels I would never leave the house in the evenings; now I am not afraid to go out after the dark to buy some necessities.

Salma is planning to build a room for herself on the roof of her brother's house. She has been part of her brother's household since her parents died. Salma is forty years old and single. She has been helping her nephews with school work because her brother's wife is illiterate. Salma does little housework; she is contributing financially to the household and therefore has an elevated status in the family. She has been facing health challenges throughout her life. Having an income and connections through her work has allowed her access to better health services.

Vivian's education and income give her a voice in her family and community. They allow her to speak up against female genital circumcision (FGC) and to pay for health, education and life expenses. She has been a victim of FGC and has been lobbying her siblings, friends and relatives to spare their daughters. Vivian's daughter will not be circumcised. Vivian is paying for her daughter's private kindergarten. Vivian was nine months pregnant during the interview and told me that she had previously had a stillbirth when she delivered at the public hospital and would therefore pay for her next delivery at a private hospital.

Aida also took part in the APC weaving programme. She lives in Zabaleen although her family is from outside the community. Her mother moved to this area because it was cheap; after her husband's death Aida's mother brought her and her sister up doing janitorial jobs, all the while encouraging her daughters to go through school until they both got diplomas. Aida experienced a rough youth as she perceived the surrounding society to be unsupportive of, if not outright hostile towards, a household of women. This perception has made her focused on security in the form of a safe family house. The house she grew up in was modest and needed lots of repairs that were badly done by contractors; Aida attributes this to the workers not taking women seriously. She wants to rebuild her mother's home and to live in it with her new husband and mother. She had been saving up for this, but her savings got used up paying for her marriage expenses. She is starting to save anew and is determined to build a strong, beautiful house. As Aida explained to me:

> It is hard to live without a father, brother or other male relative around. A neighbour tried to expand his house by taking over a publicly owned area in our alley. When I complained he attacked our house at 3 a.m. while he was drunk. I made a complaint at the police office, but what really helped me was the backing by members from the NGO in this legal complaint; with their help we were able to stop the neighbour making further attacks.

Owing to her hard circumstances Aida wanted to leave her formal education when she was at the end of middle school and join the NGO's loom business to bring income to her mother. The NGO and her mother encouraged her to work from home while continuing her studies. She finished her finance diploma and became a clerk at the NGO. Aida is now one of four women leading the recycled paper division, which produces cards, wrapping paper, writing paper and other paper goods. The finished products are sold to hotels, schools and businesses and are displayed in the NGO's shop on the premises.

Can ICT contribute to creating an alternative public sphere for women?

The examples of the Siwan and Zabaleen women's training and work run counter to the focus of the present Egyptian education and labour systems, which are geared towards females' participation in the public domain. A female has to go out into the public sphere to benefit from the system, however. The dichotomy of public versus domestic spaces has been a central issue in women's development (Gilman 1917), and to this date has not been satisfactorily resolved to recognize women's current daily obligations and restrictions (Valian 1999; Waring 1988).

The 'ideal worker versus domesticity' argument has dominated and is still dominating the landscape of women's participation in the economy. The notion of the 'ideal worker', according to Williams (2000: 1–6), is that of a full-time worker, often working overtime and unencumbered by family obligations. The 'ideal worker' was originally a man who was being supported by his wife, who stayed at home to take care of hearth and family. Domesticity is the whole package of life that does not fit into the 'ideal worker' terms of reference, i.e. raising children, household duties, social duties that interfere with paid work, and so forth (Stone 2007; Swiss and Walker 1993; Hirshman 2006).

The stories of Lamia, Iman, Abeer, Salma, Vivian and Aida show how some women's growth is assisted by taking into account the challenges and boundaries they are facing. It was easier for them to break out of society's mould by first building their capacities within frameworks that took into account the societal difficulties that females face. In contrast, when women have to first counter the imposed societal constraints to pursue their goals in the public domain, many are put off and their development suffers.

Until today, 'no country has ... created an urban fabric and an urban culture to support men and women on equal terms as citizens and workers' (Hayden 2002: 232). There is a need to experiment with life and work frameworks that offer greater access to and higher returns for education, skills development and productivity. ICT seems to be the ideal tool for a female development model, but the technologies have yet to be used in a context beyond the prevailing gender-insensitive structures. This research supports the creative quest for a more appropriate life, work and empowerment model for women using the technologies available (especially ICT) that could be employed to promote and increase alternative education and work systems.

Using adult and part-time education systems worked for Vivian, Salma and Abeer, although in Egypt these parallel education systems are considered of lesser quality by the public. This attitude was reflected in the interviews. A respondent from Aswan, Asmaa, who has a two-year commercial diploma and wanted to gain a university degree for a clerical job, found the part-time adult education so poor that she was not able to pass exams, although she took them twice:

> I gave up after two years of trying. The education I was getting during the year was not good enough to give me the needed grades in the end-of-semester exams. I have now put my CV at the government employment office in Aswan and hope to be employed with my diploma.

Asmaa does not think that the computer training she got will give her an edge in securing a government job. She says she has also forgotten a lot of what she learned because she is not using it.[3] Asmaa lives in a village and acutely feels the disadvantages of not being allowed by her family to attend college and telecentres.

Conclusion

The research examined the importance of alternative frameworks for women's empowerment through a selected sample of Egyptian crafts-women. The interviews showed commonalities in what the women deemed as important life-enhancing support. These learning–earning frameworks highlight how crucial space and geographical factors were for female development in the researched group.

Some of the main findings were as follows:

- Women benefit from participating in the activities of local NGOs that are sensitive to local customs and work around the restrictions women face.
- The continuous association with a supportive organization (such as a local NGO) made it possible for these women to sustain and consolidate their advancements.
- Nearly all the women said that their dream would have been to have a university degree, despite the fact that there are limited job opportunities for women with degrees. The importance given to education among Egyptian women harks back to the social mobility a university degree provided during the Nasser regime. It would be beneficial to offer women education and skills training that realistically reflected earning opportunities in present-day Egypt.
- Higher-quality alternative and parallel educational systems need to be put into place in Egypt. At present education outside the formal realm and hours is in most cases of lesser quality and has less value attached to it. ICT is an excellent tool for providing quality adult education in settings outside of formal structures.
- There is a need to make decision-makers aware of successful examples of women who, by finding spaces that adapted education and work needs to the realities of their lives (domestic duties and restrictions regarding participation in the public domain), were able to achieve high levels of personal development. ICT is especially suited to bridging public and domestic spaces since it enables the creation of virtual spaces that can be accessed by females and other (currently) secluded members of society, e.g. people with disabilities. To date the

full potential of ICT for education and work and as an information tool has not been explored in Egypt. ICT has mostly been used within the traditional modes of work and education, instead of being used to construct and make accessible a more space- and time-flexible learning and productivity model for the average Egyptian woman and man.

• The study proposes incorporating the traditional female spaces into an ICT-supported socio-economic framework that minimizes the need to constantly attend public spaces for learning and working. Despite the fact that ICT offers alternative ways of connection and communication, the traditional life/work framework continues to be used, depriving Egypt's economy of a vast amount of human resources.

• Policy-makers are advised to look with more critical eyes at the needs of women if female participation in Egypt's development is to be strengthened. The educational investments made in Egyptian females to date could be augmented by making education and skills development available in women's spaces. Strengthening and redesigning alternative education, skills learning and work structures with the available technological means (with ICT playing a large part) would mean women could develop and draw upon their potential to a much greater degree than currently possible in the male-dominated public domain.

Notes

1 Siwa became a tourist destination after a road was built to connect the oasis and a major highway in the mid-1980s. The opening of the oasis brought a lot of changes to it; one of them is the buying up of old silver from the oasis and the crude commercialization of traditional crafts.

2 Lately the Zabaleen community was shaken by the government's decision to modernize the garbage collection system, outsourcing it to Spanish and Italian companies. An agreement was brokered allowing the Zabaleen to work on certain aspects of the garbage collection cycle.

3 Connectivity at the village is so low that the PCs at the NGO are hardly used to go online.

References

Folbre, N. (2001) *The Invisible Heart: Economics and Family Values*, New York: New Press.

Gilman, C. P. (1917) 'The housekeeper and the food problem', *Annals of the American Academy of Political Science*, 123: 127.

Habermas, J. (1989 [1962]) *The Structural Transformation of the Public Sphere: An Inquiry into a Category of Bourgeois Society*, Cambridge, MA: MIT Press.

Hayden, D. (2002) *Redesigning the American Dream: The Future of Housing, Work, and Family Life*, New York: Norton.

Hirshman, L. (2006) *Get to Work: A Manifesto for Women of the World*, New York: Viking.

Spain, D. (1992) *Gendered Spaces*, Chapel Hill: University of North Carolina Press.

Stone, P. (2007) *Opting Out? Why Women Really Quit Careers and Head Home*, Berkeley: University of California Press.

Swiss, D. J. and J. P. Walker (1993) *Women and the Work/Family Dilemma: How Today's Profession-al Women are Finding Solutions*, New York: Wiley.

Valian, V. (1999) *Why So Slow? The Advancement of Women*, Boston, MA: MIT Press.

Waring, M. (1988) *If Women Counted: A New Feminist Economics*, New York: Harper & Row.

Williams, J. (2000) *Unbending Gender: Why Family and Work Conflict and What to Do about It*, Oxford: Oxford University Press.

Woolf, V. (1929) *A Room of One's Own*, London: Hogarth Press.

An alternative public space for women

8 | Using ICTs to act on hope and commitment: the fight against gender violence in Morocco

AMINA TAFNOUT AND AATIFA TIMJERDINE

Change, hope, starting anew, despair, defeat, power, challenge and commitment: these are the terms with which we express ourselves about encounters with women survivors of violence and women in charge of Moroccan Counselling and Legal Aid Centres to which the former turn in their time of need.

Change is implied in the rejection, by the women survivors, of violence as a reality that is frustrating and offending to their human dignity. There is also the feeling of hope – for a better future and a different world for women in which peace prevails and women's dignity is respected. Despite the fissure that marked one part of their lives, some women were able to open up to the world again, and to head confidently and boldly towards a new experience, thus starting anew. There was also, however, despair and defeat for others who broke down under poverty and violence.

The women working in the Counselling and Legal Aid Centres exhibit the power and the desire to take up challenges, to face the prevailing culture that allows and legitimizes violence and discrimination, and to fight mentalities and a discourse that sees women as inferior to men. There is a commitment to creating new methods for defending women and a belief in information and communication technologies (ICTs), which for them are the most effective tools to expose violence and manage the centres. ICTs signify a media revolution to them – an opening up and an essential asset for development and communication.

Research context

When we thought of conducting research on ICTs from the perspective of their use by the Counselling and Legal Aid Centres and by the women who are victims of violence in Morocco, the research appeared to be of a general and descriptive nature. In the course of preparing for and thinking through its hypothetical and methodological aspects, however, some questions were raised:

- Which research approach can be adopted to address gender-based violence in a context where this constitutes an accepted part of private space, and is not recognized as an abuse of the human rights of women and a social phenomenon that needs deep study and analysis?

- Which theoretical and methodological approach can be adopted to address the use of ICTs by women survivors of domestic violence?

It became clear to us that the research question itself provoked debate on the role of ICTs as tools women can use in their efforts to counter all forms of discrimination. Presently a lot of importance is given to 'violence against women' by human rights and women's associations in Morocco. Also, because of the current focus on the use of ICT, the issue of violence against women was drawn into the discourse on change and development related to ICT.

Living in a world where information technology has become a tool for work, a means of empowering people and an avenue for entering into numerous worlds, narrowing distances and establishing relationships, we raised the following question: how and why do women survivors of violence and women working at the Counselling and Legal Aid Centres use ICT to fight gender-based violence? The answer to this question could shed light on whether women survivors of violence actually benefit from Morocco's opening up to the world of ICT.

We know that the environment in which we live and work in Morocco is marked by inequality between men and women and an absence of gender awareness. This environment is also characterized by lack of participation of women in decision-making, no efforts to eradicate digital illiteracy, and no attempt to remove the constraints that women experience related to their triple gender roles (Smyth et al. 1999: 14).

Moroccan women face numerous economic, social and cultural challenges that prevent their access to and use of (and hence their ability to benefit from) ICT. The ICT sector is characterized by disparities between men and women, and does not take into account gender and equity in development when addressing social problems. Moreover, the ICT sector also limits the possibility of the social and professional integration of women, especially those who are poor and illiterate. This is because the use of ICT requires at least an average education standard, financial means for the purchase of equipment and time for training (especially for women who assume family responsibilities). As one of our respondents told us:

> For me, I want to learn how to use it, but it is not possible now. It provides many services. It has become a necessity and the one who does not know how to use it is illiterate. I consider myself illiterate. I started learning for some time then I gave up. One needs many hours per day.

At the core of the problem is the issue of women's status in the public area in Morocco. When a woman leaves her household, she becomes subject to public norms of patriarchal moral and social control and loses whatever 'sovereignty' she has. This contributes to the fact that women and men have different existences in Internet spaces, which deepens the digital gender gap in Moroccan society (Centre National de Documentation du Maroc 2003: 104). The presence of women in some public spaces (Internet cafés) is not accepted by society at large, because such spaces are considered to be reserved for men (especially with regard to use of the Internet, since some men use it for pornography). Lamia from Meknes told us:

> In Internet cafés, men are not supervised. They sometimes use pornographic websites [...] and nobody cares about that. But the women feel embarrassed because they are watched by others who keep an eye on what they are writing or watching, even by the Internet café's owner. There is no privacy.

Our study coincided with the Moroccan public debate opening up to issues that have long been taboo, the most important of which is the issue of women's rights, now at the centre of political and civil society debate. This situation required us to position ourselves clearly. As researchers and feminists we are actors in the change that is taking place around us, with all that we are and all that we have in terms of empowerment. This study into women's use of ICTs in the fight against gender-based violence was a double opportunity for us as researchers and as women focused on women's empowerment: empowering ourselves with rapidly developing capabilities, which is a type of exploration of our skills, and empowering the women with whom we were working by bringing them into this particular research process.

Methodology

The women who took part in our research were those in charge of the legal centres (who supervise the work and coordinate with the association to which the centres belong); women counsellors and legal assistants whose task is to listen to women, assist them and communicate with other stakeholders concerned with the phenomenon of violence; and women survivors of violence who went to the centres seeking guidance, legal advice and psychological and judicial assistance.

To select women survivors of violence we sought the assistance of the centres' heads, who had access to them. These survivors are women of different ages who do not belong to the same social class, and neither do they have the same educational level. In this chapter we quote four survivors (whose real names are not used, to protect them) who reflect the diversity of those who seek the assistance of these centres. Yet our general understanding has been grounded by the conversations we had with forty women who use the services of the centres, and the directors of the six legal centres that are based in Rabat (two), Fez, Meknes, Marrakesh and Oujda.

We found that conducting a study on the relationship between gender-based violence and the use of ICT was both easy and difficult. It was easy in a sense because of the availability of data and working tools and because we had clear perceptions at the methodological level of how to address our research problem, and difficult because these women were in a crisis when we engaged with them and were also so diverse. They had come to the centres specifically to seek a solution to their problem, so it was difficult for us to get answers to our questions about a subject (ICT) that they might not consider a priority at that point.

The focus of our research was guided by the dream of a better future for women in Morocco. This dream presupposes that access to information is a right for all, and that women survivors of violence can claim their right to live in economic, social and psychological security and demand their right to access to information and its production.

Our selves and other selves

We consider the women respondents not as objects of study, and neither do we approach them solely as the interpreting subjects who create meaning in and construct the rationality of their daily lives. We see them as the actors who co-create their reality and are thus inevitably the main contributors to social change where it pertains to their lives. This perspective has led us to adopt an interactive fieldwork approach and to take a critical stance towards the knowledge construction process in the recognition that researching women who live in difficult conditions becomes even more challenging when these women have lost access to channels of self-expression. It was also our aim to develop effective action plans based on this research and then to move on to the next step, the next dream.

We were able to establish relationships with the women survivors of violence and also with the women employees at the centres/associations, with whom we could continue to work to draw up strategies and programmes aimed at denouncing violence against women and breaking the taboo and silence that encourage the aggressors to continue their acts.

In our fieldwork and our meetings with the women we tried to open up to the women and stay reflective at the same time – a combination of professionalism and intimacy. We came to know what we did about the women respondents thanks to their ability to express themselves – the right to speak is not something that is given, but something that is taken.

Findings

The women working at the centres were aware of their significance and their role in making change, and the impact of their know-how in putting on pressure, negotiating and supporting solidarity. They gain in power and ability by belonging to groups working and fighting for one goal and one vision inside and outside Morocco. This gives them self-confidence and propels them forward whenever despair sneaks in. They made effective use of the various tools of information technology (phone, e-mail, Internet), and as such the use of ICT had a positive impact on the fight against domestic violence by enhancing communication and decision-making.

ICT allows self-expression and collective action. Fatiha from Rabat, who is in charge of a legal centre, said:

> It certainly facilitates the work. For example, at the level of statistics we used to work manually, but now thanks to the network we have no difficulty in obtaining a particular result, for example by age, region, etc. For the victim in the past, we relied on the address and the landline telephone, but now most of them give us the numbers of their cell phones. As regards the files of victims, we now look for the victim's name through the computer to identify the full file in addition to other information.

Regardless of their tasks, whether as counsellors, directors or assistants, the women working in the legal centres consider ICT to play an important role, mainly in raising awareness about the phenomenon of violence and opening up new prospects for work, since it has improved methods and facilitated the exchange of information with other legal centres. Said Zakia from Marrakesh:

> It has facilitated so many things. Instead of moving to Marrakesh or Rabat in one day, the e-mail facilitates the work. I can reply to e-mails while working. I can do many things at the same time, the fax, Internet and telephone instead of sending a letter, which may take three days. For the e-mail, you get the answer instantly. Instead of doing a piece of work in one month, I do it in one day.

The women survivors of violence who opened their hearts to us told us about their lives with their ups and downs and related their experiences of violence so, we felt, that they would not forget. Some women survivors of violence also spoke about their new life, and felt like adolescents, opening up to life.

When we asked these women to tell us about ICT in a few words, we did not expect such strength and depth of expression. Some of the respondents considered the mobile phone as 'your friend in need, your brother, mother, and father', 'a solution to problems', 'brings people closer', 'a protection sometimes', 'a necessity'. Others said about the Internet: 'we will not just use it to expose violence but also for knowledge, our relationships and education'. These simple and deep words can be interpreted and linked to the conditions and circumstances in which the women use this technology.

Sanaa from Meknes: 'I was expelled from my house and I called my father asking him to visit me. I called my family to help me. If there had been no cell phone, they would not have come to me.'

Lamia from Meknes:

In the past, the situation was different from now. There was violence in a specific context. People used to live in large families. If the violence is committed by the husband, the family intervenes and provides protection. Now a crime may be committed and there is nobody to provide protection. There is God and the cell phone.

Women survivors ready for change

The women survivors of violence who were ready for change seemed full of life and vitality. The women, who were self-confident, with confidence in their own power, had restored their self-regard and reconciled with themselves by making a decision about an unpleasant situation, despite social, economic, physiological and family impacts. They had come to gain control of their lives and fate, and the lives and destiny of their families and children. They rejected violence and militated to fight against it. These women had shifted from being survivors of violence to becoming actors and militants.

When these women possessed ICT tools, such as the mobile phone, they were aware of the strategic role of these in protecting themselves and in opening up to what is happening outside their surroundings and limited milieu. According to them, the mobile phone replaces the role of the family in reporting. As one woman survivor of violence put it: 'In the past when your husband beats you, you seek help from your family who asks you to be patient, but now you can contact a legal centre which can make your problem known and thus you help other women to reject violence.'

Some of these women are using the Internet with its services, which has clearly become an important space for creativity, dissemination and information, enabling women to establish connections and become conversant with the experiences of other women in the world. These women are determined to be trained and educated in order to keep pace with technological progress, and reject exclusion and the missing of opportunities. These women survivors of violence have come to control their resources and do not need the permission of anyone to acquire or use these tools.

Access without control and determination

There were other women who rejected their condition but remained 'submissive', women who had not yet reached the level of rebelling and rejecting. Among them were those whose determination was broken. These women are seized with fear and a lack of self-confidence, but are somehow still hopeful about the future. They are as yet unaware that what they are living through and suffering from is not due to them or predestined. Among them are women who possess ICT but see it as widening the disparity between poor and rich, while knowing that we can expect more from these tools. Among them too are women who possess the technological means, especially the cell phone, but have no control over them because they can be deprived of them at any time or when their husbands get angry. Aicha told us: 'I have to tell my husband because he must agree. The man sees the cell phone as an enemy. If the man has the right to have the cell phone, the woman also has the right to have it and is in need of it.'

These women do not feel equipped to participate in the bright future that ICT 'promises' through access to knowledge and improvement of living conditions. A woman from Fez said:

> I am not convinced. The financial aspect is not the reason why I do not
> have a cell phone. I have money. I do not know how to use the cell phone.
> My brother tells me I must use the blackboard to learn because I did not
> have the opportunity to learn.

No access – yet the first step is taken

Then there were those women who were still bearing their difficult situations but who had no ability to change them. Even expressing despair in tears, however, as some of them did, can be interpreted as a rejection of the patient acceptance that is considered the best way of eventually achieving a bearable relationship with a husband. As such, the expression of their grief and anger can be seen as a major step in overcoming despair.

Perceptions about obstacles to ICT use

According to the counsellors and assistants at the legal centres, based on their experiences of their day-to-day work and direct contact with the women survivors of violence, the major obstacles to use of ICT by these women are illiteracy, poverty, 'unawareness' and their husband's authority over them.

For the centres' employees, lack of training is the first barrier to use of the Internet. The approach adopted by the associations, however, obliged them to employ people who specialized in data processing. The centres' directors saw their limited financial means as a major barrier to the use of technology. It is true that the Moroccan state has begun to recognize the role of such associations (especially women's associations and legal centres) in development and raising awareness, but this recognition is not accompanied by financial support. The centres rely on international organizations for financing projects, and are permanently looking for funds to ensure their continuation.

Conclusion

Through our research and encounters with the women respondents, it became clear to us that we cannot speak of women's access to ICT in a context characterized by the absence of approaches that take into consideration gender and the needs of poor people.

The saying 'all women are equal in violence' proved true, regardless of their age, educational standard, social and economic conditions and geographical location (rural or urban). Our focus groups comprised women of different ages and cultural, economic and social conditions. There were adults, young women, the illiterate, the literate, employees, workers, teachers, single, married and divorced women. It became clear to us that ICT plays a role in raising awareness of gender-based violence, and is also a tool for expression, opening up new prospects for work, improvement of work methods and saving valuable time.

Yet, between the blackboard in the world of learning to read and write and contemporary technology, there is a historical gap that apparently cannot be jumped by a large proportion of women. Returning to the blackboard is not possible, and nor is getting into the adventure of virtual worlds. This transforms the relationship with ICT into one of ignorance of the subject. What is the relationship here with the authority of men? Can one talk about a kind of 'phallo-technology'? As one of our respondents told us: 'the remote control is controlled by the husband or the father or the older brother'.

The development of ICT provides tremendous opportunities for women's empowerment. A study conducted by UNESCO in 2003, however, reaffirms the existence of the digital gender gap and that the priorities of intervention, in addition to equal use of ICTs by women and men, must also focus on the participation of women in decision-making, the fight against illiteracy and the removal of constraints related to triple gender roles for women.

From the opinions of the women in charge of legal centres, we concluded that ICTs are essential tools to contain the phenomenon of violence by controlling and handling information related to it. The access of women survivors of violence to ICT is, however, determined by their socio-economic situation, their educational standard, their living conditions and their autonomy. This raises the question of democratization and generalization of the use of ICT, and requires adoption of measures to reinforce the access of women to ICT. We had thought that these women would be able to keep pace with the technological progress that we see in our country, but the feminization of poverty and illiteracy seems to have reached its highest point (Association Démocratique des Femmes du Maroc 2007).

It is necessary that the policies supporting the empowerment of women take an interest in ICT as an essential factor to overcome the digital gap affecting women, especially women survivors of violence, and as a step towards breaking the silence that surrounds this phenomenon.

While it is apparent that a large number of women who survived violence are unable to take advantage of the opportunities relating to digital progress prevailing in the world, we did, however, also learn about experiences in the use of ICT which gave hope, made us optimistic and increased our belief and confidence in women's power to make use of these technologies to better their lives and bring about change.

References

Association Démocratique des Femmes du Maroc (2007) *Rapport parallèle des ONG au 3ème et 4ème rapports périodiques du gouvernement marocain.*

Centre National de Documentation du Maroc (2003) *L'implantation d'Internet au Maroc: enjeux et perspectives.*

Smyth, I., C. March and M. Mukhopadhyay (1999) *Guide to Gender Analysis Framework*, Oxfam Publishing, Arabic version.

United Nations ICT Task Force (2003) *Tools for Development: Using Information and Communications Technology to Achieve the Millennium Development Goals*, Working paper.

9 | The names in your address book: are mobile phone networks effective in advocating women's rights in Zambia?

KISS BRIAN ABRAHAM

For a long time, women have formed groups and organizations within their communities to collectively solve common problems, to network, to share experiences, and to advocate for change. These groups have been physical groups configured around church associations, community and neighbourhood initiatives and professional interests. The introduction of the mobile phone has affected the communication within these women's groups in various ways which need to be investigated.

Harnessing the potential of mobile phone communication to gather support for advocacy on women's issues presents a number of challenges. These may include prohibitive service provision costs, absence of formal and effective integration of the mobile phone in administrative networking initiatives, and the constraints (both traditional and practical) on women's freedom to access and utilize communication services independently.

This chapter is based on a study conducted in Lusaka in 2007 and 2008. I set out to explore how the communication for advocacy and change in women's groups (which are formed for that purpose) has been changed and/or affected through the use of the mobile phone.

Research process

My main sources of information are five leaders of women's groups that focus on women's empowerment (active participants in networks that comprise or are associated with the membership of the Non-Governmental Organizations Coordinating Council – NGOCC[1]), officials from the government regulating body responsible for mobile phone service provision, and representatives of mobile phone service providers. Qualitative in-depth interviews were carried out with these individuals.

Findings

Possibilities for women's networking Mobile phone communication is possible across Zambia regardless of remoteness since it uses wireless technology that demands minimal infrastructure installations for its operation, in contrast to the 'traditional' fixed-line telephone communication system. Women or women's groups that own mobile phones communicate with other women as well as men, unmoderated; the content develops as they communicate, with no one external to the conversation editing their words.

Individual users of mobile phones seem within reach of as many people as are listed in their phone book or phone address data files. Through their phone address book, users are assured of access to other users regardless of distance. Women's empowerment advocates have used this potential to channel advocacy messages to users of mobile phones. As a result, networks have formed which connect individual users on the basis of advocacy issues of common interest. These networks have turned into virtual communities where users can channel their own matters of interest to the general lists in a bid to seek support. Beyond their individual members, organizations like the NGOCC have immeasurable potential for communication through the lists of women within the phone address books of the individual members.

Women's organizations and activist networks are the structural elements that the NGOCC has utilized in achieving vast changes towards women's progress, not only within its immediate organizational environment, but also nationwide. Members of the general NGOCC network, such as Priscilla Mpundu,[2] former executive director of the Zambia Association for Research and Development, participate in NGOCC advocacy initiatives whatever their geographical location. She explains:

> I moved from Lusaka and I am now based in the Copperbelt Province [northern Zambia]. I receive updates from the NGOCC Secretariat on advocacy actions in my e-mail and on my mobile phone, but I find that the mobile phone messages reach me faster and I am quickly alerted [to] what is happening, as opposed to the Internet, which I don't check every day. I relay the messages to members of the new organization I am forming here.

In explaining how the NGOCC utilizes the mobile phone for mobilization of support, Leah Mitaba, communications specialist for the NGOCC, explains: 'We usually call our members to notify them of common advocacy measures, we send text messages to our membership on events such as the court hearings that affect us and we mobilize them to meet at court and render support to women.'

Another group that utilizes the mobile phone in women's development networking is the Chipata District Women's Association. The community association runs a mobile phone project in the Eastern Province's rural

Chipata district with the support of Oneworld Africa. It strategically bases its use of mobile phones on three principles: advocacy, livelihoods and entrepreneurship. Utilizing these principles in their use of the mobile phone, the association carries out advocacy work for women's progressive change in their community.[3] To improve their personal livelihoods and sustain their use of the mobile phone, the women generate income through the entrepreneurial provision of communication services to their community members.

The economics of mobile phone communication While it is true that communities can be created through exchanges of voice and data via mobile phones, a major factor to consider is cost. The economic status of women predetermines their position in relation to the virtual networks sustained by mobile phone communication. This consideration impacts on women's ability to communicate. According to Leah Mitaba at the NGOCC, only women with talk-time (call units) will be privileged members of the mobile community, with the ability to initiate conversations and the power to choose when to communicate. Those with no call units may be included at the discretion of those who have them. This can lead to the negative effects of such networking and exacerbate inequalities if not rectified.

Over a period of time, low-income-earning women who are part of the women's empowerment mobile-phone-sustained virtual network begin to lose their 'voice'. They become silent listeners and simply recipients of texts and alerts from more financially empowered members. They become the mobile phone virtual network's 'lower classes'. Brenda Zulu, an information communication technologies journalist based in Lusaka, laments:

> When you have names of poor people in your phone book, you will not have much access to your own development through your phone. More beneficial are names of people with resources in your phone book; that way, you can call them when you are faced with problems and they will assist you. Poor people will not call you back when you ask them to because they usually can't afford to make calls.

Beeping or paging (calling a user and hanging up before they answer the phone, which evades the call charge) and the Short Messaging Service (SMS – allowing users to communicate with others through short text messages) are coping methods in situations where users want to avoid costs, since they are almost free (SMS) and totally free (paging). These methods are becoming increasingly common as users avoid the limiting costs attached to making traditional calls. A virtual class system is emerging, however, as one user suggests: 'Members of the beepers and pagers association are a menace, they bother you with their beeps until you call them back without considering that you are using your own money to call them.'

These sentiments with respect to the 'underprivileged user' represent the 'cost irritation' attached to using mobile phones. While recipients may be inconvenienced by these practices, they are also an outreach opportunity for those in need or distress. Generally, women are the worst hit by poverty in Zambia, and one can presume that of the spectrum of women mobile phone users, a great number are 'underprivileged users'.

Formal institutions like the NGOCC, while utilizing mobile communication networks, are slow to adapt the costs of sustaining this communication system in their advocacy budgets. Leah at NGOCC believes that adaptation of mobile phone costs in organizational budgets can empower network members who are silenced by the inability to purchase call units, since the institution would facilitate mobile phone communication on a staff-to-network-member basis. She explains:

> In the advocacy department we utilize our personal mobile phones very often because members call our personal numbers and we tend to call them back because it speeds up information exchanges. Our limitation is that unlike corporate organizations that give their officers incentives for mobile communication, we don't have this policy in our organization.

Unless a 'poor' user is making calls that have more value to her than the cost of the call itself in terms of emotional comfort, economic gain or information, these mobile phone calls will entrench poverty. The risk of entrenching poverty in poor advocacy network members is very real, because advocacy does not directly generate incomes. Strategies employed to ensure that the 'silenced member' (owing to low income) is sustainably included in development conversations present a hope for equitable mobile-phone-sustained advocacy, as in the case of the Oneworld Africa District Women's Development Association mobile phone project. According to Kelvin Chibomba at Oneworld, in reference to the project:

> The women are actively using the mobile phone to advocate for women's rights and for social services. And they have developed collective mechanisms to ensure that the costs of call units are paid for through other collective income-generating activities designed for the purpose of sustaining the 'non-profit' advocacy.

Gender-based conflicts Another barrier to the effective use of mobile phone networking for advocacy is gender-based conflict over use of the mobile phone. The Zambian media's (Chakwe 2007; Batista 2002) coverage of communication by mobile phone among heterosexual couples has hinted at gender-based tensions. Reports have noted how cultural values have influenced the way women communicate and to a degree have hampered their freedom of expression and freedom to network. This perspective was echoed by the women I spoke with.

During our conversations gender-based conflicts were frequently mentioned as having occurred as a result of mobile phone use. The conflict usually occurs because of suspicion about whom a partner (whether male or female) in a relationship is speaking to. The names listed in the phone book of a woman's personal mobile phone must be dialled with caution lest she upset her partner. Leah Mitaba explains:

Based on deep cultural, traditional and religious grounds, most married couples in Zambia believe in the principle that married couples are one. This principle contradicts the ownership model of the mobile phone companies that is presented as personal and private property owned by its user.

In homes where couples are in possession of a mobile phone, the boundary of ownership is often crossed out of curiosity, suspicion and disregard for the independence of women. Partners tend to be wary about whom the other partner is communicating with, and because of the 'oneness' principle tend to claim the right to know. Conflict arises when either partner claims independence. It has been the case that females who have claimed their independence and autonomy in using the mobile phone have been victimized (Chakwe 2007). The consequences in the extreme have included abuse, death and divorce.

Discussion

Networking via the mobile phone establishes virtual communities and yields 'social capital', meaning 'stocks of social trust, norms and networks that [women] can draw upon to solve common problems' (Sirianni and Friedland n.d.; Sinha 2005). In the context of mobile phone use, the stocks of social trust, norms and networks are virtual and amorphous as they are embodied in the mobile phone book, which is a compilation of the user's contacts. These contacts are individual but can be configured to form networks to suit specific purposes. Once deliberately configured, networks of civic engagement on the issues and visions for change articulated by women are an essential form of social capital. The denser these networks are, the more likely that members of the community and decision-makers will respond to their recommendations (Sirianni and Friedland n.d.).

Sinha (2005) maintains that phone calls reinforce virtual networks and in turn generate social capital. Similarly, networks formed by women's groups or organizations for particular purposes can be linked to each other via phone calls and can subsequently collaborate to achieve changes for the advancement of women. For these organizations, this 'social capital' is a prerequisite to influencing policy and successful advocacy, according to their experiences in a number of cases where the mobile phone was used.[4]

The 'virtual class system' separating those with call units and those without negatively affects advocacy for women's empowerment, however, because it represents exclusion of the disempowered woman from these development discourses. For the user with call units, the phone book is a realistic portal through which to access social amenities, i.e. information, emotional well-being or resources, while for the underprivileged user the potential is diminished owing to their inability to afford communicating at will. This diminished potential is itself an indication of poverty. According to Amartya Sen in *Development as Freedom* (1999), poverty can be identified in terms of capability deprivation; the poor may experience social exclusion, and they cannot normally take part in the life of the community, including, in this case, the virtual community.

Adequate income, then, is a means to capabilities, and the cost of using mobile phones reduces the abilities of poor users since their financial resources diminish with every purchase of call units. It is critical to note that the effectiveness of mobile phone advocacy is reliant on constant communication, which demands constant purchase of call units. In reality, for the poor virtual network member with capability inadequacy, the purchase of call units risks being a further addition to their poverty. Mobile-phone-sustained virtual networks that are used in advocacy for women's empowerment cannot serve this purpose with the involvement of economically disempowered women unless measures are taken to deliberately empower these women economically.

For the 'poor', this train of thought thus begins to undermine the concept of 'freedom' that is synonymous with mobile phone use, making 'free mobile phone access' and 'free mobile phone communication' unrealistic and misleading concepts due to the high cost of communication.

Gender-based conflict over use of the mobile phone also influences mobile phone networking for advocacy among women negatively owing to its restriction of women's freedom to communicate and express themselves. In the book *Is Multiculturalism Bad for Women?*, Saskia Sassen, in an essay entitled 'Culture beyond gender' (1999), describes group rights as cultural rights and stresses that group rights are considered a way of protecting the importance of culture. In this context, we observe that the rights of the individual woman user may contradict the cultural principle that married couples are one. Sassen insists that it is difficult for women to both exercise their individual sense of self and attain richness of experience/norms/rituals in most cultures where women are disempowered. It is this sense of self which is in conflict with the cultural demand for women's subordination and collaboration in the patriarchal status quo. Where conflict occurs and affects women, it is often because the woman sacrifices the group rights that generally uphold patriarchal values, in favour of her individual rights.

The current gender conflicts over mobile phone use expose women's resistance to cultural restrictions that limit their freedom of expression and freedom of networking. Women in situations of conflict arising from their new-found independence linked to use of the mobile phone are faced with the dilemma of either adapting their use of the mobile phone to fit with their constant cultural/traditional subordination, or of adapting it to their desired or self-elected emancipation. In effect, the mobile phone presents itself as a culturally revolutionizing tool, bringing to the fore long-standing but unresolved injustices.

Conclusion

Returns from the efforts of women's mobile-phone-sustained advocacy networks are more immediate when the networks are dense. Depending on the strength of this density, social networks are formed and potential social capital for change can be realized. This social capital can be a useful prerequisite for women's progressive change.

The incapacity of disadvantaged women participants to afford to sustain their participation in mobile-phone-hosted developmental discourses represents poverty and inequality among women. It also represents the risk that mobile-phone-enhanced advocacy may ignore the voices of 'poor' women if deliberate measures are not put in place to include them on the basis of the recognition of their absence and the circumstances thereof. Furthermore, women must elect to uphold their individual and collective rights as women amid the patriarchal society in which they live and resist the traditional gender norms that limit their freedom of expression and networking.

Only when these two barriers are overcome will 'the names in the address book' have substantial meaning in networking for women's rights in Zambia.

Notes

1 The NGOCC is a non-governmental organization (NGO) that serves as a women's organizations umbrella body, coordinating and strengthening its member NGOs and community-based organizations addressing gender and development through capacity building and networking.

2 Those interviewed agreed to use of their real names in this chapter.

3 They, in collaboration with their community radio station, run a phone-in radio programme on which they invite local leaders and create a forum where developmental questions can be asked and answered. They also use these phones for network linkages for development issues for women's empowerment in their community.

4 Other programmes in which the NGOCC implements mobile phones in its work include:

a) Sixteen days of activism against gender-based violence: Members text reminders to commemorate the days and also text advocacy messages in commemoration to the general public.

b) Election into public office of women: There has been a steady rise of elected women officials, owing to an extent to text message campaigns by members of the NGOCC advising members of the general public to remember to vote for women.

c) Court case appearances: The organization supports women victims of human rights abuse and alerts members en masse to turn up at court hearings as a show of solidarity to victims and as a publicity effort for mass education.

d) General information dissemination and receipt: The organization is increasingly using the mobile phone as a tool of dissemination of general information related to the well-being of women (Leah Mitaba, NGOCC, January 2008).

References

Batista, E. (2002) 'Cell phones: the marriage breaker', *Wired*, www.wired.com/gadgets/wireless/news/2002/06/53452, accessed September 2008.

Chakwe, M. (2007) 'Marriages in a cell phone era', *The Post*, 22 April, postzambia.com/post-read_article.php?articleId=25563, accessed March 2008.

NGOCC (2004) *Beijing +10 Shadow Report on the Situation of Women in Zambia*, Lusaka: Zambia Association for Research and Development ZARD/Non-Governmental Organization Coordinating Council (NGOCC).

Sassen, O. (1999) 'Culture beyond gender', in S. M. Okin, *Is Multiculturalism Bad for Women?*, Princeton, NJ: Princeton University Press.

Sen, A. (1999) *Development as Freedom*, New York: Knopf.

Sinha, C. (2005) 'Effect of mobile telephony on empowering rural communities', Conference on Digital Divide, Global Development and the Information Society 2005, www.irfd.org/events/wf2005/papers/sinha_chaitali.pdf, accessed March 2008.

Sirianni, C. and L. Friedland (n.d.) 'Social capital', Civic Renewal Movement, www.cpn.org/tools/dictionary/capital.html, accessed March 2008.

THREE | Using ICTs: making life better?

10 | Mobile phones in a time of modernity: the quest for increased self-sufficiency among women fishmongers and fish processors in Dakar

IBOU SANE AND MAMADOU BALLA TRAORE

The evolution of information and communication technologies (ICTs) is upsetting the long-standing socio-economic and cultural landscapes of human societies. They push the boundaries of human action, and are often regarded as a panacea for various ills of humanity, particularly in countries in the South, leading to associated hopes and fears. ICT is redesigning the architecture of our world with a speed and intensity unprecedented in the history of human societies.

These days it is widely acknowledged that the quality of ICT is an influencing factor in building and strengthening economic and social development in the North and South. In African countries there is an urgent need to look for appropriate ways to fill the technological gaps that separate them from developed countries (Mottin-Sylla et al. 2004).

Today, the influence of ICT brings up several questions. These technologies give rise to phantasms of all kinds, creating dreams in millions of women and men around the world. Some analysts attribute to them excessive powers to transform societies, while others declare that ICTs do not have the power to change society but simply accompany a general and widespread movement which is witness to worldwide economic and cultural exchanges. It is the more optimistic reading of ICT which seems most widely accepted in the literature (Flichy 1991).

Neglected for a long time by economic development theorists as a transforming factor in socio-economic relationships, ICT is now considered a tool that can contribute to the creation of wealth for nations. It can act as a lever to accelerate growth and development by facilitating social exchanges and economic activities. It is this 'developmentalist' concept of progress through ICT which is now regarded in all African countries as a way to solve the serious problems of underdevelopment and poverty among their citizens (Commissariat général au Plan 1991).

In Senegal interest in ICT is primarily in the Internet and mobile (cellular) phones (Chéneau-Loquay 2001). Here the use of mobile phones is predominant but lack of economic means among most of the population, widespread illiteracy and a low level of schooling in French are obstacles to more generalized use of ICT.

With the massive eruption of women into the popular economy in Senegal – elsewhere known (incorrectly) as the 'informal' economy and here called the 'popular and solidarity economy' – as elsewhere in Africa, we are observing unprecedented growth in the use of mobile phones.[1] This process is part and parcel of the socio-economic changes that generate new behaviours linked to the capitalist world economy, which forces women and men to fit into the economic fabric of the country. With economic pressures impacting on a significant number of people, women are getting more involved in income-generating activities. Through this entrepreneurship women are tending to strengthen their creative skills while affirming their financial self-sufficiency, and subsequently are setting in motion a process that questions the traditional power of Senegalese men in the home.

ICT plays an important role within this quest of women to strengthen their self-sufficiency. For women fishmongers and fish processors in Dakar – the group we focus on in this chapter – mobile phones are the preferred tool for commercial transactions, making their profession less difficult because this technology increases their control (contraction) of time and space.

The focus of this chapter's analysis is to clarify the efforts of these women entrepreneurs in Senegal (and in so doing give more visibility to them) as they are in the process of liberating their creative potential for the purpose of social change. In other words, our work positions itself within the gender and development discourse whose objective is transformation of the social relationships between the sexes.

Theoretical framework and methodological approach

It might be useful to underline here, if only summarily, the assumptions that lie at the heart of our chapter. Faced with the multiple difficulties that African states have to contend with in trying to modernize based on imported development schemes, at the outset of our research we located our contribution within a framework of economic development and endogenous social change. We justify this positioning based on our refusal to use general development theories whose abstractions do not take into account the perspectives of the social actors affected by these or the relevant gender relations. (Which no doubt explains why these imported development models have not produced the expected results.)

As part of the scientific information-gathering necessary for this research, a series of meetings was held with heads of the main national structures responsible for the fisheries sector: the Regional Oceanographic Service and the Maritime Fisheries Division. These agencies are involved in the realm of halieutics (fish) production, which is mostly dominated by economic operators such as fishing companies, women fishmongers, women micro-fishmongers and fish processors (men and women). We also had to seek permission from and the help of these authorities to be able to meet women at the sites of our study, and to determine with them a discussion framework.[2]

The second step in preparatory information collection was a series of meetings with women involved in the fisheries sector at the main fish-landing sites in the Dakar region: Soumbédioune, Hann Yarakh, Penthium Thiaroye and the *Marché central au poisson* (central fish market).

After preliminary discussions with the women entrepreneurs at these sites it was possible to secure their involvement in our study, and to develop with them the terms and conditions of this research. It was also useful to explain our research project to the heads of the groups of women that we met.

Our investigations were difficult because they took place during the winter, and flooding had displaced the population, who moved to other centres and temporary lodgings. The survey that we carried out allowed us to address two groups of people: women members of the Groupement de Promotion Féminine – Group for the Promotion of Women (GPW), who own and make effective use of mobile phones as part of their commercial transactions, and those who do not have them or use them only occasionally. From this, we were able to get a sense of the population we needed to question in order to obtain a credible sample which met saturation principles.

A total of sixty people were interviewed in Wolof, the main national language in Senegal, addressing economic living conditions of Senegalese women, women's entrepreneurship and use of mobile phones. Three focus groups were set up involving women of different ages and belonging to different economic interest groupings (EIGs). These groups considered women's sociocultural environment, social relationships between the sexes, family relationships (husband–wife–relatives), working and impact of groups on the promotion of women and EIGs, use of mobile phones, and training needs. We also recorded life stories and practised participant observation.

In increasing our understanding of the women fishmongers and fish processors of Dakar who tried to strengthen their entrepreneurial success by using mobile phones, we refused to consider ourselves as 'tourists' on the outside of the phenomena to be studied. Positioning ourselves within the principle of engagement and distancing, we strove throughout our stay among the women in our sample to 'objectify objectification'. In fact, given the complexity of the fisheries sector (well known for its traditions and rites), only full immersion in this environment, anthropologically speaking (i.e. participation and sharing common interests), enabled us to overcome the barriers generally faced by observers coming from outside this environment. Obstacles would usually be related to lack of trust, perhaps because of the women's reluctance to provide information considered taboo (since it concerned, for instance, the social relationships between the sexes). By creating conditions of meaningful conviviality we were able to build close relationships with women fishmongers and fish processors – to such an extent that our presence gradually became virtually invisible to them as we proceeded with our study.

This choice of methodology allowed us to witness phenomena (such as the hard realities of their trade) that were less skewed by our presence, and to get a better grasp of the meaning and sense that these players give to their entrepreneurial actions. By proceeding gradually from a position of limited knowledge of the facts under study to a position of growing understanding, we tried to avoid the usual ambushes and biases of classic investigation methods. These tend to favour at times *Homo economicus*, an individual who is supposedly totally rational, selfish and calculating; and at other times *Homo sociologicus*, an individual who maintains quasi-static standards. We preferred *Homo situs*, who rebels against such a reductionism of ordinary science. The latter operates with the help of a 'composite and situated rationality, whose descrambling requires more complex models than the one provided by the regular economic rationale' (Zaoual 1998).

We were sensitive to the harsh working conditions of women fishmongers and fish processors, who, depending on fish landings at the wharf or incoming orders, may work anywhere from four hours to twenty-two hours a day in areas where the norm was a lack of safety, aggression from organized crime, and lack of appropriate basic equipment. We were also amazed by their strong determination to ensure the well-being of their families, faced by the harsh effects of the economic crisis affecting most Senegalese citizens since imposition of structural adjustment programmes in the 1980s.

Despite our research attitude of alternating engagement and distancing, we are aware of the multiple biases that any research is incapable of avoiding completely, such as distortion of the collected data, emotional biases and extrapolation.

Socio-economic and political context of the research

In analysing Senegalese society in terms of gender relationships, two main trends of thinking can be discerned. The first underscores invisibility of the essential activities of women in managing the economy and the environment, their absence in labour statistics, in economic or food production; their marginalization and the lack of consideration of these activities, regardless of their significance at the economic level; and the devaluation of their status and roles in an economy grounded in the concept of monetary income. The second insists on the need to take into account these roles that women play (Sow 2004: 50).

We tried to identify the main factors that form the basis of the inequality between the sexes in Senegal. A study of Senegalese society reveals that the most visible characteristic of the gender relationship is the hierarchical organization of social relationships, which subordinates women to men. In traditional Senegalese society authority is manifested as a male attribute. This translates into a separation of domains, activities and characteristics between the sexes (Diop 1981).

It is in such a context, profoundly marked by the pervasive influence of ancient structures for managing men and women, that the national state of Senegal has tried to build since 1960 (the year of its independence) an endogenous modernity which remains illusory to this day. In fact, economic and social development policies undertaken – based on models estranged from the realities in this country – have shown their limits, if not their failure.

In order to redress the deteriorated economic situation and make a new start, the state has been forced since the 1980s to appeal to international financial institutions such as the World Bank and the International Monetary Fund. This meant that the implementation of structural adjustment programmes was based on the condition of borrowing from overseas; in other words, confiscation of the economic sovereignty of the state.

For Ndiaye and Tidjani (1995) the substance of structural adjustment programmes relies mainly on the search for a socio-political order dominated by market logic and withdrawal of the state from the important sectors of the national economy (water, electricity, agriculture, industry, etc.) (see also Duruflé 1988; Diouf 1992). These programmes have accelerated the deterioration of living and working conditions, and have resulted in multiple consequences: lay-offs, business closures, restructuring of the economy along purely liberal lines, wage reductions, less buying power for the workers, and flexible staff management.

Overall, everything indicates that structural adjustment programmes have been counterproductive and have increased the pauperization and marginalization of a great number of women and men, as much in rural as in urban areas. As a consequence, the disastrous employment situation in Senegal has weakened the dominant position of men and contributed to the precariousness of many families. In this context, women's associations and GPWs play significant roles in mobilizing women with a view to alleviating the economic and social constraints that weigh heavily on families. To do this they invest massively in the popular and solidarity economy.

Over the years since the 1975 proclamation of the UN Decade for Women, GPWs have undergone continuous development and expansion. The philosophy motivating them is based on the idea that it is easier for women to develop common activities and find funding as a group than individually. The significant advantage of this approach resides in the change in perspective, with the current gender approach promoting a sound strategy for the reduction (even the end) of disparities between the sexes.

Emerging female entrepreneurship in Senegal needs to demonstrate a real capacity for initiatives through active associative networks: unified community or trade groups strongly linked to the affective life of these women. In fact, on the one hand such organizational structures mitigate the material and psychological effects of the material crisis, and on the other they facilitate the financial self-sufficiency of these women by affording them opportunities to better provide for their families and resolve certain personal problems or desires. As structures that lessen the constraints linked to the role and status of women, these groups also strengthen the mobility of their members by allowing them to build socio-economic links outside the domestic circle of relatives. In a nutshell, the groups give their women members the opportunity to express their individuality through and within new spaces that are more open to their desire for emancipation.

The actual dynamics of these structures, through the material production incarnated by the EIG, allow more and more female entrepreneurs to slowly but surely free themselves from sociocultural constraints and obstacles holding back full expansion of the movement for the liberation of women's creative forces towards more self-sufficiency and freedom. Women entrepreneurs face different challenges throughout their professional journey, including discrimination, difficult access to funding and credit conditions that offer very little advantage.

Results

> ICTs are only tools, means of information and communications. By themselves, they cannot solve social problems (Mottin-Sylla et al. 2004: 140)

In the struggle for development, the Senegalese state views the telecommunications sector as a strategic element in economic and political modes of intervention. The communications variable plays a significant role in the direction and optimization of resources to be mobilized, and in the coordination of activities undertaken. Subsequently, ICT is undergoing rapid development and expansion – and this is happening practically all over Africa. The mobile phone is by far the most utilized ICT, and this corresponds with the importance given to speech in orally based African societies.

For the women who contributed to our research, the use of a mobile phone allows them to save time and significantly increase business volumes. They say that the mobile phone erases the problem of distance. Said one respondent, who is forty-four years old and a mother of six children: 'When I bought my portable, it was for my activities. Sometimes, my clients need me, but are not able to reach me. Now that I have it, I don't have to travel to solve my problems. The portable is a necessity.'

This point of view is shared by another married respondent, who is forty-one, and a mother of nine children:

> By necessity, I bought a portable. Sometimes, I have clients who call me to get news about the market ... very often, the one who supplies me with fresh fish may call me very late at night. It also happens that I have to stay at the fishing port until it's very late, and it is with my portable that I call my husband to let him know. Also, sometimes, I have urgent needs and I solve them with my portable. I am more mobile with my portable and I'm not afraid that my family might not know where to reach me if they have to. I dial my number and I answer my calls. However, I don't know how to read, nor how to send an SMS [text message].

A thirty-nine-year-old divorcee and mother of two agrees:

> Before, when I left home I did not feel fully at ease until I got back. Now, with my cellular, I can be reached fairly quickly. Once I'm at the market, I have better dealings with my clients. I don't have to travel or to announce that I have the merchandise requested. In addition, it sometimes happens that the Association informs us at a moment's notice about a meeting to be held; in such a case, in order not to worry my family, I use

my portable phone to inform them. With the cellular I am more free and I don't worry about my family any more. In addition, I know how to read and send SMSs.

Testimonies gathered from the women in our research made it obvious that the mobile phone has had many positive effects. The phenomenal explosion in the use of the mobile phone in Senegal since 1996 clearly shows that this tool is now an integral part of the modalities that make possible the work undertaken by female entrepreneurs. It greatly contributes to the increase in commercial transactions and also improves the quality of relationships with suppliers and clients. In the popular and solidarity economy the speed of development of this new form of communication offers many benefits, leading one interviewee to say that 'if the mobile phone did not exist, we would certainly have needed to invent it in order to meet the needs expressed or not by a great number of women and men around the world'.

One thing is obvious: the mobile phone has become a necessary tool in the daily life of a great number of women and men. Is it a fashion statement or a working tool? It is no doubt both of these together. Use of the mobile phone by all categories of social players in Senegal, from upper management to fisherfolk, clearly shows that this is not an epiphenomenon. There is, however, clearly a sense that this needs to be better understood through more in-depth research.

In the fish-products marketing sector our results show several advantages linked to use of mobile phones:

- a great reduction in travel;
- a new factoring of time;
- an opportunity for quick contacts; and
- increased client loyalty.

The women also indicated their need for training in various subjects, allowing them to acquire the skills necessary for efficient execution of their trade (Sané and Traoré 2008). The need for training is particularly urgent as regards their main working tool, the mobile phone, as well as in the Internet. They said that the latter would open up new opportunities for them for exports beyond the countries on their borders. Given the high level of illiteracy in the French language among them, they also want a better functional literacy adapted to their particular needs, and an introduction to accounting and financial management.

Changes in socio-economic relationships within society and families in urban environments

The development of urban zones in Senegal was linked to implementation of the colonial administration and economy, and accelerated after the country's independence in 1960. Looking to promote economic and social development, the new state undertook a series of reforms, seeking to break away from the colonial model at political, economic and institutional levels. The new structures of production were addressed in the Land Reform Act (1964), the Local and Territorial Administration Act (1972) and the Family Code (1973).

The proliferation of urban areas from 1960 to the 1980s is explained by the emergence of new opportunities (jobs, trade, industries) that cities offered, particularly in the Dakar area. In response to the erosion of the rural economy traditionally marked by peanut crops, an influx of rural men and women headed to the urban centres in search of income-generating activities. One should recall that the migration of rural populations towards cities is a dimension of the gradual rupturing of social, cultural and moral values caught in the tension between tradition and social changes.

In order to better understand the current dynamism of Senegalese women, it should be noted that in traditional Sahel societies hierarchical organization is founded more upon lineage links than upon the conjugality that is a trait of the present modernity. As already mentioned, traditional organization favours the separation of the functions of production, consumption and residence. In such a context men and women have access to distinct resources and also assume different responsibilities.

It is such a social model (currently reconstituted) which to varying degrees is a source of self-sufficiency for women. In the Sahel countries generally and in Senegal in particular, spouses maintain individual ownership of property. They rarely hold common goods and capital, and they assume different roles and responsibilities in terms of expenses. The feeling of self-sufficiency that this creates for women is another reason for the development of female entrepreneurship. This wise custom throws into stark contrast the current pervasive power of patriarchal standards.

These days women are assuming new roles with the reconstitution of the traditional family model, the ongoing nuclearization of the family, changes in value systems and the questioning of the predominance of lineage and its underlying hierarchical relationships. This march towards the 'liberation' of women has had the side effect of increasing the divorce rate and the emergence of women as heads of family, as much in the country as in the cities.

As previously indicated, the crisis of the imported development model, and its inability to produce credible alternatives to the current situation where productive forces are underdeveloped, results in the absurd saturation of the 'official' labour market and the insignificant volume of available jobs to absorb the abundant labour force. This explains why a great number of men and women try to escape from insecurity and poverty and try to find ways of making a living within the popular and solidarity economy.

In the current socio-economic crisis severely affecting Senegalese families in general and women and young people in particular, we observe the increasing incapacity of heads of families (men) to fully provide for the essential needs of their household by themselves (Antoine et al. 1995). It is this situation of rupture with the fairly recent past which explains why women are coming out of their domestic universe to get involved in the economic universe in search of new income-generating opportunities. From this point on, the work of women outside of their family becomes a vital necessity.

The life stories we recorded indicate that the daily lives of women fishmongers and fish processors are an interaction between family life and professional life. Like other women involved in the popular and solidarity economy, they hold traditionally incompatible roles, i.e. as simultaneously spouses and substitutes for their husbands in the sense that they have become their families' breadwinners. In urban areas this tendency progresses farther and upsets the architecture of the traditional family. This unexpected situation profoundly challenges masculine superiority in the management of household affairs. Practically all of the women interviewed were forced to assume an essential role in supporting the family, either because their husbands were unemployed or because they have had to retire.

Hence, socio-economic changes that profoundly affect society contribute to the social power of the women involved in the popular and solidarity economy. Faced with increasingly difficult living conditions (as much in rural as in urban areas), women have demonstrated great self-organization and adaptation skills. They have set up multi-faceted structures (GPWs, EIGs, tontines, etc.) aimed at fostering activities that are both lucrative and support solidarity among themselves. This evolution is no doubt more obvious in urban areas by virtue of their deeper immersion in the capitalist world economy, pushing many women to search for social and political emancipation outside the patriarchal sociocultural structures. For them education and training become an aspiration and a means of social advancement. This growing determination by women to get out of the domestic sphere (Mbow 2005), while seeking a new equilibrium between the sexes within a society undergoing a transformation, is sometimes a source of tension.

The traditional ideology of women's dependence on and submission to men (in particular to their husbands), as prescribed by Islam, the religion of the majority in Senegal, is often evoked to limit the movement for the emancipation of women. Objections are generally framed as follows: activities outside the home distance women from their domestic and educational responsibilities, give them freedom and, by the same token, can lead to infidelity. Beyond such male resistance, however, evolution towards a real redistribution of the roles of men and women still manages to follow its logical course.

Conclusion and recommendations

In investigating an economic, social and societal change process, we wanted to show how some Senegalese women in the fishing sector seek to lessen the obstacles and constraints that curb their full self-realization through entrepreneurship. How did they use a working tool such as the mobile phone to maximize their commercial transactions? How did factors such as illiteracy, poverty and technical and material difficulties curb their keen desire to break with a model of society that belongs to another historicity (tradition), and whose structuring principles (discrimination, marginalization, etc.) do not correspond with the present aspirations of women (self-sufficiency, equal rights, accountability, etc.)?

There is an urgent need to achieve – on their behalf and that of many other women involved in the popular and solidarity economy – economic and social policies able to appreciably improve their living and working conditions. Such initiatives could have a decisive influence on their future behaviours and attitudes, and thus allow them to fully participate in the present endogenous modernization process in Senegal.

Considering everything mentioned above, we make the following recommendations:

- That in addition to ongoing efforts to foster the development of female entrepreneurship and organizations that support the promotion of women, the state of Senegal should contribute more as a facilitator to ensure that female entrepreneurship becomes a true structure for promotion and emancipation.
- That the social advancement of women undeniably requires a multidimensional policy of public powers that act simultaneously on the school system, on employment and on the social and cultural environment.

- Redefinition of male and female roles will be an unavoidable necessity. Such a process will call for a revaluation of the image of women more in line with the present direction of Senegalese society, which is increasingly imbued with new values of modernity – including the use of mobile phones to conquer space for increased freedom and achievement.

Notes

1 We challenge such designations as informal or underground economy. Contrary to the sector known as 'modern', i.e. official, this new sector brings together most of the active workers. The popular and solidarity economy combines three poles: the market, the non-merchant and the non-monetary. (See Ndiaye 2005.)

2 The women are assisted by public services. It was therefore important to inform the authorities so that meetings with them could take place under appropriate conditions.

References

Antoine, P. et al. (1995) *Les Familles dakaroises face à la crise*, Dakar: IFAN-ORSTOM.

Chéneau-Loquay, A. (2001) *Les Territoires de la téléphonie mobile en Afrique*, available online at www. africanti.org/resultats/documents/ACL_mobile.PDF.

Commissariat général au Plan (1991) *Technologies de l'information et performances économiques*, Paris.

Diop, A. B. (1981) *La Société wolof. Tradition et changement. Les systèmes d'inégalité et de domination*, Paris: Karthala.

Diouf, M. (1992) 'La crise et l'ajustement', *Politique Africaine*, 45.

Duruflé, G. (1988) *L'Ajustement en Afrique*, Paris: Karthala.

Flichy, P. (1991) *Une Histoire de la communication moderne. Espace publique et vie privée*, Paris: La Découverte.

Mbow, P. (ed.) (2005) 'Hommes et femmes entre sphères publiques et privées', Série genre [Gender Series] no. 5, Dakar: CODESRIA.

Mottin-Sylla, M. H. et al. (2004) *Citoyennes africaines de la société de l'information*, Dakar: ENDA.

Ndiaye, A. I. and B. Tidjani (1995) 'Mouvements ouvriers et crise économique', Dakar: CODESRIA, Série de monographies [Series of monographs], pp. 3–95.

Ndiaye, S. (2005) *Economie populaire et développement local en contexte de précarité. L'entreprenariat communautaire dans la ville de Saint-Louis (Senegal)*, PhD thesis, University of Quebec, Montreal.

Sané, I. and M. B. Traoré (2008) 'Femmes et technologies de l'information et des communications au Sénégal. Cas des transformatrices de poisson et mareyeuses de Dakar, Senegal', Report available at: www.GRACE-Network.net.

Sow, F. (2004) 'L'analyse de genre et les sciences sociales en Afrique', in M. I. Ayesha, A. Mama and F. Sow (eds), *Sexe, genre et société* [Sex, gender, and society], Paris: CODESRIA/Karthala, p. 50.

Zaoual, H. (1998) 'Le besoin de croire: une nouvelle énigme pour les sciences sociales du développement', *Culture et Développement* [Culture and Development], 33, Brussels.

11 | Women entrepreneurs in Nairobi: examining and contextualizing women's choices

ALICE WANJIRA MUNYUA

Throughout the world billions of people are purchasing mobile phones. A 2007 International Telecommunication Union report estimated that 3.305 billion mobile phones were in use. Rapid adoption of this technology raised hopes that people in the developing world would benefit from it (Gamos 2003).

In Kenya the demand for mobile phones is huge and continues to expand; many mobile users do not own a landline at home or at work. A 2005/06 Communications Commission of Kenya annual report showed that landline subscriptions had continued to decline, remaining below 300,000 subscribers, whereas mobile telephone usage had risen from 4.6 million to 6.4 million subscribers during 2005/06. 'A substantial proportion of small businesses use mobile phones as their only means of communication' (Vodafone 2005: 51). This confirms that in Africa the mobile phone is used as a substitute for rather than to complement a landline (Donner 2007). A mobile phone is seen to offer advantages over fixed lines.

A study of Kenyan women entrepreneurs revealed that the mobile phone had indeed affected the effectiveness and efficiency of women-owned businesses (Wanjira Munyua and Mureithi 2008). Has the application and use of the cell phone to enhance entrepreneurial success also contributed, however, to women entrepreneurs' empowerment? This chapter discusses the business choices made by the women entrepreneurs who fall into different categories of capacity and size,[1] and explores how the use of mobile phones has facilitated their efficiency in managing micro-enterprises and their domestic responsibilities, and the implications for women's empowerment.

The research context

Most of the Kenyan women entrepreneurs whom we spoke to indicated that their main reasons for going into business ventures included the need for achievement, autonomy and flexibility, along with providing for and educating their children (Wanjira Munyua and Mureithi 2008). Our 2008 study in Nairobi with thirty-three women revealed that entrepreneurship is becoming an increasingly popular career choice for many Kenyans. We found that while some individuals start businesses based on their need to be independent, most of the women chose the entrepreneurial route in response to external situations, including redundancies, frustration with their current workplace and pay, or a need for greater flexibility in their lives.

In recent years the Micro and Small Enterprises (MSEs) part of the informal sector has played an increasingly important role in Kenya. According to Ikiara (2001), and a World Bank report (2001), MSEs are regarded as offering an alternative route to economic growth, especially in the context of increased poverty and unemployment, as well as the advent of economic reforms that have led to the liberalization of the economy.

A survey conducted by Wolf (2001) in South Africa, Kenya and Tanzania notes that MSEs provide employment to more than 50 per cent of the income-earning population. The study estimates that in Kenya small enterprises generate 12–14 per cent of the gross domestic product. Kenya's economic landscape also reflects the dominance of MSEs as the most dynamic aspect of the private sector (ibid.).

One significant characteristic of the sector is that as it has grown, it has also become an important employer of the female labour force in the country. According to the Kenya Rural Enterprise Programme and Central Bureau of Statistics (CBS) Baseline Survey conducted in 1999, the number of men and women owning micro-enterprises in Kenya was almost equal, at 670,727 enterprises owned by men compared to 612,848 owned by women. A great disparity is noted, however, in the type of businesses men and women choose, and the incomes generated by the businesses. Women are concentrated in community, social and personal service businesses (Republic of Kenya 1998, 1999, 2000). This survey seems to suggest that women may have opted for these types of businesses owing to the low demands in terms of new skills, capital and equipment required to operate in this segment.

Gakure (2004) found that women's productive activities were concentrated in micro-enterprises that conformed to their traditional gender roles, such as food processing and garment making. The Kenya Central Bureau of Statistics (Republic of Kenya 1999) Baseline Survey reveals that while the numbers of women- and men-owned enterprises are almost equal, women outnumbered men in services (55.7 per cent women) while men outnumbered women in manufacturing (65.7 per cent men) and construction (91.2 per cent men). The choice of sector also seemed to define the profitability of the enterprises. Male-owned MSEs had 75 per cent more income than female-owned enterprises – women earned

4,344 Kenya shillings (Ksh) for every Ksh 7,627 men earned from their micro-enterprises.

A review by the Kenya CBS in the same period indicated that more female-owned enterprises (5,585) than male (4,045) closed down (Kibas and K'Aol 2004). Of those businesses that closed down, lack of funds was common to both women- and men-owned MSEs; lack of customers and too much competition accounted for 26.8 per cent of women's business closures against 12.5 per cent of men's closures. Women also cited personal reasons, for example having to take care of children, where it became increasingly difficult to balance work with family responsibilities. Taking care of a sick family member accounted for 33.1 per cent of women's business closures, while for men it accounted for 20.3 per cent (ibid.). According to Mincer (1978) and Polachek (1981), women are generally at a disadvantage when competing with men for enterprises and job opportunities. Most societies expect women to leave the labour market for purposes of childbirth, childcare and the accompanying domestic responsibilities, skills that are undervalued and perceived as incompatible with enterprise and labour market opportunities. While government statistics indicate that, in recent years, the number of women-owned firms with employees has increased, even with this growth women remain underrepresented in terms of their proportion of the high-growth firms.

Women's business choices

As Gakure (2004) notes, most women entrepreneurs in Kenya tend to draw upon their domestic skills in their micro-enterprises. She subsequently concludes that as the skill base seems to determine the choice of the business, the choice of the business entered into is largely gendered in the first place. This is a reflection of the impact of Kenya's cultural bias in education and training on career choices. Connell (2002) indicates that much of the gender construction in schools creates very distinct notions of what it means to be a man and a woman, with polarized attributes for femininity and masculinity. Socialization in schools touches on the informal (hidden) curriculum, which is a critical dimension of schooling through which educational settings may introduce changes in social perceptions, but which generally continues to reproduce traditional values and attitudes. This socialization is achieved through a wide array of practices, ranging from administrators' and teachers' attitudes and expectations, textbook messages, peer interactions and classroom dynamics. There are also expectations in terms of the roles that students are supposed to play in the future, and these influence their attitudes, as well as behaviours practised in and outside the classroom.

A 2005 Population Council study noted that for all developing countries, approximately 10 per cent of boys and 40 per cent of girls aged between six and eleven never enrol in school. This is especially pronounced in areas where factors such as employment prospects and mothers' education are lower, and where girls are more likely to have other responsibilities such as housework and childcare, and are even required to engage in income-generating activities to supplement the family household income. This is the case especially in most Kenyan lower-middle to low-income households.

According to Connell (2002), through socialization men assume the role of income provider and identify with masculine stereotypes, whereas women assume the role of homemaker and identify with feminine stereotypes. Consequently, men and women prefer job attributes and acquire skills that relate to their gender roles and stereotypes. Furthermore, if women have internalized the belief that they are not valuable in their own right and that as such their potential professional contribution is not valued either, it may lead to the perception that meeting societal demands is more important and more valuable than their personal dreams and wishes and, in actual fact, that fulfilling their own dreams is not a real option because there is no real choice.

Many women end up adopting socially constructed gender values which devalue them, creating an inability to recognize themselves, their dreams and aspirations in the context of social norms. According to Chege (2003), women who conform to gendered societal norms are the perfect embodiment of a Kenyan woman. Therefore, those who build successful businesses or careers are perceived to be venturing into masculine roles.

Women with this 'strong female image' may still hold and transfer societal myths regarding women entrepreneurs on to their business, affecting their attitude and the ways in which they pursue business success and growth (Brush and Hisrich 1999). Further, women's socialization may affect their self-assessment about being prepared with regard to business creation. Brush (1997) notes that 'the gendered perspective of the founder influences the organising process and resultant new organisation, whether it is for high growth or not. This perspective creates unconscious biases regarding capabilities and potential.' Our study also confirmed this notion that despite the growth of women's own businesses, a large majority started small and stayed small, never employing more than ten people.

Gakure's study (2004) in Kenya sought to determine the social factors that influenced growth and development of female-operated enterprises.

This study found that the majority performed poorly. Could the control of choice to go into a particular sort of business or to go into business at all affect their efficiency and effectiveness? For most of the women (68.6 per cent) the decision to go into business was determined by people other than themselves. These included their husbands (24.6 per cent), parents (27.4 per cent) and friends (13.1 per cent) (ibid.). For the women who participated in the Wanjira Munyua and Mureithi study (2008), going into business was a way of contributing additional income to support their families, and for some it was necessary as they were the sole breadwinner. For the women who chose their enterprise, their need to combine doing business with their domestic responsibilities was a significant factor in business choice.

The motivation to go into business, as well as the type of business chosen, influences the choice of information and communication technology (ICT) or tool that can be used to enhance their business and enable them to manage their homes at the same time (ibid.). Most women chose businesses that allowed them the flexibility needed to raise a family, and the communication tool – the cell phone – that facilitated meeting the demands of their double roles.

Computers are still a relatively expensive investment for MSEs (Wolf 2001). The Wolf study further noted that MSEs usually face a comparatively uncertain environment and entrepreneurs often have a short-term time horizon. Therefore the decision to implement and appropriate ICTs depends on the intuition of the entrepreneur, which is subject to their training and experience. This could explain why not all potential users introduce the different ICTs, despite their advantages.

Is the mobile phone contributing to businesswomen's empowerment?

For most Kenyans the choice of owning a mobile phone rather than a landline is affected by many factors, ranging from the failure of Kenya's telephone corporation to deliver on its universal access obligations, a more liberal regulation environment, and increased competition in the telecommunication sector (Mureithi 2005), to the users' perception of convenience and affordability of the mobile phone. Penetration of the cell phone is high among MSEs in Kenya; Mureithi (ibid.) found in an industrial cluster in Nairobi that 93.8 per cent of the entrepreneurs owned cell phones, in contrast to 29.7 per cent who used fixed lines. Factors that affected decisions to own a mobile phone rather than a landline included the ability to communicate anywhere, any time, and subsequent faster sales of products, among other perceived benefits. The legal status of the business also seems to determine information needs and the ICT tools to use. According to Tandon (2002), small businesses usually have no option but to remain informal to avoid the challenges of taxation, reporting and licensing. Tandon's study noted that business owners consider other communication tools besides the mobile phone only once they perceive the business to have grown.

Most of the respondents in the Wanjira Munyua and Mureithi (2008) study felt that the use of the mobile phone had improved their business's performance through their ability to integrate business and family issues. They could also organize social meetings, such as those with women's groups, through features such as the calendar and phone reminders. The mobile phone allowed them to have a sense of control, even when away from their business premises, and it improved their networks with friends and clients, as well as providing the ability to transfer money through the new service called *sambaza* credit (sharing of airtime).

When asked why they purchased a mobile phone in the first place, most of the respondents spoke of encouragement from their male partners, spouses, mothers and friends. Asked what the challenges were in using the mobile phone, the women entrepreneurs cited the high costs of operating a cellular phone in Kenya, as well as concerns regarding instances where spouses and male partners sought to find out the contents of some of the conversations conducted on the phone. Some of the women felt that there was a conditional benefit of the mobile phone owing to intrusion on their privacy. When technology like the mobile phone comes into the domestic sphere it potentially brings the world with it.

The phone can indeed be a great vehicle for networking and sharing information. The flipside of the mobile phone, however, is that it can tempt the user to blur the boundaries of private spaces, and this can become another source of tension in unequal gender relations. Huyer and Sikoska (2003) found that men frequently felt that the new freedom of women to have mobile phones was destabilizing their marital relationship. In most of the cases men monitored their spouse's use of the mobile phone and Internet. Another study of women and use of mobile phones in Zambia (Wakunuma 2007) found that while mobile phones have had positive impacts for women, they seem to contribute to conflict in the household between spouses, with husbands and partners wanting to control how their partners and wives use the phone, and sometimes whether they are allowed to continue to own and use the mobile phone.

Most studies seem to point out the clear advantages of mobile phones for women entrepreneurs, but the questions can be asked whether gender inequality is being perpetuated in relation to women's access to and use of mobile phones, and whether the use of cell phones contributes to women entrepreneurs' empowerment.

In this context, what is empowerment? The case of Lillian

Lillian, one of the women entrepreneurs who participated in the 2008 Wanjira Munyua and Mureithi field study on the use of mobile phones among Kenyan women entrepreneurs, manages a family hair and beauty salon employing nine employees. Her business and situation corresponds with factors found in two categories of women entrepreneurs (see note 1), and her story provided an opportunity to explore, increase our understanding of and continue investigating the dynamics of ICTs and women's empowerment in a real-life context.

Lillian had chosen a medical career and had embarked on it, completing the first year of a medical degree in Canada. She felt, however, that she had to abandon her medical career to help her family survive the financial difficulties they were encountering. Her mother called her back home to help set up her beauty and hair business as a partner, while Lillian's older and younger brothers continued with their education abroad. Lillian decided to give up her needs for those of her family, even though this meant giving up on her dreams. She believed that as the only girl in the family it was expected of her to help her mother educate her brothers. She said: 'I did not have my daughter Wanjiku then and being the only girl in the family, it was expected of me to come back home and that is the way things are.'

When Lillian made the choice to return home to help her mother set up and manage the business, she was excited to be of assistance to her family. She felt, however, that she had lost an opportunity to study medicine, which was her dream, and which she felt she could have linked into the hair and beauty business, therefore living her dream and helping her family at the same time. This is indicative of the many ways in which fear of disappointing their families and not living up to their mothers' expectations, following habitual patterns of thought and action as well as their own low expectations for themselves, characterize many women's choices and limit their dreams for their own lives (Blau et al. 1998).

Lillian's actions seem to be at odds with her beliefs about herself and her capabilities, but they are in line with societal expectations. Nevertheless, Lillian is quite happy with her choices. Despite finding that their beauty business does not cover all her financial and professional needs, she does not consider what happened to her wrong in any way. She has accepted the option of helping out her family and at the same time getting a little money to educate her daughter. Lillian's well-being at the time depended on her evaluation of her situation, which seems to have been based in socialized preferences. She seems to have adapted to her gendered situation and her analysis reflects her understanding of what is for her own good and the good of her family. But does this translate into empowerment?

Lillian confirmed that some of the advantages of owning a mobile phone (as opposed to a landline) were that one can be reached anywhere, and therefore she can conduct her business at any time of the day or night or monitor her household at any time. This gives her a sense of control and flexibility, both needed to manage her dual areas of responsibility (Wanjira Munyua and Mureithi 2008). She was given her first mobile phone as a Christmas present and uses it to conduct her business activities. She keeps in touch with clients, organizes debt collection and coordinates activities in the salon, along with arranging social activities such as monitoring her daughter's daily activities and movements and keeping in touch with friends and other members of her family.

For Lillian the social and economic advantages of accessing and using a mobile phone for her hair and beauty business and for her domestic needs seem evident. The question has to be raised, however, whether patterns of gender socialization are being perpetuated and reproduced in the use of the new technology and choice of business, re-emphasizing the fact that technological innovation and the opportunity to become an entrepreneur do not guarantee empowerment for women, neither do they address the substantial obstacles to women's social, political and economic development.

Empowerment or gender role entrenchment?

The contemporary concept of empowerment in Kenya rests on the assumption that increases in women's access to resources like education, wealth and ICTs would transform them and, by extension, society meaningfully. It ignores the fact that women's access is often mediated by poverty, classism, traditional divisions of labour, social traditions and expectations, racism and xenophobia, and that access can be empowering only to a small minority of women. It also ignores the notion that in many circumstances, although choices play a critical role, these are usually determined by social norms and what is expected of one as a woman or girl; therefore many choices do not necessarily serve a woman's own interests and their wishes for their own lives. Lillian's choice to come back home to help her mother with the family hair and beauty business was in response to her mother's request for her to come back and help rejuvenate a dwindling family income.

Nussbaum (2000) suggests that many preferences are constructed as adaptations within a context of traditions of privilege and subordination. Seen from this perspective, a preference-based approach would tend to reinforce inequalities. When Lillian made the choice to return home she lost her opportunity to fulfil her dream. She chose to fulfil traditional expectations of her as a woman and daughter, rather than resist the norms of her context and pursue her own goals.

Nussbaum's approach to adaptive preferences challenges the view that a culture/context-based understanding of what empowerment means to women would suffice when one strives towards social justice and empowerment. Rather, having the capability to do the things that people have reason to value is identified as a crucial concept. So, rather than simply evaluating the equality of and access to resources such as income and wealth, the analysis should ideally focus on people's capability to take action (Sen 2000). According to Sen, 'individuals have varying needs for resources according to their social and physical circumstances, and the special obstacles they face, among other factors. Therefore, even when people may have the same basic resources, they may end up being unequal in their ability to perform valuable human functions.'

Most of the women in the Wanjira Munyua and Mureithi study seem to have adapted to managing a combination of business endeavours and busy households. Men in business generally can focus more time on ensuring the success of their businesses. Harkim (2006) notes that most of the men in her study are married with children and seem to have the advantage of physically and mentally working longer hours because their wives are at home with the children. So even with women increasingly engaging in enterprises, they continue to be responsible for the domestic, unpaid, work.

From a feminist perspective this gender-based division of labour is hierarchical and patriarchal and therefore an issue of justice (Knobloch 2002). Knobloch identifies three aspects of gender-based divisions of labour. The first is that men do paid work while women are responsible for non-market, unpaid work. Second, most jobs are either 'male or female' and paid jobs done by women are often lower paid than the male ones. The third aspect is that women are most often held responsible (by social and cultural norms and unequal gender relations) for caring activities around a household, even when they are employed outside the house or have businesses that depend on them. Women therefore work twice as much as men, combining both the non-market economy and market economy work, often managing what she refers to as a 'double day' (ibid.). As a result, women choose occupations that allow them to balance paid work and domestic responsibilities.

To define women's empowerment, we may need to deal with individual variability, allowing women to state which functions they care about, and examine their needs within these functions. There is a need to critically examine (Fraser 1997) the notion of women as universal caregivers and the unexamined and decontextualized acceptance of women's preferences and desires, on the justification that 'what is good for the individual is by extension good for the society'. This preference-based approach tends to reinforce inequalities, especially those internalized so strongly as to have crept into women's dreams and desires, as illustrated by Lillian's choices and her willingness to return home to a role of combining domestic and income-generation responsibilities in a traditionally female sector, and her integration of an ICT into her efforts to manage this gender-specific double role effectively. The striving towards gender equality and women's empowerment in the ICT arena seems to require thoughts and actions that can move beyond accepted gender norms, even when the norms are being maintained and enhanced by women themselves.

Conclusion

ICTs have played a positive role in promoting development of women's entrepreneurship in Kenya, and the mobile phone in particular appears to have had a huge impact on the effectiveness and efficiency of micro-enterprises owned by women. The cell phone does not, however, appear to have changed fundamental issues of gender relations. Instead, patterns of gender socialization and segregation are still being reproduced.

ICTs have been and continue to redefine gender relations in complex and multidimensional ways. The Wanjira Munyua and Mureithi study has provided insights into how the mobile phone, for example, can be utilized in ways that reinforce traditional ideas of how women and men should behave, while at the same time providing an avenue for challenging gender norms.

The study also confirms that technological invention does not guarantee empowerment. A vast majority of Kenya's population is still untouched by the mobile phone revolution. Further, the availability of physical infrastructure or being connected does not necessarily capture actual use, since actual use is affected by sociocultural and economic factors.

Undoubtedly, ICTs can contribute immensely to development, but technology needs to be specially harnessed towards social roles through active human participation and mediation. Some of the women in the

Wanjira Munyua and Mureithi study reported increased efficiency and indeed confidence when using a mobile phone for their business, and this seems to be almost universally true for different sociocultural contexts (Hafkin 2002; Gurumurthy 2004). Does this increased efficiency and confidence the women experience while fulfilling traditional gender roles, however, have the potential to change existing gender relations?

Note

1 An International Labour Organization study on women entrepreneurs in Kenya (Stevenson and St-Onge 2005) provides anecdotal evidence of a profile of such women. The study found that Kenyan women entrepreneurs are not homogeneous, but fall into three distinct categories, each with its own demographic profile, extent of previous business experience, capacity, needs, access to resources (credit, premises) as well as orientation towards growth. The first category is labelled the 'Jua Kali' micro-enterpriser. These women own their business, which is often not registered and is in the informal economy. They have little education (less than secondary level) and are constrained by lack of entrepreneurial and business know-how, access to credit, and awareness of markets and market opportunities. They are most likely to employ a few family members, operate from a home-based shed (or *jua kali* – a Swahili term for 'hot sun', referring to the open-air working conditions) with limited potential for growth. To obtain credit, they are likely to be part of a women's 'merry-go-round', a group of five or six women who combine their savings over a six-month period of time and then start lending, on a very short-term basis, to members from the pool. For communication needs they are likely to rely on word of mouth and a mobile phone using the cheapest tariff available (Wanjira Munyua and Mureithi 2008).

The second category comprises women with very small (usually six to ten employees) businesses, who have minimum education (to secondary level), with previous experience as an employee in a public or private sector enterprise. These businesses would be registered and operate from legitimate business premises. These women are likely to have access to some level of training and microfinance to advance their business, but are still constrained by access to financing. Commercial banks in Kenya still prefer to lend to large depositors, and these women are unlikely to have title deeds to meet collateral security requirements. They probably own a mobile phone and use it to manage the business. This category of businesswoman would have growth potential and perhaps even access to international markets.

The third category is made up of women who may have some level of university education; they may also come from an entrepreneurial family with experience in managerial positions. They are likely to have small, medium-sized or larger enterprises with growth potential and an opportunity to engage in export. They would keep a mobile phone as well as a fixed line to conduct business and would also most probably own and use a computer and the Internet.

References

Blau, F. et al. (1998) *The Economics of Women, Men and Work*, 3rd edn, Englewood Cliffs, NJ: Prentice Hall.

Brush, C. (1997) 'Women-owned businesses: obstacles and opportunities', *Journal of Development Entrepreneurs*, 2(1): 1–25.

Brush, C. and R. Hisrich (1999) 'Women-owned businesses. Do they matter?', in Z. Acs (ed.), *Are Small Firms Important? Their Role and Impact*, Norwell, MA: Kluwer Academic Publishers.

Chege, R. (2003) *A Curriculum of the Training of Trainers in Gender Mainstreaming*, Nairobi: African Women's Development and Communication Network (FEMNET).

Communications Commission of Kenya (2006) *Annual Report 2006*, www.cck.go.ke.

Connell, R. W. (2002) 'The globalization of gender relations and the struggle for gender democracy', in E. Breitenbach et al. (eds), *Geschlechterforschung als Kritik*, Bielefeld: Kleine Verlag, pp. 87–98.

Donner, J. (2007) 'The use of mobile phones by micro entrepreneurs in Kigali, Rwanda: changes to social and business networks', Research paper, *The Massachusetts Institute of Technology Information Technologies and International Development*, 3(2): 3–19.

Fraser, N. (1997) *Justice Interruptus: Critical Reflections on the Post Socialist Condition*, New York: Routledge.

Gakure, R. (2004) 'Factors affecting women entrepreneurs' growth prospects in Kenya', Paper prepared for the International Labour Organization (ILO), Geneva, November, www.ilo.org/global/What_we_do/Publications/lang–en/index.htm, accessed April 2008.

Gamos (2003) 'Innovative demand models for telecommunications services', www.telafrica.org.

Gamos et al. (2004) 'The impact of mobile phones in Africa', Report prepared for the Commission for Africa, www.commissionforafrica.org/english/report/background/scott_et_al_background.pdf, accessed 29 April 2008.

Gurumurthy, A. (2004) *Bridging the Digital Gender Divide: Issues and Insights on ICT for Women's Economic Empowerment*, New Delhi: UNIFEM.

Hafkin, N. J. (2002) 'Are ICTs gender-neutral? – a gender analysis of 6 case studies of multi-donor ICT projects', *UN/INSTRAW Virtual Seminar Series on Gender and ICTs*, Seminar One: Are ICTs Gender Neutral?, 1–12 July, www.uninstraw.org/docs/gender_and_ict/Hafkin.pdf.

Harkim, C. (2006) 'Women, careers, and work-life preferences', *British Journal of Guidance & Counselling*, 34: 279–94.

Hisrich, R. D. and M. Peters (1998) *Entrepreneurship: Starting, Developing, and Managing a New Enterprise*, New York: Irwin.

Huyer, S. and T. Sikoska (2003). 'Overcoming the gender digital divide: understanding ICTs and their potential for the empowerment of women', Synthesis paper presented to UN INSTRAW (United Nations International Research and Training Institute for the Advancement of Women).

Ikiara, G. K. (2001) 'Economic gloom still persists: Kenyans to continue grappling with unfulfilled expectations due to mismanagement',

Special report in *Sunday Nation*, 30 December, Nairobi: Nation Press.

International Telecommunications Union (ITU) (2007) *Key Global Telecom Indicators for the World Telecommunication Service Sector*, www.itu.int/ITU-D/ict/statistics/at_glance/KeyTelecom99.html, accessed 10 September 2008.

Kibas, P. B. and G. O. K'Aol (2004) 'The Kenyan entrepreneur: typologies and characteristics', Paper prepared for Frontiers of Entrepreneurship Research 2004: Twenty-Fourth Annual Entrepreneurship Research Conference, www.kauffman.org/, accessed March 2008.

Knobloch, U. (2002) *Promoting Women's Capabilities: Examining Nussbaum's Capabilities Approach*, Conference paper prepared for Von Hugel Institute, St Edmund's College, University of Cambridge, September.

Mincer, J. (1978) 'Family migration decisions', *Journal of Political Economy*, 86(5): 749–73.

Mureithi, M. (2005) *Factors Affecting Internet Use Among Micro-Enterprises: An Empirical Study in Kariobangi Light Industries in Nairobi, Kenya*, www.tespok.co.ke/test/Tespok_Presentation.ppt, accessed 12 April 2008.

Nussbaum, M. (2000) 'Women and human development: the capabilities approach', in *Adaptive Preferences and Women's Options*, Cambridge: Cambridge University Press, pp. 111–66.

Polachek, S. (1981) 'Occupational self-selection: a human capital approach to sex differences in the occupational structure', *Review of Economics and Statistics*, 63(1): 60–69.

Population Council (2005) *Accelerating Girls' Education: A Priority for Governments*, www.popcouncil.org/gfd/girlseducation.html.

Republic of Kenya (1998) *Economic Survey*, Nairobi: Government Printers.

— (1999) *Economic Survey*, Nairobi: Government Printers.

— (2000) *Second Report on Poverty*, vol. II: *Poverty and Social Indicators*, Nairobi: Government Printers.

Sen, A. (2000) *Development as Freedom*, New Delhi: Anchor Books.

Stevenson, L. and A. St-Onge (2005) *Support for Growth-oriented Women Entrepreneurs in Kenya*, International Labour Organization (ILO).

Tandon, N. (2002) *E-commerce Training with Small-scale Entrepreneurs in Developing Countries: Some Findings*, Paper presented at the DfID meeting: Poverty Elimination and the Empowerment of Women: Strategies for achieving the international development targets, London: DfID.

Vodafone (2005) *Africa: The Impact of Mobile Phones: Moving the Debate Forward*, Vodafone Policy Paper Series no. 2, www.vodafone.com/etc/medialib/attachments/, accessed February 2008.

Wakunuma, K. (2007) *Mobiles Reinforce Unequal Gender Relations in Zambia*, www.id21.org/insights/insights69/insights69, accessed 28 April 2008.

Wanjira Munyua, A. and M. Mureithi (2008) *Harnessing the Power of the Cell Phone by Women Entrepreneurs: New Frontiers in the Gender Equation in Kenya*, Final report for the Gender Research in Africa into ICTs for Empowerment (GRACE) Project, www.GRACE-Network.net/.

Wolf, S. (2001) *Determinants and Impact of ICT Use for African SMEs, Implications for Rural South Africa*, Bonn: Centre for Development Research/ZEF, www.zef.de/, accessed April 2008.

World Bank (2001) *Engendering Development: Through Gender Equality in Rights, Resources, and Voice*, World Bank Policy Research Report, Oxford: Oxford University Press.

12 | Internet use among women entrepreneurs in the textile sector in Douala, Cameroon: self-taught and independent

GISELE YITAMBEN AND ELISE TCHINDA

According to a 2005/06 estimate of the African Development Bank (2005), women entrepreneurs own approximately 38 per cent of the 7,100 small and medium-sized private enterprises (SMEs) registered in Cameroon. A large number of these SMEs in the region of Douala and a few in Yaounde have ten to fifteen employees.

These women SME entrepreneurs are mostly engaged in the ready-made clothing sector and dressmaking; this sector creates the most jobs in Cameroon. Three modes of production coexist in this sector: industrial uniform production; ready-to-wear; and traditional (independent tailors and garments made to measure). The women who participated in our study were involved in ready-to-wear clothing manufacture.

This chapter explores whether women heads of enterprises use the Internet access services provided through the multimedia centres of the Chamber of Commerce, why some do not, and if they do use the Internet, for which purposes do they use it?

To enable enterprises to take advantage of the multiple opportunities in the field – the liberalization of world trade in the textile sector, strategies put in place to attain the Millennium Development Goals, the African Growth Opportunity Act (AGOA), and programmes of the Tokyo International Conference for African Development, the Cameroon Chamber of Commerce, Industry, Mines and Crafts (CCIMA) started a multimedia centre with funding from several partners in development. Apart from providing economic operators with services including training, counselling, useful information on the socio-economic environment, and facilitating access to foreign markets, this centre places at their disposal an Internet access space with a capacity of thirty machines and a bandwidth of 128 megabytes (MB). It is in this centre that a support programme for women entrepreneurs in the textile sector and clothing arena is being developed with a view to preparing them to conquer the North American market within the framework of AGOA.

Background

The 1995 WTO Agreement on Textiles and Clothing brought with it a quota system governing international trade in textiles and clothing. The ending of this agreement in 2005 meant that developing countries such as Cameroon, which do not usually export large quantities of clothing, would have more and more difficulty entering or remaining in world markets.

Thanks to the renewal of the AGOA of 2001, however, opportunities do exist. Textile production in countries affected by this agreement will continue to be exempt from customs duties. According to the *Washington Post*, through AGOA the value of textile exports to the USA rose from $600 million in 1999 to $1.5 billion in 2003. Also in 2003, imports from thirty-seven countries, including Cameroon, grew by 55 per cent compared to the previous year.

Several programmes are to be developed to strengthen the capacity of entrepreneurs and help entrepreneurs in the clothing sector organize themselves to better penetrate the US market. In these programmes there is a special place for companies owned or managed by women. The potential is enormous. The African designs are attractive, and certain American retailers seek to obtain supplies from Africa. Market studies have shown that Afro-Americans are more sensitive to products that express their ethnic heritage. This market, estimated by the World Bank in 2003 as worth potentially between US$200 and US$270 billion, is a very promising niche for African exporters in the clothing sector (Biggs et al. 2003).

Information and communication technology (ICT) means that export is no longer reserved for large companies. ICTs have significantly reduced transaction costs and thus opened up entry into the international market. A series of publications from the International Trade Centre (Knappe 2005; Hirsch 2005) have highlighted the advantages of the Internet for entrepreneurs in the clothing sector of developing countries, which include:

- monitoring goods that could improve the competitiveness of producers;
- speeding up delivery, reducing costs and improving services;
- integrating design and development of products through access to virtual prototypes of clothing and 'tests' in real time which can simulate the appearance and adjustment of a new model in two or three dimensions, considerably reducing costs of research and development;

- developing solutions in collaboration with buyers or simply using their system (Knappe 2005);
- 'internal security' and other customs protection;
- receipt by manufacturers of data on outlets in an almost instantaneous way – they may start production and ship replacement stock without waiting for orders from the retailer; and
- short delivery times and reduced inventory costs.

Thus, according to these authors, although the use of e-applications is not in itself a guarantee of success, e-commerce (envisaged in the broadest sense and not as a synonym for online sales) can enhance business efficiency while reducing costs and delays.

The Internet seems to be unknown, however, to the large majority of women entrepreneurs in Cameroon. Like other African countries (Chéneau-Loquay 2002), Cameroon is characterized by limited access to and use of the Internet (Tankeu 2005). A report by the International Telecommunication Union (ITU) in 2006 underlined the lack of ICT infrastructure in Cameroon and the high cost of bandwidth and lack of adequate local content, making participation of women in Cameroon in e-commerce difficult.

Cameroonian government actions to encourage the use of the Internet are embryonic and barely visible. The Internet is used by only 0.16 per cent of the population. Objectives in telecommunications and ICT have either not been achieved or are experiencing considerable delays. These objectives include increasing fixed-line tele-density from 0.7 per cent in 2005 to 30 per cent in 2015, and were intended to make available to the public an offer of access to 2 MBs in all cities with a digital centre before the end of 2007.

Methodology

Process and techniques for data gathering Our study was essentially quali-tative and exploratory. When developing an understanding of the situation for women clothing entrepreneurs we used individual interviews, group discussions and life stories. We started with a series of meetings with members of organizations supporting women and entrepreneurship, and with fashion designers and women entrepreneurs.

Another meeting, organized under the auspices of the CCIMA, gathered forty fashion designers together. This was followed by a meeting with women entrepreneurs (including the designers), in which we asked whether and how they used the Internet. We also carried out thirty-four semi-structured interviews with women in the clothing sector. We limited ourselves to Douala, the economic capital of Cameroon, where diverse activities take place, including the fashion, design and ready-to-wear industries. Its proximity to the Atlantic Ocean and the existence of an international airport near by makes this town the hub of international trade in Cameroon.

Individual interviews were carried out at the respondents' job sites. We asked about their use of the multimedia centre of the CCIMA; their knowledge of the Internet; their use of the Internet; obstacles they experience in relation to usage; and their needs for training.

Findings

Use of the multimedia centre of the CCIMA Of the thirty-four women interviewed, seventeen were members of the CCIMA. Six knew of the existence of the multimedia centre, but only two have occasionally used the Internet at this centre. When asked why they did not use this resource centre, the following reasons were given:

- Lack of information, even from the CCIMA to its members, of the existence of this resource centre (which was put in place in 2001). According to Edith,[1]

  In reality, I am not even informed of the existence of this centre, and we hold regular meetings in the meeting hall of this institution. I would have at least visited it once to see. As I know of it now, if I have time, I will go there.

- The fact that this centre is not at the site of the institution, but is situated in a residential quarter with difficult access.
- The opening hours (8 a.m.–4 p.m.) from Monday to Friday are not convenient even for those who wish to frequent it. These hours correspond to traditional working and schooling hours:

  It is by luck that I learnt of the existence of the multimedia centre of CCIMA. I have been there twice. I found mostly students there. There was nobody there to help me carry out my research. Moreover, the opening and closing times of the centre are not to my convenience. (Claudia, a fashion designer)

- The fact that it has never organized sensitization activities for women on the uses of the Internet.

Moreover, in looking into the training programme of the Chamber of Commerce, we found that there was no programme on how to use the Internet.

This centre, created at the behest of the development partners, is an example of the many expensive projects decided on abroad, without dialogue with the actual beneficiaries.

Despite the fact that this centre is not useful to them, they have taken the personal initiative to learn about using the Internet and essentially are self-taught, using the Internet as a support tool for their entrepreneurship initiatives.

Knowledge of the Internet Most of the women we spoke to acknowledged that they knew about the Internet. As Jeanine said, 'I know the Internet very well, for at least five years my uncle [a senior staff member in a private company] had Internet in his office. When I went there, very often, I found him busy reading or sending mails. I profited from consulting my mailbox.'

The women entrepreneurs acknowledged that the Internet could be of great use to them in the search for customers, correspondence with family and partners, and access to sites communicating useful information for their market studies. Three women used the Internet for greater visibility for their activities by means of virtual boutiques. Seven others thought it could improve their creativity and capacity to innovate. The women knew of the Internet as a communication and information search tool. Certain services, however, such as discussion forums, and the capacity to undertake collaborative work via the Internet, were not known to them.

Use of the Internet by women entrepreneurs Thirty-two of the thirty-four women interviewed and using the Internet did so for social or professional reasons, as outlined below.

Professional reasons

1) To communicate. Women used the Internet to communicate in real time with others and for rapid access to the immense resources that abound in this medium. For two of the thirty-two, the Internet enables them to become informed on current fashion and to improve their creativity and competitiveness:

> The world of fashion changes often. Trends, colours, and styles change from one season to the next, from one country to the other. In my case, I have a varied clientele, in Cameroon, but also outside the country. So, in order to be up to date, I dip into the Internet, I find out what's changed, and even about emerging trends. This allows me to be in phase with my clients. (Nicole, a fashion designer who exports her products to the USA)

Two women said that they use the Internet to communicate with their suppliers. Rachel, who has an export and import business, uses it this way:

> You know, sometimes I don't always have the possibility of travelling. So, if I have an order to send, I send an e-mail to my supplier and I specify what I want. It has happened a few times that I was not completely satisfied with what he sent me. Since I've been working with him for quite a while and we know each other, everything usually goes well. I'm glad that the Internet is here.

On the other hand, Florence, another entrepreneur, specified: 'I prefer to deal right on the spot because you are not always sure if you buy through the Internet that you will get good-quality merchandise.'

The Internet also enables them to make their enterprises visible; four of the thirty-two women interviewed used the Internet to communicate with their clients.

Rose, a fashion designer and married mother of two, was recruited after university to be a senior staff member in a local private enterprise. A number of years later this enterprise went bankrupt and she found herself jobless. With her severance benefits she decided to learn dressmaking. She had in the past learnt how to sew from her seamstress mother, and sewed dresses for her colleagues, who appreciated her talent. She went to Paris and a year later, on return to Cameroon, opened her dress-making workshop. Since then she has been participating in fashion fairs at national as well as international levels, and has won several prizes. Rose told us:

> I am a proprietor of a website. It was created for me by one of my Canadian partners, during a sojourn in Canada; I participated in a fashion parade and fair. Thanks to this site, you can imagine, I was found by one of my great American clients that had for long had difficulties contacting me. The Internet enables me to communicate with my customers. I have a lot of other customers out of Douala, and even out of the country.

2) For training. Three women declared having used the Internet for training. Françoise holds a baccalauréat. She is married and has three children. Her passion for the Internet was born during the course of her training:

> I got to know the Internet when I was still a student. When I started training as a fashion designer, I was pleasantly surprised to find on the Internet some sites of foreign dressmakers and their designs ... I got

inspired by them during my training, and I have designs that are very much appreciated by my customers, that I created, with inspiration from these sites. I do not frequently visit them, but when I do visit I am prepared to give up some hours of my time. I get a lot of ideas. All that I regret is not being able to have Internet in the house.

Contribution to competence and knowledge at the professional level Competences and knowledges declared to have been developed by the participants through the use of the Internet covered the domains of communication, training and information.

1) Communication and training. The women used the Internet to access their accounts, write, edit and send messages, chat, and scan and send photos of family events to friends and parents abroad.

Diane, who holds a First School Leaving Certificate, is married and a mother of five, is a member of an association affiliated to the Chamber of Commerce. She took several training courses there in entrepreneurship, and then took part in computer training provided by the Association pour le Soutien et l'Appui à la Femme Entrepreneur (ASAFE) based in Douala. It is thanks to her son, who always accompanies her to the cybercafé, that she learnt to use the Internet: 'In the beginning, the Internet was a real curiosity to me. But so long as I go there, I learn a lot from it. The speed with which I work with the Internet is increasing. I know how to open my mailbox. I can download documents. I would not have believed it two years ago.'

2) Information. Seeing the Internet as a source of information, women respondents use it for searching for information (on prices and brands of dressmaking equipment, fashion sites, fashion trends), sharing of information with foreign partners and colleagues, and watching fashion parades. Claire declared:

> Through the Internet, I have learnt to search for information on suppliers of sewing equipment; on the trends of fashion. I needed an over-sewing machine. As I could not find the brand on the market, I launched a search on the Internet that enabled me to locate some suppliers abroad that were selling them. I contacted them at the same time that my sister stayed in that location. She put me in contact with the one in her location, and I negotiated and was able to acquire my r̶ ̶ ̶ ̶providing me with so much fame in my trade.

3) Other uses. Some other ways in which the Internet wa

useful included the creation of designs, improvement of creativity, access to cutting courses and downloading from relevant sites.

Olga, one of the women we spoke to, holds a Higher National Diploma in Dressmaking obtained years ago. Based in Douala, she has opened shops at the airports of some European countries. She has participated in numerous fairs and fashion parades in Cameroon and abroad. Every two years she organizes a fashion parade in which renowned fashion designers participate. She confessed that she built her reputation on the quality of her products and on their originality, and said:

> The Internet has brought so much to me. It is a source of inspiration for me. When I visit fashion sites I get myself always versed with news in the domain of fashion, and that gives me a lot of ideas. Our sector is one of those that witnesses a lot of mutations. These trends change frequently, new designs appear while others eclipse. I make European fashion design, therefore in ready-to-wear. One must always be up to date in order to retain or win other customers. Often I have found patterns that I adapted to come out with original designs that have earned me awards. Today I have customers in all the provinces of Cameroon and in Europe. I have the luck of belonging to a dynamic association. We have a partner abroad that placed at our disposal a website where we expose our designs. I was recently contacted by an American trader dealing in ready-to-wear. Negotiations are under way and on course. I have hope.

What becomes clear is that the Internet is turning out to be a powerful business tool for these women. Learning through the Internet has contributed to enhancing the dynamic competence of quite a few of our respondents, enabling them to acquire knowledge for themselves and for their enterprises. E-learning can indeed reinforce communication and computer competencies, media attitudes and self-motivation. It is therefore suitable for women in general and particularly for women entrepreneurs who are creating their own businesses.

Social reasons All of the women who use the Internet said that they use it to communicate with their relatives:

> I only use the Internet to receive and send mails. I have family abroad, and as they have Internet at their home, they have obliged me to get used to the Net. At times when they have things to tell me, they call and the telephone does not go through. It is in the cybercafé that I consult or send my mails. (Yveline)

Seventeen of the thirty-four women entrepreneurs we spoke to used the Internet for professional reasons. Thirty-two of the thirty-four used it for social reasons. Those who use the Internet for professional reasons were self-trained.

Conclusions and recommendations

The multimedia centre of the CCIMA dispenses important resources that are unfortunately not used by its members. The location of the project renders its access very difficult, and its opening hours did not permit the women entrepreneurs who were interviewed to go there. The multimedia centre appears to have been conceived and put in place under the recommendation of donors. The beneficiaries of this project were never consulted, either during formulation or implementation. In other words, its objectives, strategies and basic principles did not take into account the specific situation of the local women entrepreneurs, nor their particular needs.

Hence, it is important that a vigorous information campaign is undertaken by the CCIMA to inform its members of the availability of these resources, if the situation regarding their use is to change.

The activities of this centre ought to be redirected, starting with a dialogue with women that takes into account their needs and specific situations. The authorities of the organization need to be aware of the issues associated with the intended users of the centre.

As for the state, it is desirable that it puts in place a coherent training and incentive policy and creates programmes for women entrepreneurs to access ICTs. The state must also put in place a framework for making the acquisition of computers and the cost of access to the Internet more affordable for women entrepreneurs. The capacity of the bandwidth must also be improved in order to facilitate efficient use.

For programmes to be useful to women entrepreneurs in Douala, it is recommended that the programme designers learn from what the women have put in place already, taking note of the emerging Internet knowledges and practices. Only when women are consulted about their needs and realities pertaining to Internet use will Internet support programmes be developed that will enable women entrepreneurs to enhance their lives and their contributions to the Cameroon economy.

Note

1 We are not using the real names of the women entrepreneurs with whom we spoke.

References

African Development Bank (2005) 'De l'entrepreneuriat féminin au Cameroun', Financing project, Cameroon: Stean and Associates.

African Growth Opportunity Act (AGOA) (n.d.) www.agoa.gov/, accessed 30 September 2008.

Biggs, T., M. Miller, C. Otto and G. Tyler (2003) 'Africa can compete! Export opportunities and challenges for garments and home products in the European market', World Bank Discussion Papers, World Bank.

Chéneau-Loquay, A. (2002) 'Modes d'accès et d'utilisation d'Internet en Afrique: les grandes tendances', *Africa and the Mediterranean*, 'Africa and the digital divide' dossier, 41, December.

Hirsch, S. (2005) 'E-management – suppliers become closer partners', *International Trade Forum*, 3, www.tradeforum.org/news/fullstory.php/aid/924/E-management_-_Suppliers_Become_Closer_Partners.html.

Knappe, M. (2005) 'Get connected', *International Trade Forum*, 3, ITC, www.tradeforum.org/news/fullstory.php/aid/925/Get_Connected.html.

Tankeu, R. (2005) 'Fracture numérique de genre au Cameroun: quelle ampleur?', ENDA/ANAÎS.

Tokyo International Conference for African Development (n.d.), www.ticad.net/fra/dossier2008/2008YokohamaDeclaration-fr.pdf, accessed 30 September 2008.

Washington Post (n.d.) 'L'Agoa est prolongé jusqu'en 2015: l'Agoa III a été adopté par les sénateurs américains', www.afrik.com/article7424.html, accessed 30 September 2008.

13 | ICTs as agents of change: a case of grass-roots women entrepreneurs in Uganda

SUSAN BAKESHA, ANGELA NAKAFEERO AND
DOROTHY OKELLO

Current literature emphasizes the active role of information and communication technologies (ICTs) in the development process. It has been widely argued that ICTs have enormous potential for reaching rural populations to provide them with education and training, job opportunities, access to markets and information important for their economic activities, as well as facilitating their participation in political processes. The poor, however, especially women, have limited access to and utilization of ICTs in their daily activities. This is primarily due to limited infrastructure and near to total absence of ICT access points in rural areas (Hafkin and Taggart 2001). The Uganda Participatory Poverty Assessment Process (MFPAED 2002) revealed that women are still regarded as property by their husbands owing to dowry payments and, as such, men have control over women's lives, including their time, access to information and participation in politics, social groupings and training.

Our research team set out to explore the factors that facilitated the uptake and utilization of information provided on a CD-ROM entitled *Rural Women of Africa: Ideas for Earning Money* by women entrepreneurs. The CD was intended to improve their businesses in particular and lives in general.[1] The CD-ROM project was proposed by the International Women's Tribune Centre (IWTC) in partnership with the International Development Research Centre/Eastern and Southern Africa Office (IDRC/ESAO), Nairobi, and implemented in Uganda by the Uganda National Council of Science and Technology (UNCST) in partnership with non-governmental organizations including the Council for Economic Empowerment of Women in Africa – Uganda Chapter (CEEWA-U), Media One and Uganda Development Services (UDS). The CD-ROM was pioneered in 2001 at three telecentres in the rural areas of Nakaseke and Buwama, and Nabweru in the peri-urban area.

In order to access the information, women would meet at their respective telecentres at scheduled times and together with a facilitator browse the CD-ROM. At the end of each session, the facilitator would guide them in a discussion relating to what they had learned and how it applied or could be applied to their daily activities.

Field findings revealed that although most of the respondents appreciated the information provided on the CD-ROM and had a fair understanding of business enhancement and expansion, translation of this information into knowledge and applying it to achieve the desired impact remained a challenge and varied according to one's marital status, individual attributes and location. It came out clearly, however, that given the opportunity, women are quick to form social networks aimed at creating their own spaces where they feel appreciated and wanted. The use of role models in promoting or hindering access and use of ICTs was also explored.

Sampling of respondents

Our research team undertook pre-research visits in order to introduce the study to the project managers at the respective telecentres. The project managers were instrumental in identifying the respondents of the study. Respondents were interviewed between September 2005 and February 2006. Purposive sampling was used during the initial stages of selection, targeting the leaders of women entrepreneurs who had attended the CD-ROM sessions at the three telecentres. After identifying the lead women, other respondents within the local communities were invited to participate through word of mouth. A total of sixteen women were interviewed. In addition, interviews were held with the officials who implemented the project. These included Rachael Mijumbi Epodoi, the project local consultant, Gorretti Zavuga Amuria, Rehema Baguma and Daniel Semakula, former project managers at the Council for Economic Empowerment of Women in Africa – Uganda Chapter (CEEWA-U), Martin Nsubuga of the United Nations Educational, Scientific and Cultural Organization (UNESCO) and Anne Walker of the International Women's Tribune Centre (IWTC), who was also the project's international consultant.

Data collection and processing

Qualitative methods of data collection were employed in order to explore the in-depth dimensions of the subject. Interviews and focus group discussions were held, each at the respective telecentres, with the project beneficiaries and with the telecentre management committees. All the interviews were taped to ensure accuracy and comprehensiveness.

Field visits to the telecentres, homes and places of work where the respondents run their businesses were undertaken. This enabled the research team to observe and compare the information given by the respondent with the state of their businesses. Respondents shared stories about how they used the information on the CD-ROM to improve their businesses. To analyse the data and sort them into thematic areas and identify the factors that affect women's access to and use of information on the CD-ROM, the Nvivo qualitative software program was used.

Field findings

Uptake of the information on the CD-ROM and self-discovery Prior to the CD-ROM project, most women included in our research identified themselves as poor, timid and lacking confidence to speak and get involved in public affairs. For those who were in business, the issue of enhancing their business for better returns was not much embraced. They were found to be resigned to the little money they got from the small businesses, which they spent on buying household necessities, with limited focus on business expansion and other investments, as reflected in the quotations below.

My income was low as well because of the low quality of products. I could not invest the little income that I earned from the products back into the business to ensure continuity and profitability.

I was keeping poultry on a small scale; I had only twenty chickens. I had a feeling that big businesses were for the rich. By then, there was an increase in the number of poultry farmers, which increased competition. Eventually I lost some of my customers to the new suppliers. My income drastically reduced and I was miserable, almost giving up. But yet I did not know what to do for my survival.

With the advent of the CD-ROM project, women accessed new information and ideas on how to improve their businesses, identifying business opportunities and discovering their potential. Those who had land started using it for commercial purposes such as cultivation of cash crops. Others diversified their businesses and ventured into new business areas. As a result, they developed new identities, from housekeepers to entrepreneurs, with others taking up skills training courses such as tailoring. Subsequently, most women moved away from personal or family subsistence to marketing their goods. They developed into confident citizens and one, who was widowed, won an elective political position within her community. Thus, at the end of the project, women had another story to tell.

Economic empowerment: liberating or otherwise? Empowerment of women was conceptualized in our research as a process through which women's enterprises and their personal lives progressed to better levels of performance, and the question was raised as to whether and in what way

145

empowerment could be attributed to the use of the information accessed through the use of the CD-ROM. In relation to business, the respondents shared their experiences based on information they acquired:

> After learning about customer care, my attitude towards my customers changed. I realized that my customers were my bosses and I needed to talk to them well in order to attract them.

> The information about packaging and storage of products helped me a lot. My hygiene improved significantly. For instance, before I used to pack the chicken eggs in the trays without first cleaning them and very few people would buy them. But now I carefully clean one by one before packaging and now the sales have gone high. The income levels have improved. I can afford to cater for the family needs including paying school fees.

It was evident that these women experienced an increase in their income as a result of improving the quality of their products and services. It was also true that, as they earned more income, they tended to spend a considerable amount of it on family welfare, and some noted that this was an important factor in maintaining a good relationship with their husbands.

You cannot sacrifice life in favour of business Owing to increased responsibilities, most women could not make any meaningful progress in their businesses as they used all the profits and sometimes part of the capital to meet the needs of their families, including buying food, and paying school fees and medical bills. As a result, most of their businesses were either in a state of stagnation or on the verge of collapsing. The business knowledge acquired had not been translated into personal economic enhancement owing to conflicting gender roles and expectations.

Florence shared her experience when asked why her business had not made any considerable profits despite the fact that she had received the information on entrepreneurship development.

> INTERVIEWER: You said that you have operated this business since 1999. Is this correct?
>
> RESPONDENT: Yes.
>
> INTERVIEWER: Why is it that you have not been able to expand your business in terms of space and capital?
>
> RESPONDENT: Uh, yes, see, I use all the profits to take care of my family's welfare, including school fees, healthcare and food.
>
> INTERVIEWER: Isn't your husband supportive?

RESPONDENT: He is, but he cannot do everything. And besides, there are things that affect our children and it is easy for the father to ignore but not the mother. For instance, my second daughter got pregnant last year before completing school; unfortunately, the man responsible for the pregnancy abandoned her. Of course, her father (my husband) was not impressed. I had to meet all the health costs during her pregnancy and delivery, which was difficult. She had a Caesarean and almost died. I used almost 300,000 shillings (Can$180) to save her life. That meant that all my profits and obviously part of the capital [were] spent on the medical bill. You cannot sacrifice life in favour of business. A human being lives once, but a business can collapse and revitalize again. And now I have decided to take her back to school. Her father refused to pay her school fees because he is still angry with her. But as a mother, I don't want her to drop out of school; I want her to continue with her education. She made a mistake and I hope she learned a lesson. If I refuse to take her back to school, she will become a much bigger problem in future.

The above case demonstrates the complicated nature of economic empowerment among women. The main purpose of the CD-ROM project was to enhance women's entrepreneurial skills, and thereby increase their incomes and hence their economic status. Indeed, most of the respondents had either started other income-generating activities (IGAs) or improved the existing businesses. For many of them, however, their business returns did not correspond with the efforts invested. This was partly because most of the profits were spent on family needs rather than being reinvested into the business. There was a general concern among respondents that their husbands abdicated their family obligations upon realizing that their wives were expanding their businesses. Such women, however, were not ready to confront their husbands because of their desire to preserve their marriages. Besides, being able to take care of their children's needs was more fulfilling than demanding equal responsibility from their husbands.

This corresponds with the theory of adaptive preferences by Amartya Sen quoted in *Women and Human Development: The Capabilities Approach* (2000) by Nussbaum, who observed that 'women and other deprived people do not desire some basic human good because they have been long habituated to its absence or told that it is not for such as them' (p. 139). In this case, several of the respondents in the study did not take a when their husbands suddenly abandoned their family respo some when they realized that their wives were now capable of income. To some women, improvement in their relationship

147

husband was preferred to making personal savings. 'Now I can contribute to household expenses and this has improved my relationship with my husband,' one woman said. It seemed that women's reproductive household work was still not recognized because it did not have an economic value: only when these women earned an income and ventured into income-generating activities outside their homes were they appreciated by their spouses. Yet although most of the respondents had thus not made any tangible investments owing to household expenditures, they were contented and convinced that they had made a positive step in the right direction.

When social arrangements depart from standard practice The story seemed different for the two widowed women. There was a shared pattern between them. In both cases, they were fully dependent on their husbands before the unfortunate situation of widowhood. When their spouses passed away, these women had no one to turn to for support. Luckily,[2] both women had inherited the property, including land. As a means to secure their survival and that of their children, they started engaging in income-generating activities inspired and motivated by the information accessed through the CD-ROM.

Being independent enhanced their mobility and they were free to join different entrepreneurial development initiatives for support. Attending the CD-ROM sessions at the telecentres became one example of the kind of support they were looking for. They used the knowledge to start or expand their businesses as well as save and make more investments. Being in charge of their income and having the ability to decide how to use it seemed to make them more active and progressive than their married counterparts. Lydia of Nabweru and Juliet of Buwama described to the study team how they used the information provided on the CD-ROM to improve their businesses and life in general. Juliet explained:

Since I joined the CD-ROM sessions at Buwama telecentre, my income increased tremendously. I can manage my family well even though my husband died. At least I am earning more than 200,000 Uganda shillings (Can$120) per month. Using the profits from my business, I have managed to construct a four-roomed commercial building and acquired a *bodaboda*[3] that has made transport for my commodities required in the business easy. I make four jerricans of passion fruit juice every day and sell them. My line of business has expanded from a retail shop and local cattle to two shops, including one in Kampala, a *bodaboda* motorcycle, livestock and milk, piggery and rental income from the house in Jalamba. My life has changed for the better; I have identified other income-generating opportunities, and can currently cater for the requirements of my family, including paying school fees for the children. I pay tuition fees for my son at the university.

The case of Lydia Nabagala is quite revealing. Lydia was in her thirties, a widow with two daughters. Before she was widowed, Lydia was a housewife who depended on her husband as the sole provider. When her husband died in 2002, Lydia continued to depend on her family members (mother, father and siblings) for survival. Her husband's family could not provide any support for her. She had no hope for the future and thought she would die soon.

One day, one of her sisters made a comment that became a turning point in Lydia's life. In the middle of one of the conversations they usually had, she said, 'Lydia, we are looking after you and your children as long as you are alive; when you die, we will not continue doing the same ...'

Lydia said that the comment caused a lot of pain to her but marked a defining moment in her life. She was compelled to think critically about herself and the plight of her children, which she called 'awakening'. At around the same time, her friends invited her to attend computer classes that were taking place at Nabweru telecentre. The classes were taking place in the afternoons and this was a convenient time for her. Eventually, she developed ideas on how to improve her condition and stop depending on her family. She decided to drop the identity of dependency and create her own survival. She shared with us how she had progressed since taking the decision to fend for herself and her family.

I realized I had plenty of space. I decided to use the garage to raise chickens as well as sell water to earn an income. I am able to pay for the water bills and use the profits generated for domestic requirements like buying food, paying school fees and paying for transport for my children to school. I also realized that I could make use of the extra land on my plot to put up some rental housing.

At the time of the research, Lydia had been elected to chair one of the community-based organizations providing support to widows and orphans. This was because the community recognized her as an enterprising, confident and responsible woman. This corresponds with Mageo and Knauft's (2002) assertion that 'one's identity is determined by the process of self-experience' – in other words, what one experiences as an individual in turn determines how s/he identifies herself or himself within a given environment. Lydia's desire to be self-reliant and independent developed from her experience as a dependant on her family after the death of her husband. Before her husband's death, she had been confined in the home and was comfortable with her position as a housewife doing domestic chores. When her husband died, however, and her family members indicated that they would not take care of her children into infinity, she was compelled to redefine her position and take on the responsibility of taking care of herself and her children. At this point, she chose to change, to no longer be dependent and reshape her position and identity by exploring her personal power to take charge of and control her environment, thus re-creating her own world. By attending classes at the telecentres, she was able to access information about business entrepreneurship which raised her consciousness about the available opportunity to improve her condition using the resources at her disposal. In addition, joining classes at the telecentres enabled her to relate with other women and learn how to express herself in public.

Lydia's and Juliet's cases were similar to those of most of the respondents in that their experiences had been largely influenced by the patriarchal values inculcated in them through the socialization process. What made their situation different was that they were widows and had acquired access to land. Being widows increased their ability to explore their potential and take decisions regarding the use of the resources at their disposal to improve their economic status as well as the welfare of their families. Before then, the women fully depended on their husbands and had limited business skills. Lydia's and Juliet's cases revealed that given the right information and opportunity to access and control productive resources like land, women can exploit their potential and improve their economic and social status.

Amartya Sen notes that 'whenever social arrangements depart from the standard practice of male ownership, women can seize business and economic initiative with much success' (1999: 201). This corresponds well with Lydia's and Juliet's situation: not only did the state of widowhood raise their consciousness, enabling them to grow out of the victim status, they also took control of their lives and successfully engaged in new business initiatives to fend for themselves and their children. This shows that given the right information and freedom to manage their affairs, women have the ability to make useful contributions to the development of their families and their communities.

They also proved that poverty is not solely income related, but includes deprivation of capabilities to enhance one's potential. In this case, Lydia and Juliet were both widows left with no money in bank accounts. They had some resources, however, such as land, at their disposal. Using the right information provided by the CD-ROM enhanced their entrepreneurship skills, which in turn expanded their abilities to engage in more productive activities to earn an income.

Women and networking As women gathered at the telecentres, they formed new relationships with each other and became more acquainted with the trainers with whom they shared experiences and challenges. Before then, all these women had led individual lives mainly centred on their immediate and extended families. In areas like Nakaseke and Buwama (which are rural), households are as far as 5 kilometres apart. With the introduction of the CD-ROM project, the telecentres became a meeting place not only for the training sessions, but also for interaction among the trainees. Before and after the training sessions, women could find time to chat and share experiences among themselves. Consequently, new groups (both formal and informal) were formed to continue the relationships established at the telecentres. These included, for example, the Nabweru Revolving Fund, the Twekembe Women's Group and the Nakaseke Women's Development Association (NAWODA). These groups were based on self-help principles whereby a pool of resources would be collected to raise money for start-up capital and to boost the existing businesses.

From the telecentres, some women learned of and eventually joined other existing informal groups, such as the '*Nnigina* groups', after realizing the benefits of group formation. The word *Nnigina* literally means 'be happy and feel appreciated'. *Nnigina* groups were an initiative of women in the capital city, with the aim of creating a forum where women, especially those in the informal sector, would meet, share experiences, appreciate each other and exchange gifts. The gifts were not necessarily intended to provide business capital for the recipient but were a way of showing appreciation and value for the individual in the community. It was noted as an empowering process; *Nnigina* enables women to organize themselves, share experiences and provide an environment in which to enjoy themselves without external support.

Role models The issue of role models emerged as an important factor affecting access to and use of information. Respondents from Nabweru and Buwama revealed that they were prompted to attend computer lessons at the telecentres after observing other women perceived to be of high repute in society doing the same. In Nakaseke, the main attraction in the telecentre was an elderly lady called Anastasia Namisango, popularly referred to as Nasta. Nasta, over seventy-five years old and illiterate, had unwavering enthusiasm and determination to learn how to use a computer. Her popularity within Nakaseke and beyond surpassed her wildest dreams when she was selected to attend an international conference in New York to showcase the role of ICT in improving women's livelihoods. Because of her old age and illiteracy level, Nasta surprised everyone when she was selected to represent women in her community at the conference. Upon her return, she became a role model to many in Nakaseke. Suddenly, everybody in the community wanted to come to the telecentres and attend computer lessons. Because of the long distance to the centres, some women would organize themselves into groups in different locations and invite Nasta to offer them training sessions. Some of the respondents shared their experience in this regard:

> When Jaja[4] Nasta was taken abroad, I realized that it is possible for anyone to learn how to use a computer. I asked myself, if Jaja Nasta, as old and illiterate, can learn and teach, how about me, a young woman. I then joined and became one of her students and she would teach us how to move the mouse and the computer would start talking and teaching. I also joined because I wanted to learn how to type my name.

> When I learned that Anastasia, an old woman of eighty years, could use the computer, this challenged me to attend the lessons to see how the computer could help out.

It should be noted that the use of role models can be counterproductive as well. This was the case with Nasta. Although she inspired many in her community to desire to learn how to use a computer, many of her admirers, though able to access information on the CD-ROM, were not able to apply this information for improved business success. In this, they were following her example. At the time of the study, Nasta had no business enterprise in place and a visit to her home had nothing to show in relation to entrepreneurship. She was living in abject poverty as before. She had stopped at the level of interpreting the information and passing it on to others and had never translated it into knowledge to empower herself and those around her. This could partly be attributed to her advanced age, and failure to comprehend the purpose of the project. For a role model, however, this was counterproductive, since this shortcoming was reflected in all her followers, the Nakaseke respondents.

Conclusion

By providing grassroots women entrepreneurs with information, the CD-ROM project aimed at enhancing their enterprises, thereby empowering them economically. The study revealed that although the women used the information to improve and expand their businesses, most of them could not make significant progress as they spent much of the proceeds on household needs and their children's welfare. The widowed women, however, illustrated a situation of self-discovery, moving from the status of dependency to that of independent and economically empowered individuals. They used the acquired information to make significant improvements in their businesses, made profits to take care of their families and also contributed positively to the development of their communities.

Notes

1 The CD-ROM used a simple browser navigating system with graphic interface and spoken text. With its simple-to-use features and spoken text in the local language (Luganda), the CD-ROM required minimal technical know-how to operate. It offered direct access to entrepreneurship-related information for grassroots women. The topics covered included: using what you have to create a business, quality of the product or service, customer care, quantity of the product or service, market research for the services or product, pricing for the product or service, storage of the product, packaging and working capital.

2 In most Ugandan cultures, when a man dies, his relatives have a right to share his property without consent from the widow. In the worst cases, the widow is chased away from her marital home or asked to return to her parents' family. The Succession Act also allows women to share only 15 per cent of the family property if their husbands die. The remaining 85 per cent is shared between the children and any dependants under their husband's care.

3 The word *bodabodas* is used to refer to motorcycles used for commercial purposes. Since culturally women are not allowed to ride motorcycles, they hire young men to undertake the business on their behalf.

4 Literally translated, grandparent or elderly person.

References

Hafkin, N. and N. Taggart (2001) 'Gender, information technology, and developing countries: an analytic study', Academy for Educational Development, available at ict.aed.org/infocenter/gender.htm.

Mageo, M. J. and B. M. Knauft (2002) *Power and the Self*, Cambridge: Cambridge University Press.

MFPAED (Ministry of Finance, Planning and Economic Development) (2002) *Uganda Participatory Poverty Assessment Process: Second Participatory Poverty Assessment Process Report (UPAP 2): Deepening the Understanding of Poverty.*

Nussbaum, C. (2000) *Women and Human Development: The Capabilities Approach*, Cambridge: Cambridge University Press.

Sen, A. (1999) 'Women's agency and social change', in *Development as Freedom*, New York: Anchor Books.

14 | The mobile payphone business: a vehicle for rural women's empowerment in Uganda

GRACE BANTEBYA KYOMUHENDO

The introduction and proliferation of mobile telephones in Uganda in the past decade has sparked an information revolution that is especially apparent in the rural areas. The level and intensity of women's participation in this revolution are quite amazing. My attention was drawn to the mobile payphone, particularly to the women who have exploited this novel technology to become self-employed, freelance payphone operators. It is these innovative, resilient women who became my research participants.

The engagement of the women in a new and unique business venture quite naturally presented a multitude of complexities. My focus, however, is not on these complexities per se, but on the internal factors that the women experience within themselves which might be the result of internalized cultural images of proper womanhood[1] and the implications of holding these value systems for the women's empowerment and gender equality.

In striving to address this question, and within the broad focus on gender and empowerment which informed the wider GRACE project, my analysis draws on the responses and experiences of eight women who prior to engaging in the mobile phone business were living ordinary lives. Through close observation of the women I became aware that commercial telework, its numerous benefits notwithstanding, may have created new and unique tensions, especially in the women's domestic lives. I became concerned about the effects of socially and culturally constructed gender roles and relationships on the capacity of the women to operate their phone business effectively and derive empowerment.

When I reflected on the phone business, and the women's daily realities, words, responses, perceptions and meanings vis-à-vis their life and telework experiences, my own thinking and conceptualization of empowerment and gender, especially in a rural Ugandan ICT context, was reshaped. I realized that although empowerment is mainly about increased ability to make strategic life choices as a result of increased access to and control of resources, not much is known about the nature of the choices women make and how their choices affect or are affected by the entrenched gender inequalities in their communities.

This situation raised the question of whether the introduction of the mobile payphone and the associated business opportunities/employment gains for the women can translate into meaningful empowerment and gender equality in a setting where gender-based inequalities are being reproduced and perpetuated. I became curious about the degree to which gender discrimination undermines women's gains and potential for realizing empowerment in the existing rural Ugandan ICT context, seeing this as a central question in contemporary debates focusing on women's empowerment and ICTs.

Methodology

The research was conducted in Hoima district, mid-western Uganda. Located 200 kilometres from Kampala, Uganda's capital city, Hoima is known to be predominantly rural, and although its ICT status is not exactly known, it is well served by various mobile telephone networks. As a result of the latter, mobile payphone businesses have been established, and these are mostly operated by women.

This qualitative study involved extended semi-structured interviews with eight purposively selected women teleworkers. Owing to interruptions from the teleworkers' clients, the individual interviews, which were in the form of a dialogue between the researchers and the women, were conducted in a multistage manner.

The multistage nature of the interviews yielded a number of advantages. For instance, the breaks in structured interviews allowed the researchers to accord the respondents respectful and genuine attention, which turned out to be not only a novel experience for the women, but also an empowering one, in which they lost all inhibitions about sharing personal intimate gender- and work-related experiences with us.

Whereas the formal interview dialogues encouraged the women to express, elucidate and disclose their teleworking experiences, the informal dialogues during the breaks in the interviews allowed them to unfold and express their ideas, thoughts, feelings and impressions freely. All the eight women told their respective stories and, by the end of the interviews, we were not only friends with our respondents, but also their close confidantes.

For the purpose of this chapter, our analysis of the interview transcripts sought to identify the tensions between the women's need or desire to work and the restrictive social pressures they face. The focus brought to light the meanings they make of this combination of forces in relation to their sense of empowerment.

Findings

Despite a rocky start, all the eight women registered impressive financial success through participation in the payphone business. As a result of increased income, all the women reported not only making substantial contributions to meeting domestic, personal and other expenditures, but also saving and reinvesting the profits in the business. This chapter considers how the women interviewed responded to this financial success, especially the impact on their power and status within the home and community and their inner feelings about their self-worth.

Case 1, Zaituni,[2] said that ever since she started making substantial financial contributions to her family's upkeep, courtesy of her phone business, her abusive husband had stopped battering and verbally abusing her: 'I feel my husband respects me though he does not openly show it. He stopped beating me and doesn't quarrel as loudly as before.' In the wider community, Zaituni feels that her status has been elevated as a result of her better financial position; 'my friends and relatives see me as a financially stable woman [*mukazi was sente*]. I'm happy that I'm capable of managing my own life.'

Case 2, Monica, the most senior but relatively poor compared with the rest of the interviewed women, had a different view. She emphatically asserted that irrespective of a woman's financial or other contribution, her status and power within both the home and the community cannot exceed a certain threshold. She laboured to explain that a married woman cannot exploit her financial success to make empowering choices without jeopardizing her marriage and status in the community. Monica regarded herself as a woman of high status both within the home and the community, not as a result of her increased domestic financial contributions, but because of her stable marriage in which her husband appreciates and approves of her telework: 'I am held in much esteem by the community I know, and this has nothing to do with what I contribute to family upkeep – which is modest in any case. I am contented with what I am, so long as my husband appreciates what I do.'

Case 3, Oliver, who lives alone, could not talk about her status in the home. She felt strongly, however, that women teleworkers, by virtue of their profession, are incapable of commanding respect in the community irrespective of their enhanced incomes:

> I know I am making more money and living relatively comfortably. However, I am sure that my work does not earn me respect in any way. The phone business is seen as work for failures in life. Some people see us as disguised sex workers. However, I am comfortable with what I am doing

so long as my survival is assured. Status and power cannot feed and pay rent for you.

Case 4, Sylvia, had similar sentiments to Oliver's. She felt uncomfortable and declined to talk about power and status since she did not see herself as capable of acquiring any currently or in the future.

Case 5, Florence, said that ever since starting her now successful phone business, she had not experienced any changes in her status or domestic power relations. Like Monica, she was of the view that a wife's financial contribution does not matter and is not commensurate with her power either in the home or the wider community. She remarked:

> The phone business was a good idea and it has boosted our grocery shop and general welfare. My husband's attitude towards me, however, has not changed. He still makes all major decisions, monitors the phone business closely, and dominates me to the extent that he has refused [to allow] me to own a personal cell phone, though I can comfortably afford it.

Case 6, Phionah, felt that when she opted out of paid employment, and engaged in freelance telework, her social status declined. Supporting Oliver's sentiments, she acknowledged that the moral conduct of some phone business women leaves much to be desired, a factor that does not augur well for their status and power at any level.

Case 7, Eva, sadly noted that prior to engaging in the phone business, when she was poor and married, people respected her; but when her business succeeded she lost the marriage and all the associated respect. Though she continued working and had more freedom, she did not feel motivated to utilize her phone business to make empowering choices. Demoralized by her estrangement from her husband, which apparently resulted from tensions over her phone business, Eva had this to say about her situation:

> I am free, making and controlling whatever I earn from my phone business. However, all this is meaningless without my husband. How can you talk about [being] or feel empowered when you have been deserted? Does freedom to do what you want have any meaning when you are living alone? Empowerment starts with having a husband – someone to exercise your power over at least.

Case 8, Melanie, was of the view that the success of her phone business has elevated her position at all levels. Her acquisition of a husband, which she attributes to her improved financial circumstances, she noted, has increased her self-confidence and given her inner power as a married woman. Unlike most of her colleagues, Melanie feels that acquisition of financial stability and not marriage is the starting point for empowerment. She acknowledged, however, that gender tensions are not conducive to viable phone business operations. She remarked:

> My husband knows the value of my phone business and does not complain about my prolonged absence from home and exposure to the public. This alone gives me inner strength and confidence, and resilience to continue with such work despite my Islamic faith, which does not condone such work, especially for married women. The fact that I am working against such odds makes me feel empowered.

The mobile payphone: a vehicle for women's empowerment and gender equality or mere economic getting by? None of the eight phone business women, despite variations in their social and economic circumstances, could be described as financially stable prior to engaging in commercial telework. Although most of the women were in marital relationships, many of them were not receiving adequate financial or other support from their husbands. Like their wives, the husbands were financially disadvantaged, and could barely meet their traditional roles, responsibilities and expectations as family breadwinners.

Against this background, the launch of the mobile 'village' phone came at the most opportune time for the poor, cash-strapped women. Despite the business start-up difficulties, including raising enough capital to purchase the phone set, securing suitable working premises, obtaining their husband's approval and lack of business experience, the nascent businesses flourished. Substantial monetary gains by local standards were realized in record time and the women reported improvements in living standards both for themselves and their families.

The mobile phone business was acknowledged and appreciated by the women as being unique, not like any other business. Apart from the direct monetary benefits, it provided the women operators with a physical and digital address, which had the effect of reducing their hitherto social and physical isolation. Further, the business required them to be smartly dressed and presentable, and to interact freely with their potential or real clientele.

The ability of the women to set up and profitably operate the payphone business, to generate and control their money, contributed substantially to improving their own and their families' well-being. Several of the women, when talking about the future of their phone business, exuded internal strength and a strong sense of resilience and self-determination, implying that they were in a better position to control their own destinies:

> Some people are saying that this type of business is for failures, that we will moreover soon compete ourselves out of business. Of course this cannot happen since the demand for our phone services is increasing daily. Soon we shall spread out even to the remote trading centres.
> (Oliver)

One might assume that as a result of increased access to and control of financial resources, courtesy of their booming businesses, the women had the potential to reverse the disempowerment imposed on them by the prevailing patriarchal system, and the social and economic subjugation they experience both in the domestic and the community domains. The findings, however, indicate the contrary. It is evident that although the women's participation in commercial mobile telephony created new choices which they could exploit meaningfully to empower themselves by challenging the social structures that disempower them, especially at household level, hardly any of the women seem to even attempt to utilize their expanded choices to assert themselves as key decision-makers within their respective families.

None of the eight women mentioned being motivated by their new positions as financial contributors in their households, for instance, to effect or initiate changes in gender roles and responsibilities, gender identities or even the routine gender activity profiles. Even with the potentially increased choices and power at their disposal, any action or behaviour seen as diverting from the existing gender status quo of male domination in households was undertaken only surreptitiously.

When asked what the effects of their businesses were, some of the women's responses included being battered or verbally abused less often by their husbands, feelings/assumptions of increased respect on the part of their husbands, deliberate under-declaring of business profits to their husbands, making secret savings, reinvesting profits in business ventures such as buying plots of land, *bodabodas* (motorbikes commonly used for short-distance transport), livestock and retail shops, among other effects. Some of the women talked of assisting their relatives and being able to utilize hitherto financially inaccessible contraception methods (to regulate their fertility), secretly.

For the few women who chose to fully enjoy the unique and liberating effects of the mobile phone business, such as evading domestic drudgery and staying at their work premises for long periods of time, even after dusk, dressing smartly and interacting freely with real and potential customers, controlling their profits and above all attempting to become key decision-makers in the home, the consequences tended to be dire. As a result of real or imagined threats arising out of their wives' increased choices, the husbands' identities as de facto family heads became increasingly and irreversibly undermined. Tensions increased between spouses, and more often than not physical and psychological violence ensued. Separation and divorces arising out of unresolved, gender-related phone business conflicts became common in the case of the few women who took this route.

The women who experienced gender-based violence and/or marital break-ups, despite feeling bitter and betrayed, saw their situation as the inevitable opportunity cost of their phone business activities. Several opted to continue with their businesses as both an economic and a psychological coping mechanism. As a result of their new (single) marital status, they reported being less restrained by domestic obligations and therefore able to operate freely and subsequently make more money: 'Either you sacrifice your marriage and succeed in the phone business, or you prioritize your marriage and either operate at a mediocre level or collapse altogether' (Oliver). Echoing Oliver's view, Eva had this to say:

> The long absence of my husband from home, which preceded my estrangement, gave my business, which had deteriorated due to my domestic instability, a much-needed boost. I spent more time at my kiosk, which attracted back my old customers and new ones; and my business, now my only lifeline, boomed.

They felt less restrained by domestic obligations and therefore able to transact their businesses freely and subsequently generate more money. These women acknowledged, however, that this was at the expense of their sense of social status both in the home and the wider community. The dominant thinking among all the women is that social status is derived from marriage and how stable that marriage is, as articulated by Eva, Monica and Florence.

Analysis of the findings

There are many conflicting views to date about the development of ICTs and women's empowerment. With the proliferation of ICTs especially in rural settings, concern is being raised that although ICT development is an area women can actively participate in, if the socially and culturally constructed gender roles which play a cross-cutting part in shaping the capacity of women and men to participate on equal terms are not addressed, the marginalization of women will continue (Sharma 2001).

Other authors similarly observe that where women have used ICTs for their own purposes, they report increased knowledge and self-esteem: this is apparently universally true in different social and cultural contexts. This empowering process, however, has the potential to destabilize existing gender relations (Hafkin 2000; Gurumurthy 2004). Hafkin envisioned that women in Africa will take advantage of the medium and bring it into their economic, social and cultural context to empower themselves. She noted, however, that the new technologies are not gender neutral, and if women do not grasp the opportunities, then societal forces will prevail and they will be left farther behind.

It is thus apparent that the impact of ICTs on women's empowerment requires a broad consensus on the understanding of the construction of the sense of empowerment, which varies in different contexts. The Swedish organization Kvinnoforum, for instance, is of the view that empowerment has no set definitions; that focus should be on empowerment not given by someone else, but starting within (cited in Alsopa and Heinston 2005: 41). In the male-dominated society of Hoima the concepts of women's empowerment and gender equality are recent and not well defined. Consequently there was no broad consensus among the interviewed women teleworkers on the concept of empowerment. For women like Zaituni, Oliver, Phionah and Sylvia, the liberating effects of the phone business per se are seen as giving them economic power, autonomy and the rare chance to break free of the constraints imposed on them by the prevailing behaviour norms in the community. Irrespective of the gender tension and subsequent estrangement from their husbands, which some of these women experienced as a result of their phone businesses, they remained resilient and against all odds continued to work.

Zaituni, for instance, feels not only economically liberated (*mukazi wa sente*), but also in an empowered position owing to her increased respect in the community and, overall, her ability to manage her own life. Oliver, Phionah and Sylvia, despite variations in their marital circumstances, also feel the same way (empowered) in the sense that they are not bothered with the acquisition of power or status, which is associated with women in stable marital relationships in their community. They are not bothered with conforming to the expected norms of behaviour, such as being respectably married and not venturing out to work, whereby their fellow community women derive social status. What bothers these women is economic survival, and not social status, which can neither feed them nor pay their rent. An interesting case is Melanie, who attributed her marriage to her improved financial circumstances. She links the fact that she, supported by her husband, is able to 'work against' the social and religious expectations regarding her behaviour as a married woman with empowerment.

For these women, the sense of freedom from the inhibitions and structures imposed on them by the prevailing patriarchy was seen as a position of empowerment. How they were perceived by society, especially from the moral or religious point of view, remained irrelevant so long as they continued operating their phone businesses and were at least getting by economically.

For other phone business women, however, empowerment is not related to shifting the balance of power in the family domain. Monica, Florence and Eva were of the view that the commercial use of modern ICTs (mobile telephony) and the resulting economic gains do not have a significant impact on existing domestic gender relations. Their sense of empowerment is closely related to their social status, which is derived from marriage. Business success outside a stable marriage, in the context of the prevailing social values, is actually even seen as a potential indictment.

This category of women, prior to engaging in the phone business, was aware of this dominant thinking in the community. They were conversant with the social costs of venturing out of their domestic environments to work, particularly as roadside payphone operators, a business not seen as dignifying in any way, especially for women, even by the women teleworkers themselves. In other words the women knew that, despite earning much-needed money through operating their payphone business, they would inevitably forfeit their social status since the nature of their work and the entrenched thinking regarding domestic virtue[3] in the community are incompatible. The tough but rational choice was between acute poverty with dignity, and financial well-being devoid of virtue. The women, except Monica, apparently chose the latter and aggressively continued with their business operations.

This category of women teleworkers, nevertheless, are to a large extent striving to be seen as operating within the existing cultural framework. For instance, all of them sought husband approval and/or cooperation prior to engaging in the phone business. This can be seen as a strategy, at least at an interpersonal level, to show that they are not rebelling against their husband's authority in particular, or domestic-virtue thinking in general, which does not tolerate their participation in such work. The reluctance of these women to utilize their phone business success – to assert themselves in their homes at least, and challenge the existing power imbalances – can be seen in a similar vein as an attempt to operate as good women within the prevailing sociocultural context. Melanie, attributing her marriage to her phone business success and her inner strength to 'working against the odds' of her Islamic faith, with her husband's support, has obviously created a different domestic situation grounded in a different type of gender relationship to what the other women have.

The teleworking women whose sense of status was derived from their marriage made it clear that, despite being able to establish and operate successful phone businesses, and potentially increase their choices, they were aware of their limits. Going beyond the 'limits' – that is, utilizing their expanded choices to redefine their positions or goals, and challenge existing gendered power relations – posed formidable social costs. Thus deciding not to utilize their new opportunities to transform existing gender relations and promote gender equality was not a matter of choosing to devalue their self-worth by perpetuating themselves as hapless victims of existing gender inequalities.

The behaviour of this category of women can be seen as a rational attempt to operate successfully in the prevailing ICT context and at the same time retain their marriages, from which they derive their status and respect as women. In a nutshell, what these women are doing is avoiding rather than enduring the social costs that are inevitable when rural women in Uganda strive to empower themselves.

Despite operating within the confines of domestic-virtue thinking and sustaining their marriages and social status, the overall effect is that the new choices resulting from these women's phone businesses, by remaining unutilized, serve to bring to the fore the glaring, hitherto latent gender-based inequalities that keep women subjugated in society. These women, however, can be seen as pursuing empowerment, which for them means working and gaining economic independence while at the same time being respected by their husbands, families and society, in the existing ICT context in rural Ugandan settings.

Conclusions

The study has shown that understanding the impact of the use of modern ICTs such as mobile telephony on women's empowerment requires a deep insight into the construction of the sense of empowerment, which appears to vary among individuals in similar contexts. Broadly, empowerment is understood as the ability of individuals to make strategic life choices in a context in which they did not have this ability previously. The ability to choose, in other words, is regarded as central to the concept of power. Prior to engaging in the payphone business, the women interviewed were severely cash strapped, a situation that was presumably disempowering in the sense that it limited their access to and control of resources, and the ability to question the existing gender power imbalances in their families and to control their lives or destinies. A rational assumption would be that the substantial economic gains made by the women through the operation of their phone businesses would eliminate the disempowering factors and pave the way for the women's empowerment as we understand it. This, however, was not necessarily the case, implying that the women's sense of empowerment is determined or shaped by a multiplicity of factors, including their individual circumstances and realities, needs, aspirations and the social context in which they operate.

As a result of their phone business success, the women found themselves in different, hitherto unexpected domestic situations. The majority of husbands, including those who had directly or tacitly approved of their wives' businesses, could not cope with the realities of their success. The ability of the women to generate and control their money, the physical and social exposure they enjoyed and their long absences from home did not go down well with these men. Inevitably gender tensions ensued, and for some of the women these attained crisis levels. It is the way in which women coped or tried to cope with their respective situations which defined their sense of empowerment. Whereas for most women the battlefield included the domestic and the social environment, both Monica and Melanie felt completely supported by their relationship with their husbands. The difference between these two women was that Monica had internalized the social expectations pertaining to her behaviour as a married woman and framed her relationship with her husband within these parameters. Melanie, on the other hand, had found in her relationship with her husband the strength to stand against these social expectations.

The estranged women who coped well without husband support and/ or control, and resiliently continued to operate their businesses successfully, viewed themselves as in a position of empowerment. The women who liberated themselves from the inhibitions of the existing societal norms of behaviour, and continued against all odds to operate their businesses in the face of negative societal attitudes, also saw themselves in a strong position of empowerment. And those phone business women who chose not to jeopardize their marriages by declining to take advantage of their newly gained economic gains to define their own goals, bargain or negotiate for increased control of key household resources, or question existing gender inequalities, including decision-making power, also felt a strong sense of empowerment derived from their enhanced social status as respectably married women in spite of their telework, which does not fit with domestic-virtue thinking.

Whereas it is indisputable that all these categories of the phone business women experienced a sense of empowerment, this was at an individual level, without necessarily transforming the restricting social structures of patriarchy and gender inequality, which remained intact in the communities. This is definitely contrary to my understanding of the sense of empowerment, and I feel there is a need for a comprehensive inquiry into the extent to which the empowerment the phone women experienced is sustainable.

Notes

1 A proper woman should marry, provide services for her husband, including sex, be a mother and provide and care for her children. She should fulfil practical duties within the household, grow food for the family and do other necessary care work. She should be submissive and deferential to her husband, his male relatives and other men in the community. She is not a decision-maker in the family. For details, see Kyomuhendo-Bantebya and Keniston McIntosh (2006: 79).

2 The names being used are the real names of the research participants.

3 Regarding the domestic-virtue model, see Kyomuhendo-Bantebya and Keniston McIntosh (2006: 65–85).

References

Alsopa, R. and N. Heinston (eds) (2005) 'Measuring empowerment in practice; structuring analysis and framing indicators', World Bank Policy Working Paper 3510.

Gurumurthy, A. (2004) *Gender and ICTs Overview Report*, Bridge Institute of Development Studies.

Hafkin, N. (2000) 'Convergence of concepts; gender and ICTs in Africa', in E. M. Rathgeber and E. O. Adera (eds), *Gender and the Information Revolution in Africa*, Ottawa: IDRC.

— (2004) 'Globalization and the economic empowerment of women; defining and building a gender responsive information society in the ESCAP region', UNESCAP.

Kyomuhendo-Bantebya, G. and M. Keniston McIntosh (2006) *Women, Work and Domestic Virtue in Uganda (1900–2003)*, Oxford/ Kampala: James Currey/ Fountain Publishers.

Sharma, C. (2001) 'Using ICTs to create opportunities for marginalized women and men; the private sector and community working together', Paper presented at the World Bank, Washington, DC.

FOUR | **Creating new realities**

15 | Professional women empowered to succeed in Kenya's ICT sector

OKWACH ABAGI, OLIVE SIFUNA AND
SALOME AWUOR OMAMO

This chapter is based on a study that investigated how professional women in the information and communication technology (ICT) sector in Kenya have accessed and are appropriating ICT. The open-ended, in-depth and interactive interview approach gave researchers and key informants the opportunity to discuss issues of gender and ICT in Kenya. Focus group discussions and in-depth interviews were used to capture the respondents' 'voices', experiences and interpretations of their experiences. This was supplemented by a review of existing literature.

The study is based on the premise that ICTs have become a potent force in transforming social, economic and political life globally (Hudson 2001; Thioune 2003: 1). Even with this potential, issues of social inclusion and exclusion have emerged as a dimension of the range of critical issues that need more research and debate as we progress into the twenty-first century. In particular, there is a need for practical interventions that will shed more light on the linkage between ICT utilization and the concept of human development in general, and on the interface between ICTs and women's empowerment in particular (UNDP 2002; Rathgeber 2000; Adeya 2001). This chapter and the research it is based on set out to increase our understanding of this latter interface.

The study relied on purposively selected professional women in ICT careers, either as owners, CEOs or technical persons, working in various organizations and companies in Nairobi, Kenya. Table 15.1 indicates the educational background, training and current positions of these respondents.

As shown in Table 15.1, our respondents are well educated, trained and occupy high positions in their respective organizations/institutions. In terms of education, eight are graduates with bachelor degrees and four hold diplomas in ICT-related courses, including computer science, information systems, information technology and web designing. All of them except two studied at Kenyan universities (Moi University and the Jomo Kenyatta University of Agriculture and Technology) and the Kenya National Polytechnic. One holds a BCom. Engineering from a

TABLE 15.1 Key informants in the study

KI*	Education	Professional training	Current position
1	Bachelor of Arts degree in Sociology	Marketing course	Managing director
2	Certificates in Computer Science (marketing bias)	Corporate Governance, Collective Index, customer service and marketing courses	CEO
3	Degree in Management Information Systems	Computer Programming, Management, Systems Analysis and design, Java, computer packages manager	Territory partner
4	Degree in Information Science (IT option)	Computer packages	Systems administrator
5	Bachelor of Commerce degree (Management Science option)	Systems and Database Administration and Accounting	Assistant manager
6	Bachelor of Commerce degree and diploma in Computer Studies	Computer packages	Assistant manager
7	Bachelor of Science degree	Networking, Systems Administration and Information Technology	Systems administrator
8	Diploma in Information Systems	Secretarial	IT support officer
9	Bachelor of Commerce degree (Accounting option)	E-link, MS Office, Visual basics and certificate courses in Accounting	Application support assistant
10	Marketing degree – Technology in Management Studies	Computer packages and programming	Managing director
11	Diploma in Information Technology	Computer programming and systems management	Technician/support officer
12	Diploma in Web Designing	Computer Science and programming	Web designer/developer

* Key informants

university in the United States, where she studied and also worked in ICT for some time. All four career women with diplomas have enrolled at the University of Nairobi for a degree course – mainly in marketing and business management.

These career women hold senior technical and management positions in their organizations. Some of them are board members of various national and international organizations, for example the Internet Corporation of Assigned Names and Numbers (ICANN), an Internet policy-formulating body, and the Institute of Directors of Kenya (IODK).

The gender gap in education in Kenya

Nothing is more revealing to those committed to gender equity in development in general and in education in particular than the clear message conveyed in available education statistics for the time period since Kenya's independence in 1963. The gender gap in education has been consistent and appears in every sub-sector of education (Chege and Sifuna 2006; Abagi 1997; Abdi and Cleghorn 2005; UNESCO 2006). In the last decade, although nationally the Net Enrolment Ratio (NER) at the primary school level has been about 51 per cent for boys and 49 per cent for girls, the regional statistics show gender disparity in each of the eight provinces in the country. For example, in North Eastern Province the NER between 1990 and 2001 has been 16.5 per cent for boys and 9.8 per cent for girls. In Nairobi Province, the NER is 43.3 per cent for boys and 42.2 per cent for girls.

In the same period the NER at secondary school level by gender has been 52 per cent for boys and 47 per cent for girls. It is estimated that at the secondary school level there are 118 enrolled boys for every 100 girls enrolled. The gender gaps are even wider in North Eastern, Rift Valley and Coast provinces, where incidences of poverty are high and cultural-religious factors work against the schooling of girls. For example, even after the declaration of fee-free primary education in 2003, the primary school Gross Enrolment Ratio (GER) in North Eastern Province has remained at 31 per cent and 16.9 per cent for boys and girls respectively. In Kenya, women are also under-represented in higher education. Since 1981, only about 30 per cent of university students in Kenya's eight public universities have been female.

The imbalance in access to education is attributed to the cultural factors and socialization patterns in various communities in Kenya. Among various groups, especially in the rural areas, where over 80 per cent of the population lives, men are still regarded as the owners and controllers of resources and the breadwinners, while women are seen as homemakers (wives, caregivers) and dependent on men. Education of the girls, as compared to that of the boys, is generally not regarded as important by many households in many parts of rural Kenya. Such perceptions result in intensive differentials in socialization programmes and different behaviour patterns for males and females at home and in learning institutions. While such attributes as independence, aggressiveness and competitiveness are associated with and rewarded in males, those of dependence, passivity and compliance are rewarded in females.

Recognizing gender as an organizing principle is fundamental to understanding the ways in which we are socialized and educated, and interact with each other, and generally to the ways in which our public and private lives are shaped and organized. In Kenya, this has resulted in the gender gap in education being substantial, especially at secondary and tertiary levels.

The extent to which this 'gendered prophecy' is tackled by women and recognized as social conditioning is at the core of women succeeding in any male-dominated field, including ICTs.

Socialized beyond gender stereotyping into ICT careers

Our study has indicated that women are under-represented in ICT careers, and when they are represented, they are primarily in stereotypical roles (Abagi et al. 2006). The twelve key informants in our study demonstrated, however, that they managed to access and succeed in ICT-related careers because of two interrelated factors.

First, the social environment in which our respondents were brought up and socialized did not adhere to discriminatory gender norms. The twelve career women we had discussions with had parents who were middle-class professionals. Their parents did not adhere to gender stereotyping regarding their daughters and their daughters' education. The support our respondents received (encouragement, freedom to choose careers, appropriate advice, financial support to seek higher education and training and follow-ups) from their parents and close relatives played a major role in their education, training and careers. The parents and mentors were a major factor behind the success of these ICT career women. Other important attributes include the fact that all the women were raised by parents who were middle-class – working as teachers, administrators and managers in both public and private sectors in urban settings. Out of the twelve women, only two women had a father or a relative working in the ICT sector. None had a mother or woman relative working in the ICT industry.

Positive parental attitudes towards girls enabled the respondents to grow as individuals with 'confidence and vision in life that goes beyond just marriage and offering care and support services at home and in society at large' (respondent, ICT CEO). It was found that parental attitudes towards these women empowered them from an early age. The parents thus encouraged their daughters to work hard and excel in school, yet they did not push them towards any particular academic discipline or career. They were 'liberal' parents, who exposed their children to many things, provided an empowering environment where education and career development were highly valued, and supported the development and pursuit of the girls' own interests.

The respondents were very conscious of the roles their parents played in their success, as indicated by the following research participant:

> My parents were gender sensitive in practice and socialized us in the family as their children and not as boys and girls. They did not discriminate against girls. According to them all children needed the same treatment, thus girls were given full support to realize our potential, just like boys. I was encouraged all the way. They are my role models [and] I owe them a lot for my success in life. (Internet support provider CEO 1, 2005)

Another participant had this to say:

> My dad was selfless in the sense that he never ever made a decision for me. My decisions were mine to make and the consequences were mine to deal with. That was very clear. ... And I think that was the beginning of my self-actualization, to deal with myself in terms of making my own decisions and the best decisions for me. And I think that for me this is the most successful thing in my life. (Internet support provider CEO 2, 2005)

The respondents identify parental support, positive attitudes and exposure and access to the world of schooling and work as what enhanced their confidence and made them independently search for useful information and career openings. The specific nature of their upbringings was considered the basis for their self-actualization and sense of empowerment.

The second factor in why the respondents managed to access and succeed in ICT-related careers was their self-motivation. Our respondents' personal motivation and focus during training and at work played a major part in helping them to venture into male-dominated subjects.

Some of the respondents' personal motivation was evident as they talked about the challenges they face as women in the ICT sector:

I hear people talking about the ceiling, and when they are talking about the ceiling they are saying they believe there is something up there that stops you from moving. My belief is different. My belief is that if there is something above you that is stopping you from moving, you either decide to break it or avoid it. Actually if you can't break it you can't jump, so you either break it or you step away from it and you create another path. (Internet support provider CEO 2, 2005)

I committed myself to succeed in life and to do what interests and satisfies me. This explains why I did many courses in different countries in Europe and North America before settling here in Kenya to manage an Internet service provision company. I feel good about it and I am a role model to many Kenyan women who are interested in joining the ICT sector as professionals. My parents and friends do not mind me doing what I am doing right now career-wise. (Internet support provider CEO 1, 2005)

Through focus group discussions, the respondents revealed a number of factors and characteristics that they connect to their success in the ICT sector and their sense of empowerment. With the above understanding of individual empowerment, our respondents were able to transform their thinking, practice and perceptions of the role of women in society in general and regarding participation in the ICT sector in particular. They were able to 'break' the gender stereotyping regarding the roles of women and men in society and thus ventured into male-dominated careers. They connect their success in the ICT sector and their sense of empowerment with the principles and guidelines they use in their work. These include the following:

- having a vision – a professional dream;
- being focused and following your dream;
- having the right skills;
- being confident;
- having a commitment to work and to succeed;
- fighting for career space as a right;
- being dynamic;
- hard work;
- risk-taking;
- seeing gender not as a barrier but as an opportunity;
- continuously seeking more knowledge and skills;
- not becoming bogged down with thinking about marriage at the expense of building a career;
- going for what one wants career-wise without being inhibited by

gender stereotyping (i.e. challenging the existing gender stereotyping and discrimination in society in general and the ICT environments in particular).

Our respondents indicated confidently that they are able to make informed decisions in their careers and workplaces because they have the above characteristics (they feel empowered). They believe that as professional women in ICT they use their knowledge, skills and experience to fulfil their assignments efficiently and effectively.

According to our respondents, development entails empowering individuals (in this case women) to develop confidence in themselves over time, and to become informed and knowledgeable in society. According to them, empowerment means 'being able to make informed decisions in life and positioning oneself strategically to acquire and responsively apply knowledge and skills learned at home, in school, in society and in the world of work' (Internet support provider CEO 1, 2005). It comprises 'a situation where a girl or woman is able to challenge gender-biased stereotypes and discrimination, and pursue any career of choice without being forced by her parents, friends, the government or working environment' (Internet support provider CEO 2, 2005). Empowerment is associated with acquisition of the right knowledge, skills and attitudes to enhance one's chances of excelling in chosen careers and leading a healthy and comfortable life – being able to access basic needs and life services, including food, shelter, education, healthcare and clothing. It is also related to being able to fight discrimination of any kind, including that based on sex or gender.

Stereotyping within ICT careers

Studies in many countries in sub-Saharan Africa have indicated that women are under-represented and stereotyped in formal education and even in school textbooks, particularly those in mathematics, science and engineering subjects (Obura 1991; KNEC 2003, 2004, 2005; Abagi 2005). Our study of career women in ICT indicates that stereotyping is not only making women hesitant to access the sub-sector, but even those who access and are trained in ICTs find themselves stereotyped and/or discriminated against. The consequence is that some find themselves, despite their ICT knowledge and skills, placed in 'female'-oriented service jobs. For example, instead of providing technical support, a trained woman technician ends up working in an ICT firm as a public relations or marketing officer.

Our respondents indicated that they know bright young women

with degrees in Computer Science or Information Technology who quit working with ICT firms as technicians or programmers and are just public relations officers or secretaries in some of the private firms in Nairobi. They have been completely 'swallowed in the male-dominated work environment and are wasting their knowledge and skills in ICT because they are doing irrelevant things' (respondents, 2005). The professional women in ICT we talked with hold the view that public pressure for women to be seen smartly dressed, welcoming and smiling all the time tends to discourage young women technicians in ICT from staying with their careers and progressing in them. Wearing an apron and carrying screwdrivers and spanners is seen as a man's thing, and women should avoid it.

Currently, there is a mushrooming of colleges in Kenyan towns offering ICT-related courses. Our respondents reported, however, that most women tend to enrol for secretarial/customer care courses such as those in word-processing and office management. On the other hand, most men apart from going for word processing courses, will be doing technical work in ICT – computer maintenance, web design and programme development, among others. Men enrol for technical aspects of ICT, while most women prefer 'soft' areas, which they see most of their women friends and relatives in. The professional women in ICT are clear that this gendered experience emanates from societal perceptions that science, mathematics and technology are supposed to be male domains. As a result, it seems to be expected that girls will perform poorly in mathematics and science subjects and shy away from technological-oriented careers.

Gender-biased perceptions and attitudes are transmitted to women who enter the ICT sector. Generally, such women are seen as being in the 'wrong' profession.

The challenge I face is the fact that I am a lady, and this is a line where people believe that men are the ones to be doing this thing. Somebody sees me carrying a screwdriver and begins wondering what I am doing with it. As you try to open a machine, somebody wonders if such a machine will really work in the end! (Informant 4, 2005)

Let me tell you something ... as you might be aware most people never believe in women working in technical areas. Let us say a client has a problem somewhere and then I am asked to go and sort it out for him/ her. When you get there, the general impression is that, since it is a lady who has come to deal with the problem, it is unlikely to be sorted out! In some cases, clients are daring enough to ask, what do you know about this problem? (Informant 9, 2005)

During discussions our respondents pointed out that some ICT owners and operators, who are men, are also biased against women as they see them as 'intruders' into the sector. Women's entry into ICT is hampered right from the interview stage in most organizations dominated by men. Some of our respondents reported that there are many male chauvinists within organizations who do not hide their feelings right from the time a woman is invited for an interview in an ICT-related job or promotion. During interviews, women tend to be asked questions that relate to their family lives – for example, 'If and when you take your maternity leave, how will the IT department function in your absence?' There are also questions relating to being away from duty because of other family engagements, such as 'What will happen to your work when your child is sick?', 'Is your husband going to allow you to work late or travel?' Generally, men are not asked such questions. Their questions tend to be focused on their professional skills and experiences in ICT as related to the job at hand.

Gender discrimination in job mobility for professional women in ICT was raised by a good number of women in the study. It was reported that it is more difficult for women than men to get promoted in an ICT profession. This is largely because the sector is dominated by men and the few women who are there are in non-technical jobs (support services). Besides, some bosses have very little regard for women and that makes it difficult to be promoted.

Since the sociocultural environment is highly male dominated and discriminatory, our respondents indicated that if a woman does not build her own confidence and competence, and does not demand her rights, even if she has a master's degree in ICT, she will still be pushed out of the sector or be relegated to pursuing a career that is traditionally considered to be a woman's. Women must be focused and fight discrimination.

If [a woman] is not focused, strong and does not have confidence in what [she wants] to do and where [she wants] to go, definitely she will give in to unnecessary male-motivated pressure. In my case, I knew what I wanted in life and I went for it. I face many challenges as a professional person, not just as a woman. But I do not allow women/men issues that are based on stereotypes and in most cases just mere men's arrogance to put me down or derail me from my work. (Internet service provider CEO, 2005)

Discussing the implications of the experiences of professional women in ICT

It is ironic that, as the pace of ICT growth is increasing very fast in every sector, and awareness about the sub-sector's role in the country's development is high, few women are exposed to opportunities that encourage them to pursue ICT careers. If girls and women are left out of the ICT professional sector, then their marginalization in development in Kenya will continue and their active participation in various sectors of the economy will be affected negatively.

In most communities in Kenya there is still a strong perception that when it comes to anything electronic and/or technical, this is a man's business. This kind of thinking is not just widespread in the public sphere such as in workplaces, but is also prevalent in the private sphere, in people's houses, where, for example, when a bulb blows or a radio's batteries are to be changed, a male figure (man or young boy) and not a female figure is called upon to come and fix it. There is an assumption that technical tasks, including those in ICT, have to be performed by men. Women have been socialized by society and their parents to stay away from such tasks. Those who dare to venture into them are seen as 'strangers' who are going against the existing culture or practice.

Our study has indicated that women's access to professional ICT careers and their progress in the sector is attributable to parental support and stands against gender stereotyping in terms of their daughters' self-motivation, and the extent to which women themselves 'disregard' and/or shed the gendered perceptions and attitudes that are entrenched in Kenyan communities. A determining factor in promoting women's access to and selection of ICT careers is the extent to which girls/women and boys/men change their perspectives and knowledge of the world and careers to counter the apparent 'norms' shaped by male domination. It will continue to be difficult for women to develop professional careers in the ICT sector if the patriarchal value systems and practices in Kenyan societies are not dismantled in a systematic and sustainable way.

The respondents in our study are bold, focused and committed women who were determined to excel in the ICT sector. Despite their venturing into a male-dominated field, the challenges they face in and out of the sector as women have not dampened their spirit or determination to succeed. This is because they were socialized to disregard gender stereotypes that perpetuate discrimination against women. Besides, these professional women took a stand to show practically that there is no sector/profession in Kenya that is a preserve of men only, as many people, men in particular, would like to believe.

In a country full of gendered expectations and perceptions, our respondents are striving to be good role models to the girls and young women who are still struggling and undecided about what kind of career they should pursue. The message they send to girls and young women is that one has to decide what s/he wants to be and do in the future career-wise. Apart from being socialized positively to excel, the respondents argue that girls need to be focused and passionate about what they want to do. With the mainstreaming of ICT in various development sectors in the country, if one – a girl or boy – is committed to excel in the ICT sector nothing can prevent them from doing so.

Based on what we discussed with and observed from the professional women in ICT, it seems apparent that from an early age girls must be socialized by their family members and existing social and political institutions to take charge of their destiny by challenging the existing gender gaps and stereotypes. This is an empowering process which, in the final analysis, would result in girls being informed, brave and ready to venture into a career of their choice based on personal interest or responsive mentoring/role-modelling.

Indeed, socializing the young (both boys and girls) to challenge the existing gender stereotypes and biases is crucial to breaking the current stereotypes in careers and workplaces in Kenya. Our key respondents reflected on their own experiences and all agreed that the foundation that was laid by their parents and the exposure to various social environments made them confident and able to succeed in the ICT sector. Their own motivation, however, was the engine that drove them to succeed in the male-dominated ICT sector. They see themselves as professionals, who can compete with other professionals – men or women anywhere in the world. The confidence, pride and vision these women have is what makes them effective in running and/or working in ICT companies.

The above findings have implications for what 'education for development' should be put in place in Kenya. The experience of our respondents means that if the rest of the people (men and women) in the country, from an early age, are exposed to the situation and opportunities afforded to the respondents in this study – gender-sensitive parents, socialization that challenges gender stereotypes, a financially advantaged upbringing and freedom to excel in their areas of choice – both women and men would be able to excel in any sector of the economy, ICT included.

Socialization and education for development start with reconceptualizing and redefining the concept of 'development' to focus on empowering people – women and men. This is a process of creating an enabling environment for enhancing women's participation in all sectors of society, including ICT professions (Anyango and Abagi 2005; Makgoba 1999; Ayittey 1991; Nyerere 1962; Oruko 1981). In this direction, from an early age, girls and boys need to be socialized and empowered to challenge gendered myths, perceptions and stereotypes that are currently perpetuated in the family, in the school system, in workplaces and in places of worship.

Conclusion

This chapter has been inspired by career women in Kenya who have ventured into the fast-growing sector of information and communication technology. Based on their own experiences, these women can be role models to young Kenyan girls and youth who need to build their careers and be effective in their workplaces. They have indicated that gender stereotypes, gender bias, sex role socialization and discrimination against women in general need to be challenged and dismantled if equity in the workplace is to be enhanced.

The Kenyan government, and relevant ministries such as those of education, gender, youth, planning, finance and communication, need to put in place policy and legal frameworks that will empower young girls from an early age to change their mindset about careers and employment. Without this only a minority of women will be in a position to draw upon their families, their motivation and their determination to counter gender discrimination and participate in all sectors working towards the development of the country.

In a nutshell, a gender-sensitive policy environment needs to target the elimination of gender discrimination against women in Kenya. Specifically relevant policy and legal frameworks need to be developed (and operationalized), targeting the following:

- Enhancing girls' participation in education at all levels, thus reducing (eliminating) the gender gap in education in terms of access, achievement and transition from one level to the other.
- Empowering girls and women to acquire appropriate knowledge and life skills that will assist them in making informed decisions about their education and careers.
- Ensuring that workplace policies and the environment in general do not indirectly or directly discriminate against women by perpetuating gender stereotyping.
- Raising awareness in existing educational, social and political institutions of the need for a process whereby girls and women learn to take charge of their destiny by challenging existing gender gaps and stereotypes.

- Enhancing access and equity in the appropriation and use of ICT for personal and the country's development.

References

Abagi, O. (1995) 'Gender equity as a challenge for implementing EFA: recounting gender issues in the provision of education for all in Kenya', *Basic Education Forum*, 6: 35–42.

— (1997) *Status of Education in Kenya: Indicators for Planning and Policy Formulation*, Nairobi: IPAR.

— (2005) 'The role of school in Africa in the 21st century: coping with forces of change', in A. Abdi and A. Cleghorn (eds), *Issues in African Education: Sociological Perspectives*, New York: Palgrave Macmillan.

Abagi, O., N. Sifuna and S. Omamo (2006) *Career Women into ICT in Kenya: Progression, Challenges and Opportunities*, Research report of the GRACE Project funded by the International Development Research Centre (IDRC), www.GRACE-Network.net.

Abdi, A. and A. Cleghorn (eds) (2005) *Issues in African Education: Sociological Perspectives*, New York: Palgrave Macmillan.

Adeya, C. N. (2001) *Information and Communication Technologies in Africa: A Review and Selected Annotated Bibliography*, www.inasp.org.uk/pubs/ict/index.html.

— (2003) *ICTs and Poverty: A Literature Review*, Ottawa: IDRC.

American Association of University Women (AAUW) (1995) *How Schools Short-change Girls. The AAUW Report*, New York: Marlowe.

Anyango, O. and O. Abagi (2005) *Schooling, Education and Underdevelopment: The Paradox of Western-oriented Education in Africa*, Nairobi: Romix Services.

Ayittey, G. B. N. (1991) *Indigenous African Institutions*, New York: Transnational Publishers.

Bornstein, R. (1982) 'Sexism in education', in M. P. Sadker and David M. Sadker (eds), *Sex Equity Handbook for Schools*, New York: Longman.

Chege, F. and N. Sifuna (2006) *Girls' and Women's Education in Kenya: Gender Perspectives and Trends*, Nairobi: UNESCO.

Furtado, C. (1977) 'Development', *International Social Science Journal*, XXIX(4): 628–50.

Government of Kenya (2003) *Economic Recovery Strategy for Wealth and Employment Creation 2003–2007*, Nairobi: Government Printer.

— (2005, 2006) *Economic Surveys*, Nairobi: Government Printer.

Hafkin, N. (2000) 'Convergence of concepts: gender and ICTs in Africa', in E. M. Rathgeber and E. O. Adera (eds), *Gender and the Information Revolution in Africa*, Ottawa: International Development Research Centre (IDRC).

Hudson, H. E. (2001) *The Potential of ICTs for Development: Opportunities and Obstacles*, Telecommunications Management and Policy Program, University of San Francisco, www.usfca.edu/facstaff/Hudson/.

KNEC (Kenya National Examination Council) (2003, 2004, 2005) *KNEC Newsletters*, Nairobi: KNEC.

Lipsey, R. G. et al. (1979) *An Introduction to Positive Economics*, 5th edn, London: Weidenfeld & Nicolson.

Makgoba, W. M. (1999) *African Ren-
aissance: The New Struggle*, Cape
Town: Mafube Tafelberg.

Nyerere, J. (1962) *Ujamaa: The
Basis of African Socialism*, Dar es
Salaam: Government Press.

— (1968) *Freedom and Socialism:
A Selection from Writings and
Speeches, 1965–67*, London:
Oxford University Press.

— (1974) *Man and Development*,
London: Oxford University Press.

Obura, A. (1991) *Changing Images*,
Nairobi: ACTS Press.

Ocitti, I. (1994) *An Introduction to In-
digenous Education in East Africa*,
IZ/DVV Supplement to Adult
Education and Development.

Oruko, H. O. (1981) *Practical Philo-
sophy: In Search of an Ethical
Minimum*, Nairobi: East Africa
Publishers.

Rathgeber, E. M. (2000) 'Women,
men and ICTs in Africa: why
gender is an issue', in E. M. Rathgeber and E. O. Adera (eds), *Gender and the Information Revolution
in Africa*, Ottawa: IDRC.

Thioune, R. M. (ed.) (2003) 'Opportunities and challenges for community development', in *Information
and Communication Technologies
for Development in Africa*', vol. 1,
Ottawa: IDRC.

UNDP (2002) *Kenya Human Development Report*, Nairobi: UNDP/GOK.

— (2003, 2006) *Human Development
Report*, Washington, DC: UNDP.

UNESCO (2006) *EFA Global Monitoring Report 2006*, Paris: UNESCO.

Ward, H. (1989) *African Development
Reconsidered: New Perspectives
from the Continent*, New York:
Phelps-Stoke Institute.

16 | Reflections on the mentoring experiences of ICT career women in Nairobi, Kenya: looking in the mirror

SALOME AWUOR OMAMO[1]

Two interesting issues that continue to be raised and discussed in research and articles on the low participation of women in information and communication technology (ICT) are those of mentoring and IT expert portrayal. In the past, it has been shown that girls had very few female ICT experts to look up to or to desire to be like. Looking into the field and seeing a male-dominated arena did not attract girls in the least. Despite the success of various education initiatives in the past several years, however, there is little doubt that the shortage of women in technology begins in the playground, where gender stereotyping is already under way. As such, many industry leaders and experts believe the long-term solution to the gender imbalance in IT lies in women technologists going back to school – way back, to high schools and even elementary schools, to mentor young girls, who too often give up on maths and science at an early age (Nobel 2007).

Education, training and skills development are critical for women who want to enhance their career potential through the use of ICTs within as well as outside the ICT sector. Learning practices (learning through practice from the classroom to the workplace to the high-technology office and other forms of learning through remembering and activity) should be extended to girls (and women), made gender sensitive (women-specific training, ongoing user support, and mentoring in the communities where women live) and deepened for women as not only users but technicians, programmers, ICT policy-makers and advocates.

A recent study in Kenya came up with findings that indicate that women are highly optimistic, embracing ICT as a practical mechanism for achieving entry into the labour market (Mbarika et al. 2007). They perceive significant structural barriers, however, such as public policies that fail to facilitate the development of the ICT sector, gender discrimination by employers, and training that provides them with insufficient technical skills to enable them to effectively perform in the workplace. These findings are largely confirmed by similar studies conducted in other countries (AAUW 2000).

The following factors slow down women's career progression in ICTs:

- Lack of role models and career advice – there are few female lecturers and tutors, few female fellow students, 'invisible' successful career women, stereotypical career impressions and a lack of information about computing as a career (Camp 1997; Cohoon 2001; Crombie et al. 2001; Teague 2002).
- Inadequate institutional support – lack of special programmes that would enable females to learn computer jargon and help them feel comfortable around computers; lack of encouragement and mentoring on the part of the lecturers; lack of institutional support of gender-sensitive teaching (Cohoon 2001; Crump 2001).
- Lack of peer support groups – lack of interaction between, and lack of support networks among, female students (Springer et al. 1999).

There is therefore a need to open the ICT field to women and eliminate the gender inequalities that currently leave women in stereotypical occupations, by building capacities and providing opportunities for girls and women.

It is for the above reasons that recently numerous non-governmental organizations (NGOs) and development agencies have been trying to encourage the use of mentoring so that girls can see and connect with other women, with similar dreams and aspirations, who have actually succeeded in this field. More awareness about the nature of the ICT domain exposes them to the reality that ICT experts are not necessarily male (AAUW 2000).

Women mentoring and being mentored in the ICT sector

This chapter arises from an investigation into how career women in ICT have accessed and are appropriating ICTs, and have been empowered career-wise.[2] A significant theme that emerged was the role of mentors in the lives of the twelve ICT career women interviewed in Nairobi. While the women involved in the research were sharing what they had gained from being mentored, they spontaneously started speaking also about what they had gained from being mentors to others. Therefore, although other mentoring articles do not, to my knowledge, include what mentors themselves are gaining from the mentoring process, I decided to include this aspect with regard to my respondents as well as with regard to myself.

Their experiences and thoughts on the role of mentoring, learning and support in relation to their ICT careers mirrored my own experiences of being mentored and of being a mentor to others as a reflexive qualitative researcher in the ICT field. This chapter thus explores what being mentored, and being a mentor to others, has meant in relation to the career paths we have followed and the barriers we have overcome.

From the experiences described below, mentoring to the respondents and to me is a relationship in which a mentor gives personal and professional support and in turn gains from mentoring others and being mentored. This support comes in the form of lessons and demonstrations, observations, feedback and consultations that are facilitated by books, Internet interaction and face-to-face meetings, all of which are provided by the mentor. The mentor is to those s/he mentors a role model, an adviser, a guide and a counsellor.

ICT career women's experiences of being mentored

Through mentorship, learning and support experiences, women have been able to:

- Develop technical and professional skills, knowledge and understanding.

    My manager is a great mentor to me. He advises me on several issues including which courses I should take so that I can advance my career in IT. You know, like he tells me, you see, if you concentrate on this you won't go far, so why don't you try this. ... So he always gives me information from the perspective of a manager and somehow I get prepared in advance. (Systems administrator, 2005)

- Develop self-esteem, self-confidence, and self-reliance, a questioning of discriminatory assumptions, and a sense of determination.

    My mother was a role model to me and was very powerful. When I talk about power I don't talk about it in the context that most people understand it. I talk about power in the context of capacity and ability to survive. Observing her power has helped me in the sense that I don't take any challenge for granted; I also don't take a challenge as a bottleneck. I take a challenge as something that I analyse, identify what it is and then I come up with a critical mission of overcoming it and move on. (ISP manager, 2005)

- Gain greater understanding of career options.

    I took a computer course and started a computer beginners' class. The professor in that class became my mentor because I enjoyed the course and asked him which career it led to. He sat me down and told me that

I could be a systems analyst. He gave me a whole range of careers that I could do and explained to me exactly what career path each would take and I took interest. So from there I declared my major as management and information systems. (IT company manager, 2005)

There is this club I belong to, the Soroptimists club. The president of the club, who is a mentor to many of us women in the club, came and encouraged us to go and learn IT. She talked to us and organized management training for the members of the club. (IT support officer, 2005)

• Gain valuable feedback and different perspectives.

Yah, I have got very many mentors, but the most important is my A/C Manager (Africa Central). What I really like about him is that irrespective of whatever I want to do, he can sort me out with my problems. He can actually listen to my problems. When I tell him I cannot go to Zambia simply because I have children here and my husband is busy doing business, he will be very OK with that and try to advise me to ensure that I support the Ugandan office, which is nearer or something of the sort. (Systems administrator, 2005)

• Gain support systems.

I am now fifty years old so when I was getting to forty-eight years old I asked myself, who wants an old secretary? So I went back to school. At that time my son was also doing his first degree in IT at United States International University (USIU), so we worked together – when I was doing my assignments he was also assisting me. So he gave me that support. (ICT support person, 2005)

The sources of this mentorship, learning and support have been family members, teachers, networks, friends, ICT forums, organizations and bosses.

Mentorship from colleagues has instilled a sense of determination even in the context of gender discrimination and stereotyping, which women in the ICT field experience:

Normally there are two colleagues in this department, the head of department and the programmer we work with. Every time I feel down and feel that I should just switch from IT to something else they always tell me that there are ladies out there who have done it, what makes me think that I am different? They question why I want to go down right now when I have come this far, and assure me that they are always there to support me. And they really do! (Systems administrator, 2005)

ICT career women as mentors

Most of the women interviewed have been mentors to several young people and women moving up in the ICT field. They described the benefits of being mentors.

- Gaining a great sense of satisfaction, giving back and seeing the one you are mentoring grow and develop.

We have talked to girls about careers and all of us talk about what we are doing. We went to Nairobi Primary and we talked to Class Eight children about what to expect. We are actually planning to go and see girls in the rural areas, so that we can tell them that there is more to look forward to in future. Then we have another project called 'Take my daughter to work'. We take girls from the rural areas and stay with them for two weeks, bring them to our offices and show them what we are doing. That is part of the programme that we have. (IT support officer, 2005)

- Building key skills in providing effective feedback and basic coaching skills which are useful in preparation for leadership positions.

What I do is usually talk to the students, especially the ladies. We [the lecturers and personnel in the IT department] recently launched a club for our students where at least we hope that in the future they will help us in some of the things we are doing. Unfortunately in that club, out of the six officials there is only one lady. That really made me a little bit mad and I was telling them, come on, ladies, you can do it, why is it that we only have one person in the list of officials who is a lady and we have a group of ladies, why do you want to sit at the back? So at the end of it all they were asking me why out of all the people who are interested in the club I am the only lady. I told them that there is always a starting point and if they can see me there, they can also be there. And then also when I get to the labs to fix some of the machines I always call the ladies to come and see how I am doing it just to know that they can actually fix these machines. (Network administrator/lecturer, 2005)

- Building interpersonal skills (effective questioning, active listening, reflecting and communication).

I am the coordinator for international goodwill and understanding for the Soroptimists club. Just being a member of this club exposes you to a lot. We deal with a lot of problem areas, including education. We normally invite girls to come and stay with us during school holidays and expose them to our daily lifestyle, including work environment. We also cover human rights and the status of women. There are also

Reflections on mentoring experiences

six programme areas which deal with the advancement of the status of women, high ethical standards, human rights equal to all, development and peace, international goodwill and understanding and friendship. We also have exchange programmes and sponsorship for women to do courses. (IT support officer, 2005)

It became clear from our discussions with the women interviewed that mentorship received from those they regard as their mentors has supported their sense of determination, vision and passion. One also has to possess these characteristics in order to seek and attract the mentors one wishes to work with to succeed in ICT careers despite gender discrimination and stereotyping. A large proportion of the women we spoke to viewed mentoring as a fundamental aid to women's development.

You look for mentors, within the organization I sought mentors, and I think the whole development of my career has been through seeking mentors, identifying a mentor and following through. They really show you the route; they tell you what you should do with reference to the path you want to follow. (IT company manager, 2005)

My experiences of being mentored

Gender Research in Africa into ICTs for Empowerment (GRACE) has been and still is providing me with mentorship opportunities. These opportunities have different forms ranging from the yearly workshops that facilitate sharing to writing and other methods of learning that assist in gender and ICT research. There has been e-learning and encouragement by the coordinators who are my mentors and my research team leader (also my mentor), and most importantly I have gained by interacting with the women interviewed during our research. References, recommendations, demonstrations and observations from face-to-face meetings, books such as *The Vein of the Gold, a Journey to Your Creative Heart* (Cameron 1996) and *Heuristic Research: Design, Methodology and Applications* (Moustakas 1990), journals and newsletters on ICTs and women's empowerment and Internet interaction with my mentors have facilitated the mentoring relationship. All these have provided me with an array of experiences that have led to self-growth and an awakening transformation. These sources of mentorship have therefore led to improvement in my self-esteem and self-worth, self-discovery and self-knowledge, and these have collectively contributed to my professional development.

Improvement in self-esteem and self-worth Mentorship has boosted my confidence and given me a sense of freedom in terms of finding and expressing myself. I have learnt to handle my inner critic, thereby freeing the inner processes of recognizing, opening, questioning and integrating ideas, information and knowledge.

As an individual and as an ICT researcher, I am learning to find my own subjective truth in relation to my research findings and research process, and have learnt to allow that truth, even when it is not finely formulated yet, to enter into dialogue with other voices. I trust in my self and my truth. I have also found the joy of writing and exploring ideas and other forms of communication from a position of my strength in writing. I have moved beyond a sense of being limited in my technological knowledge to integrating the training offered to increase my skills as an ICT researcher.

Self-discovery and self-knowledge I have come to realize that, as a researcher, I am the most important instrument in my research, and therefore I have learnt to acknowledge personal perspectives and experiences in so far as this has a bearing on my research experiences. I work positively and consciously with who I am to accept my unique subjectivity. I have also undergone a process of internal search in which I have been discovering the essential meanings of my experiences, and I feel that I am actively awakening and transforming my own self, thereby enabling me to gain more focus in life and in my career.

These areas of self-growth are benefiting both my research journey and the experience of my respondents.

My experiences as a mentor

Through the transformation I have undergone in the areas of self-esteem and self-worth, self-discovery and knowledge, and what this has meant for my professional development, especially in the field of gender and ICT research and the use of ICT knowledge and tools, I have gained in the following fields and become:

1. A motivational speaker, especially to young girls who shy away from the field of ICTs and other science-related courses:

   Yesterday we visited Moi Girls High School, Isinya, and talked to the girls on the choice of subjects and careers. We encouraged them to develop a positive attitude towards science subjects and not limit themselves and their abilities. They were elated since they saw us as examples of women who had succeeded in science subjects while in school and pursued careers in ICT. (My journal, 2008)

2. A career guide and counsellor to family and friends, especially those who steer away from science subjects and science-related careers.

3. An adviser to young women and girls who want to take the ICT career path.

4. A role model: 'they look up to me and are always ready to pay attention to what I have to say. I have gained their trust and respect' (my morning pages, 2007).

5. An achiever: 'I am gaining self-satisfaction in giving back to young women and girls who think that science subjects and ICT careers are mainly for men and thus limit themselves' (my morning pages, 2007).

As a mentor, mentoring has provided:

- A catalyst for reflection upon my own practice as a gender and ICT researcher.
- An opportunity for developing personal and professional skills in the use of ICT tools and an avenue for further research in the field of gender and ICT.
- Opportunities to network with other professionals in ICT career fields.
- Job satisfaction in ICT research and increased self-esteem through motivational speaking, especially to young girls who often see the field of ICTs and other sciences as male domains.
- New opportunities for career and professional development in gender and ICT research.

ICT career women and ICT researchers: reflections in the mirror

The processes of mentoring for the ICT career women and for me involved both giving and receiving. The self-satisfaction derived from passing on what one has learned to someone who shares the same focus and same desires is a gift in itself. Furthermore, in providing mentorship there is also learning taking place: there are opportunities for critical reflection, independent thinking, envisioning of new realities and creativity, which are important capacities for ICT researchers and ICT career women alike. They increase one's self-esteem, self-discovery, self-knowledge and professional development, and thus lead to self-satisfaction. And these are, and will remain, very important dimensions throughout one's entire career and professional life.

Mentors provide much-needed support. This is particularly pertinent for women wanting to create a career in the ICT field because of the significant obstacles we experience. Raising self-confidence and self-esteem is important to both ICT researchers and ICT career women. We need motivation and support through the processes of learning and career progression, and this is where mentorship proves to be of great benefit.

The experiences shared in this chapter emphasize the importance of mentoring for both ICT researchers and ICT career women as receivers and as givers. These experiences aim to inspire others to explore these capacities in themselves and give themselves these experiences. And in developing new knowledge and insight, new confidence and self-esteem, both givers and receivers of mentoring will be encouraged to maintain their position within the ICT field and strengthen their relationships within this field. Thus not only those individuals experiencing mentorship will benefit from the mentoring processes, but the ICT field itself will be enriched.

Notes

1 I would like to acknowledge Okwach Abagi, research team leader, and Olive Sifuna, research team member.

2 The research report is available at www.GRACE-Network.net and the results of this study are discussed in Chapter 15, this volume.

References

AAUW (2000) 'Tech-savvy: educating girls in the new computer age', Washington, DC: American Association of University Women, www.aauw.org/research/tech_savvy.cfm.

Cameron, J. (1996) *The Vein of the Gold, a Journey to Your Creative Heart*, New York: Putnam.

Camp, T. (1997) 'The incredible shrinking pipeline', *Communications of the ACM*, 40(10): 103–10, www.mines.edu/fs_home/tcamp/new-study/new-study.html.

Cohoon, J. M. (2001) 'Toward improving female retention in the Computer Science major', *Communications of the ACM*, 44(5): 108–14.

Crombie, G., T. Abarbanel and C. Anderson (2001) 'Getting girls into tech classes', *Education Digest*, 66(5): 42–8.

Crump, B. J. (2001) 'Equity in the tertiary programming learning environment', *Proceedings of the Australian Association for Research in Education Conference (AARE 2001)*, Fremantle, Australia, www.aare.edu.au/01pap/cru01022.html, accessed July 2003.

Department of Economic and Social Affairs (2006) 'Enhancing women's global leadership through information technology', Parallel event at the 50th session of CSW.

Mbarika, V., F. Cobb Payton, L. Kvasny and A. Amadi (2007) 'IT education and workforce participation: a new era for women in Kenya', *The Information Society*, 23(1).

Moustakas, C. (1990) *Heuristic Research: Design, Methodology and Applications*, Newbury Park/London/New Delhi: Sage.

Nobel, C. (2007) 'Back to school:

getting girls into IT', *InfoWorld*, 29 January, www.infoworld.com/article/07/01/29/05FEwomen techteen_1.html.

Springer, L., M. L. Stanne and S. Donovan (1999) 'Effects of small-group learning on undergraduates in science, mathematics, engineering and technology: a meta-analysis', *Review of Educational Research*, 69(1): 21–51.

Teague, J. (2002) 'Women in computing: what brings them to it, what keeps them in it?', *SIGCSE Bulletin*, 34(2): 147–58.

17 | Our journey to empowerment: the role of ICT

RUTH MEENA AND MARY RUSIMBI

'Our research journey'

Through recording and exploring life histories we became aware of the opportunities and constraints women entrepreneurs in Tanzania identify regarding use of mobile phones and/or the Internet in promoting their business enterprises. Nine women, including ourselves, were part of this research journey, coming from diverse backgrounds, having different levels of education, and diverse life visions and passions. We all have dreams and internal strength and have faced different challenges, but none of us seems to have given up. This chapter focuses on this inner strength and sense of empowerment. Space does not allow us to tell the story of each respondent, so we have chosen to include just five of us. We do not claim to represent all nine, since we each had unique experiences such that we cannot generalize.[1]

Bahati avoided poverty by becoming a freelance hairdresser; her main sources of capital are her nimble fingers and a mobile phone. Rose Lyimo started her journey as a typist and now co-owns a school, owns a clearing and forwarding business, and engages in various business enterprises. Mary Rusimbi's passion for social work was greatly influenced by her grandmother when she lived with her for four years. Demere started questioning masculinity and stereotyping during her childhood, and now co-owns a publishing house with a feminist touch. Ruth Meena reacted against a father who did not believe in women's education. She pushed herself to the level of professor in political science, and is an activist in women's rights.

We start by exploring the varied ways in which the five women define power. This is followed by an exploration of the factors that influenced their journey to empowerment. In the context of this journey and its challenges, we explore the impact two information tools, the mobile phone and the Internet, have had on aspects of the women's chosen path.

What is power?

Each of the women in this study has her own definition of what power is. In this chapter we do not provide a functional definition of power as each of us has had a different experience of it, particularly the power within. Although there are some common threads running through all our definitions, each of us has a unique way of conceptualizing the power within. For some it represents a force within which pushes us into doing things; for others it is self-love, which also pushes one into taking care of oneself first, including listening to one's inner voice. Yet to others, it is a step-by-step process which moves one from point A to B, although the road might meander. It is also seen as an energy inside which gives one the courage to dare. The only common aspect of the definitions is that none of the women considers power as a force for controlling others, influencing others or forcing others to do what otherwise they would not have done.

Bahati

'Power', says Bahati, 'is a force within you which pushes you into doing things for your personal advancement.' Bahati is currently a freelance hairdresser. With only primary education and a few months' training in dressmaking, she escaped rural poverty by moving to an urban area to seek opportunities. She realized that dressmaking was highly competitive, so with the support of her unemployed aunt, who was being supported by her children, Bahati tried hairdressing. She found that work in a salon was exploitative and hardly sustained her. By keeping her other expenditures to an absolute minimum for two years, she was able to purchase a mobile phone. She worked hard to search for clients so that she could work independently. She has subsequently been able to purchase a piece of land in a poor suburb area and build a house while she continues with freelance hairdressing.

Putting a mobile phone to work The only start-up capital Bahati had when she began to work for herself was the mobile phone and her nimble hands. As she was doing the hair of some of her regular customers at her salon job, she started whispering to them her intention of quitting, and that she was going to work on her own. It did not take her long to get a number of old and new customers. She does not use the telephone to look for customers, but she receives calls from them.

> I think I advertise my work through doing a good job, so that whenever I do a good style for any customer, some of her friends would ask her who did her hair and how do I get her. She gives my number and the person calls to make an appointment. The only time I call is when I want to verify with my customer the type of extensions she wants to match

with the style she has chosen. I therefore hardly spend more than 10,000 [Tanzanian] shillings [US$10] per month on this telephone.

With ownership of the telephone Bahati has been able to break through a number of barriers. First, she left exploitative work. This decision required a very strong will since it can be quite risky. She was living on her own, as her aunt, with whom she was previously staying, had passed away. When she started to work on her own, she recalls working day and night.

Bahati cannot use her telephone to communicate with her family even if she could afford to do so. Her family lives in rural Ujiji, which is not connected to landlines or mobile phones. Since her arrival in Dar es Salaam she has not been able to go home, and for the two years before the interview was conducted she had received no information on the welfare of her family. This is one hurdle that Bahati cannot overcome, and reflects the rural/urban digital divide. While developments in the technology industry have created one 'global village', opening boundaries, some boundaries are widening divides.

When Bahati was interviewed she had just moved into her new house. She was planning to rent out one of the small rooms to increase her income and minimize the risks of living by herself. She is a bit more relaxed now that she does not have to work day and night to meet her basic needs. She is capable of earning a non-taxable income of 300,000 Tshs (Tanzanian shillings) per month, which is equivalent to US$300 per month, lifting her well above the poverty line of less than a dollar per day. Certainly combining her 'force within' with her mobile phone has facilitated her economic mobility.

Rose Lyimo

'Power is the ability to break through barriers to reach your life vision through a step-by-step process,' according to Rose Lyimo, who is currently a co-owner of a rural school known as Break Through, and sole owner of a clearing and forwarding company known as Te Te ('step by step'). 'I never give up,' she says, 'but I believe in a step-by-step approach in uncovering my potential. This is what power is all about.'

When asked what had encouraged her to start her businesses, particularly since she had previously been climbing the professional ladder, Rose said,

Basically, there was something which was driving me out of formal employment. I just found myself not satisfied however high I moved in my profession. As a child I had dreamt of being a doctor but I did not make it well in those subjects which are required for a degree in medicine. So I ended up being a typist, and secretary. Even when I joined the UN as an administrative secretary, I was not satisfied. There is a power within me which has been pushing me to go for business.

Rose's journey took her through some major steps, the final one being her current civic engagement: she is a board director for a national bank, chairperson of the Tanzanian chapter of All African Travel and Tourism, and a member of the Rotary Club.

What was the influence of ICTs in this process? Rose's current businesses and her involvement in multiple civic activities demand a high level of communication. In a clearing and forwarding business, for instance, you need information from exporters and shipping and importing agencies. Any breakdown in the information flow will cost the client a substantial amount of money for storage at the habour, and can potentially wreck a business. According to Rose, for this business to make a profit, 'you have to be on your toes, otherwise you will find it difficult to solicit clients as there is also big competition in this field'.

Rose manages the school from two premises. She has to use her company office in the city for many school-related activities because the school does not have electricity. Photocopying and secretarial services are carried out in the city office. Had connectivity not been a problem, she could have been communicating with the school manager via Internet chat and e-mail, hence reducing the cost of the telephone bill and the time involved in running to and from the school. The school is a boarding school, which admits some young children from the age of thirteen onwards. The need to communicate with parents cannot be underrated. When such children have a problem, either she or the school manager has to communicate with the parents. Alternatively parents call now and then to check on the progress of their children. Without the telephone some parents would not have chosen the school, and this would affect the business.

Additionally, the school is co-owned and co-directed with Rose taking more responsibility in the day-to-day management. She regularly communicates with her business partner on progress and any matters needing their immediate attention. Rose also has a dream of expanding the school to include primary school students. This requires extensive communication with potential clients, individuals in the same business and her co-director.

Business requires resources, both financial and material. One needs information on available credit facilities. Belonging to a number of business networks has given Rose some comparative advantages in relation to sourcing funds for expansion and diversification of her enterprises. But this also requires information-sharing with financial institutions and other business partners. It is not easy to compute the actual amount that it costs Rose to maintain communications with her various partners. She allows a budget of 400,000 Tshs per month for the school telephone. She has not yet tracked the costs of the other items. She finds the mobile telephone is very expensive, but necessary for her businesses.

Mary Rusimbi

'Power is about being able to make choices and interrogate choices made on your behalf,' says Mary Rusimbi, feminist activist, trainer with participatory and group animation skills, adult educator, gender specialist, and single parent with two sons and a deceased daughter. She was also executive director of a very powerful activist feminist organization, the Tanzania Gender Networking Programme (TGNP), when this research was being conducted. Born into a middle-class family, with supportive parents, Mary was exposed to opportunities and was able to make 'choices'.

Mary attributes her commitment to equality, her desire to work with people, her pro-poor ideology and her commitment to empowerment and human rights to experience gained from early childhood when she spent four years living with her grandmother. 'The village has had a great influence on my life and the way I look at things. My attitude towards people, my understanding of poverty and my belief in issues of social justice and equity are very grounded in the years I stayed with my grandmother,' says Mary.

The childhood network and support systems that existed in her grandmother's community instilled in Mary a sense of respect for all people regardless of class. 'Above all, it has given me a deep understanding of what material poverty is and the wealth in the hearts of poor ordinary citizens in our communities. My urban-raised siblings missed this, and this is what distinguishes me from them in many things.'

Her road to education was smooth because her father wanted her to get a good education, unlike many other girls who experienced patriarchy as an obstacle to their schooling. Mary entered university in 1973 and majored in adult education, history and languages, subjects that gave her a grounding in analysis, language and adult education methodologies, including participatory approaches. She continued her studies to master's level. She has been inspired by two great thinkers, J. K. Nyerere, the politician and educationist, and Paulo Freire and his philosophy of education for empowerment and consciousness-raising. 'The *Pedagogy of the Oppressed* has had an empowering effect on my life together with other texts, such as Rodney's book on *How Europe Underdeveloped Africa*. In feminist scholarship, I adore Maya Angelou's writings. These texts have shaped my ideology and a belief in people's empowerment.'

Mary worked in several embassies before joining TGNP as an executive director. Working with the embassies exposed Mary to new ways of working, including use of ICTs. After a while, however, she became disillusioned with the whole idea of external support as a major strategy to overcome poverty and gender inequalities: 'It was this disillusionment that made me want to work more with civil society organizations fighting for justice, fairness and equality in distribution of national resources.' This is what made her leave the embassy job for civil society engagement.

Use of the telephone and Internet and their effects on Mary's life In her many roles and identities, Mary uses both telephones and the Internet extensively. 'I do not know how I would have survived without these gadgets,' she says. She considers both the telephone and the Internet working tools which have facilitated management of her personal life and her immediate family, as well as the TGNP.

> When my son was in Australia, I would spend 150 dollars per month to get in touch with him. Having gone through the trauma of many deaths in the family, my son developed some fear, fear of death, fear of losing me, the only parent he had, and probably fear of life. Although I spent a good portion of my earnings on telephone calls, this was a kind of therapy for my son as well as for myself. He was far, we bonded through telephone conversations, and later e-mails.
>
> My youngest son is now studying in Swaziland, and I do the same. I bought him a telephone. He texts me if he needs my support, and at least every week we have a long conversation. Indeed, at a personal level, the telephone has enabled me to do the mothering role from a distance, enabled me to establish bonds with my two sons, and build lasting friendships.

Mary calls her mother on a daily basis, as she is not able to visit her as often as her other sisters because of the nature of her job. Her mother understands. She also communicates with her sisters, regarding family matters, daily. This is in addition to keeping in contact with her friends, including network members.

Mary says Internet websites have been a good source of information and knowledge for self-development. Although a full-time employee of TGNP, she also does consultancy work on the organization's behalf, and during her holidays she engages in private consultancy work. As a trainer, she updates her training resources and gender-training skills through web searches and texts available on the Web. The Information Generation Department within TGNP has been very instrumental in providing the necessary technical support in searching for this type of knowledge.

As chief executive of a feminist networking and advocacy organization, Mary finds enhanced internal communication vital for its survival. Within the organization they have established an electronic communication system that enables employees to exchange notes and memos, carry on discussions and clarify many issues that otherwise would have entailed moving between offices. This has transformed the way they do their work. 'Although this communication strategy has not replaced staff meetings, it enables us to be more focused in strategic matters of organization,' says Mary.

Demere Kitunga

'Power is the energy within oneself which enables one to reflect on one's own life, and question the social construction of our identity,' says Demere Kitunga. Demere is a dynamo – a publisher and one of the first women co-owners of a publishing house, an artist, a feminist activist and a mother of three. Working with determination, passion, a sound financial plan and in a conducive business environment, she was able to counter stereotypes and be successful. Having been exposed to various cultural traditions and expressions has had a tremendous impact on her life journey. 'I was raised by two strong women who have had a tremendous impact on my life,' she says, referring to her mother and grandmother.

From my mother, I learnt to defy stereotypes and challenge gendered constructions of roles and sexuality. From my grandmother, I learnt to love folklore, and admire cultural heritage and storytelling. Travelling with my father from one rural site to another exposed me to a variety of languages and dialects, and enhanced my understanding of diversities of cultural heritage. The primary school and national service challenged my sexual identity, as the institutions attempted to instil [in me] and teach me patriotism within the context of patriarchy and hierarchy, hence failing to distinguish between nationalism and personal identity at a time when I was [on] a dire quest for self-worthiness.

Demere had an exciting childhood. Although raised in a rural area with traditions and norms that socialized girls and boys into gender-specific roles, Demere questioned and refused to conform to the stereotypical norms from her early childhood. She loved whistling and climbing trees, which were constructed as inappropriate behaviour for girls. When Demere asked her mother why it was considered inappropriate for her to whistle or climb trees, her mother said to her, 'If you have talents in these areas go ahead and use them as talents are a God-given gift.' This counters the perception that we tend to have concerning rural, uneducated women and feminist consciousness. She certainly influenced Demere's attitudes towards her own self-esteem, her sexuality and her worthiness.

The other woman who influenced Demere's life was her grandmother, with whom she spent part of her childhood. Her grandmother would narrate stories to her, and expose her to local folklore, lyrics and initiation rites. This wealth of knowledge and experience must have had a lasting impact on Demere's life. She is a prolific writer, particularly of children's books, she composes poetry and popular lyrics, and is a very passionate admirer of traditional music and culture.

Secondary education enhanced Demere's talents. She joined reading, debating and writing clubs. She also met girls who had an interest in and a passion for arts, languages and culture. It was at this level that her reading, writing and language skills were actualized. These have been lifelong assets in her career and business life.

Demere's ICT connections For Demere and her co-director, Elieshi, electronic communication is central to their day-to-day editing and publishing work. They keep a database of clients, produce orders, and have a lot of e-mail communications with printers, staff and others. According to Demere:

> In the publishing industry, your communication is a vital lifeline for such a business. You have to communicate with authors of books or articles which you edit, you need to contact printers, and you also need to search for markets. Additionally, you need to advertise yourself, as well as access information and knowledge in the publishing industry. But as an activist, you also need to be part of networks, and engage with others, at times through e-mails. And as a mother of young adults, you need to communicate with them, for support which is mutual. It is not possible to think of a publishing industry today without ICT gadgets.

Ruth Meena

'Empowerment is self-confidence, self-determination which pushes you to move with your life against all hurdles,' says Ruth Meena. Ruth is a political scientist, feminist, human rights activist, mother of four, grandmother of four, and a friend of many. When this research was being conducted she was preparing herself for retirement from her university career, and planning to set up a centre of learning, which she will manage. Her new centre has a high school as a core business and other short-term learning activities targeting young people. The high school, which is a preparatory stage for university education, is going to utilize ICT tools extensively.

Ruth was born into a polygamous family with twelve children, ten girls and two boys. When her eldest sister got married, Ruth (then aged five) was 'given' to her sister to support her. She was raised as a first daughter of her own sister, with lots of responsibilities, including domestic chores, such as taking care of her sister's children, cleaning the animal shed, fetching water and firewood, and cooking, as her sister was busy with farm work. Ruth feels her father sent her away to her elder sister to be socialized into being a hard-working woman performing tasks that were constructed as women's work.

As Ruth combined her domestic roles with schooling, she did not perform well in her Class 4 examination. Luckily for her, she had a brother with a greater vision for girls' education, who decided to take her away from her sister and put her back in school, where she repeated Primary 4. She passed with flying colours and was one of two girls in her class who were selected for a boarding school. This is what opened doors for her further schooling, up to university level, without a break.

Asked what had motivated her to pursue her education up to this level, Ruth says:

> I was actually motivated by my father in a negative way. My father never wanted to have his daughters go beyond Primary Four, while he was determined to support the two boys up to whatever level they wanted. This made me very angry. Had it not been for the pressure from my father, I could have ended up at Class 8 and gone for a teaching career or nursing [like] my two other sisters, but I was just determined to prove my father wrong, and as long as he said no more to further education, I just went on without a certain focus or ambition for a career or university education.

During her A-level studies, Ruth started enjoying learning. 'This is when the push for higher learning was no longer through negative motivation of patriarchy resistance, but a love of learning.'

In 1968 Ruth was among the very few women selected to join the then University College of East Africa, which in 1971was transformed into the University of Dar es Salaam, where she graduated. When she joined the university she started 'soul searching' regarding what she then wanted to do with her education. 'Honestly, I was scared to just major in economics as I did know how demanding a career is in this field!' There was no career counselling in secondary school and at the university there was an assumption that the students who had completed their educational journey up to this level ought to be informed! Back in the 1960s, there were no computers to search for relevant information on career paths. Since she had teachers as career models, Ruth decided to change her field to education. Lack of information closed one career path, and probably opened the door to her teaching career, which she seems not to have regretted.

She therefore had three majors – political science, education and history. This combination exposed her to very powerful transformative professors, and leading intellectuals in political economy and history. The late Walter Rodney was a very distinguished scholar who exposed her to the political history of colonialism, imperialism and underdevelopment. John Saul and Lionel Cliffe exposed her to the socialist debates and the philosophy of '*Ujamaa*' and Marxism. The public lectures organized by some of these scholars in the 'revolutionary square' which engaged imperialism and neocolonialism further enhanced her political consciousness of theories of oppression and underdevelopment. While she says that 'the university education was inspiring and empowering', ironically this very revolutionary knowledge did not expose her to feminist knowledge and consciousness. Nevertheless, it 'created a foundation for my activism, and instilled a fighting spirit in me!' she says. Her feminist consciousness was gained through experiential learning and enhanced through self-exposure to theories of feminism.

On ICT connections Ruth describes herself as having been a consumer of ICTs for a very long time. As her life story reveals, access or lack of access to vital information has had a very critical impact in her life. Accessing information on scholarships through word of mouth enabled her to pursue secondary education. Since then, the Internet has been a very useful source of information and knowledge. She accesses various knowledge gateways to order texts for teaching, as well as training materials on gender. All her children except one are living abroad with their own families. Ruth connects with them through e-mail and SMS messages on a weekly basis. She is connected to a broadband service and chats with her family. This has reduced the cost of telephone calls, which she says are unbearable. But she also uses the mobile phone extensively in communicating with her friends and fellow activists.

General observations on power and information

From the five cases presented above, it can be seen that power is perceived as an inner strength, an inner push, something which is not tangible but which is then facilitated by the external environment. Power within is that inner strength which made Bahati move from Kigoma to Dar es Salaam to explore opportunities, and further made her take decisions that freed her from perpetual dependence and deprivation. It is a force that made Rose Lyimo leave formal employment for self-employment with very little capital. It is the driving force that made Ruth search for a scholarship fund after primary education, and a force that enables Mary Rusimbi to lead a very dynamic organization at the same time as she balances her triple roles. It is the inspiration that drove Demere Kitunga to venture into a male-dominated business.

This is the force and energy that has enabled each individual to transform obstacles into challenges, and enabled them to discover the opportunities within a very constrained business environment. In this context, power is something that is not always tangible: it is difficult to quantify, but is actualized by tangible aspects within the external environment of the individual. This inner strength is in each one of us, but most of us (women) do not recognize it, or if we do we tend to fear it. Most women have this inner strength, which allows all of us survive under extreme forms of deprivation and oppression, as we suffer silently with smiles on our faces.

Power within has not only helped individuals make choices, but has pushed some to examine choices made for them in the context of patriarchal norms and practices. All the women profiled made certain choices which moved them one step forward on the road to empowerment, while questioning the accepted norms and practices. All the profiles demonstrate self-love, self-worth and self-pride, which push the women into challenging marginalization, social exclusion and low positioning. It is this self-love which pushed Bahati into refusing to subject herself to exploitation and drove her to purchase a tool that has facilitated her business growth.

Equally important in the process of empowerment is the ability to listen to your inner voice, that voice which tells you to pay attention to your passion, your creativity and talents. It is this inner voice which directed Mary to quit a better-paying embassy job for less prestigious work with an activist organization. Demere responded to her inner voice in terms of choosing the right type of education and skills development for herself. Women need to learn to listen to their inner voice, as this is what enables them to question choices made for them without their consent. Many times women refuse to pay attention to this inner teacher, and hence engage in activities that perpetuate dependency and marginalization.

Despite the strength we have, our self-love and the ability to make choices, the extent to which we can fully recognize, appreciate and listen to our inner voices, make choices and actualize our dreams, are also shaped and sometimes defined by the environment in which we live.

Our external environment

Our external environment shapes the way we define power and the road it takes us on. We are located in a continent that has benefited the least from the information technology revolution, a continent that is the only one which entered this century with increasing levels of deprivation and poverty. This poverty carries both a rural face and a woman's face. It is also a continent where the 'digital divide' is extreme, and where network readiness is still at a very early stage of development compared to other regions of the world. It is a continent that has suffered greatly from global inequalities in terms of accessing some of the ICT tools, with an estimated mere 21 million of its 816 million citizens having the privilege of accessing mobile phones, the majority of whom are located in either North or South Africa.

Being a woman located on the African continent, and in sub-Saharan Africa in particular, you are bound to be subjected to lots of disempowering elements. You are bound to share poverty with sisters, nieces, cousins, friends, and so forth. If you are an activist, you are bound to share the agony of deprivation of basics such as food and water, and face the challenges of maternal deaths, and so forth. This consumes a lot of our energy, and at times reduces the quality time one would have spent in using information technology for furthering a feminist course, or in development. Even the privileged few with access to information technology are bearing higher costs owing to its underdevelopment. Women in Africa are paying a higher price for the technological revolution than their counterparts in the rest of the world.

In addition to the socio-political dimensions of our environment, education has had a powerful influence on the road to our empowerment.

With limited education, Bahati has had very limited life choices. She first tried the dressmaking industry, but realized that for her to make a living out of this industry, it required more investment in self-development. She could not afford this during that particular period so decided to join the hairdressing industry, which was equally saturated by semi-skilled young women and a few men.

Mary's training in adult education and her exposure to gender studies have given her a high level of understanding of the dynamics of oppressive social systems, which she is working to transform collectively with other women in the movement. Similarly, Demere's education and training enabled her to further advance her career path in an otherwise male-dominated business. It has enhanced her confidence and self-esteem, and she has achieved a great capacity to examine mainstream processes.

Being grounded in one's power within

Our journey to empowerment has been like climbing a thorny, rocky and rugged hill. While a few of us feel that we have reached what we individually consider to be an apex or breakthrough, the majority of us are still staggering to reach what each considers the terminus of our journey. Regardless of our varied backgrounds, some of us have been able to conquer some hills, some need extra effort and others are still pushing. But all of us have been on a journey to 'empowerment'. There are multiple complex factors which have contributed to the varied levels of empowerment that we have attained, as discussed here. These include but are not limited to: our geographical positioning, access to or lack of information and its cost implications, level of education and, above all, the individual will to recognize and listen to the inner voices that push us to explore opportunities, transform constraints into challenges and move on with life.

From the experiences of the women presented in this chapter, as we understand them, it becomes evident that ICT tools have the capacity to facilitate economic well-being, provided they are harnessed by women who are grounded in 'their power within'.

Note

1 The full research report shares the wealth of knowledge generated in the course of the research, at www.GRACE-Network.net.

Reference

Meena, R. and M. Rusimbi (2008) *Our Journey to Empowerment: The Role of ICT*, Research report, www. GRACE-Network.net.

Epilogue

INEKE BUSKENS AND ANNE WEBB

The relationship between women, their empowerment and the use of ICTs in Africa is complex; there are no simple summaries or solutions. Women's access to and use of ICTs cannot be understood in isolation from their gender positions and identities and how these positions and identities interact with their political-economic situation. Even women's struggles to overcome the limitations of their positions and identities through the use of ICTs have to be understood from within this context, and likewise their victories in overcoming such. Certain issues have become very clear:

- That we have to realize ICTs in and of themselves do not empower, that it is the use of them which can be empowering or not. For there to be sustainable change and 'real empowerment', women have to be the agents of their own processes, in charge of and in control of their environment, and in charge of and in control of their process of change and empowerment. That is why women's agency is key, and it is the key.
- That a woman using ICTs is not only performing an individual act, but is engaged in a process that involves all the contexts that are affected by this act. As women are participating in various contexts simultaneously, and many of these contexts are grounded in gender inequality, women's processes of change and empowerment will affect these contexts directly and immediately and may evoke tensions, disruptions and even lead to chaos. Sometimes the dynamics within these contexts are not apparent; the effects become clear only when somebody changes something. Hence women themselves will be best able to decide to what degree they can push their existing ceilings; they have to be the agents of their own development and empowerment. This is not to say that women cannot be challenged on their preferences when these preferences are an expression of having adapted to limitations, injustices and untenable situations. Even then, a woman's choices, albeit not consciously made, have to be understood first.
- That women contribute immediately to their environment and share

their gains, even at the level where they have the fewest options because of general deprivation of basic necessities (such as electricity). This finding is coherent with general predictions that women's empowerment is one of the major mediators of social and economic change (Sen 1999).

It may, for the majority of African women, still be a long walk to freedom, to the type of self-determination that women in Africa want to have, a self-determination that only they can define, using ICTs to enhance their lives and the lives of those they love. Their journeys cannot be seen and understood in isolation from the power of the global market economy and the pervasive gender images, and without recognizing the immense inner strength they are drawing on. And that is what the authors who have contributed to this book have tried to accomplish: to make women's choices visible and understandable, and to show how women's power is not always the most obvious, their choices not always in line with economic priorities, but immensely rational when understood in the context of women's triple responsibilities and their own priorities. And the way women use ICTs often reveals exactly where they are at on their journey towards empowerment.

It is against the background of this complex web of adversities that the marvel of what women in Africa have accomplished in relation to ICTs becomes clear layer after layer. It is also very apparent that ICTs are touching and influencing the lives of women in even the most rural settings. But as the meaning and relevance of 'access' are shown to be highly varied and in many cases constrained by patriarchy, the importance of confronting gender inequality in the information society cannot be overestimated. As described by Mitter, 'it is the same age old rationale: women's inferior status in the society gives them unequal access to all resources including to ICTs' (2005). The potential of ICTs to enhance our human lives in an equitable society is tremendous. Yet for this to occur the rapid spread and pervasiveness of these technologies need to be regulated in the interests of pursuing the development of a non-discriminatory society, and to be accompanied by efforts to reduce regional and North–South disparities.

Enhancing women's access to and use of ICTs requires therefore a transformation of people's mindsets and knowledge of the world that have been shaped by gender inequality and, more particularly, by male domination. The male perspective that has shaped African societies and the role of women in the labour market and in the domestic sphere is a key variable of empowerment and disempowerment in the ICT sector.

With the rapid changes in technologies, the question of sustainability also arises in relation to the type of society that is being perpetuated, now with the assistance of these new means of communication. The digital divide with its North–South dimension and its gender dimension reflects the skewedness of our economic model. Crucial contributions by people from the South and by women globally are rendered invisible and thus unrewarded and unacknowledged. Furthermore, not only are the technologies themselves raising health[1] and environmental concerns, but we are realizing more and more that our planet is under threat because of our short-sighted attachment to an unsustainable economy (UNEP/GRID-Arendal 2006).

As ICTs increase the sense of being globally interconnected as a species inhabiting this planet together, perhaps this recognition will enable us to make a stand to prevent ICTs from creating new spaces of exclusion, and thus poverty and isolation, within countries and between countries. And that is actually what the authors contributing to this book, in all their diversity, stand for.

We want to recognize the challenge engaged by the authors. Maintaining a reflexive attitude can be very demanding and anxiety-provoking for researchers because of the element of self-directed critical awareness that is part of all reflection. Furthermore, reflection of this nature inevitably stimulates change in the researchers which, even when welcomed, can become stressful in itself.

Hence the crucial importance of those willing to take on such a journey: in the quest for defining the parameters of the knowledge construction processes that define Africa, its ICT future and the empowerment of its women, not only are women's truths at stake but also the potential to create new realities.

Note

1 There are a number of studies linking health concerns to the use of mobile phones, for instance. For a recent example, see Khurana (2008).

References

Khurana, G. (2008) 'Mobile phones and brain tumours – a public health concern', www.brain-surgery.us/mobph.pdf.

Mitter, S. (2005) Interview, available at gender.developmentgateway.org/Content-item-view.10976+M5 47c1b5fa07.0.html?&L=0.

Sen, A. (1999) *Development as Freedom*, New York and Toronto: Anchor Books.

UNEP/GRID-Arendal (2006) *Planet in Peril: Atlas of Current Threats to People and the Environment*, UNEP.

Notes on contributors

Okwach Abagi holds a PhD in Sociology of Education from McGill University and is a director of the RESEARCHWEB Centre based in Nairobi. Okwach is a monitoring and evaluation/institutional development specialist, with vast professional experience in the social sector (education and health). He is a gender-responsive researcher and policy analyst and has offered technical assistance to governments and various organizations in the eastern and southern Africa regions.

Kiss Brian Abraham is a Zambian civil society social change activist. He is actively involved in the development of the Zambia Social Forum process (the goal of the forum is to create a space for meaningful debate and alternative thinking). He is a member of the Media Institute of Southern Africa and sits on the Africa Social Forum Council.

Susan Bakesha currently works as a consultant with Development Alternatives Consult (DAC). She is a gender specialist with wide experience in gender research and training, policy analysis and advocacy. She has participated in mainstreaming gender in government policies as well as a number of development projects aimed at improving the status of women. She is affiliated with a number of women's organizations in which she has been actively engaged on various projects, including the National Women Candidates' Training, Gender Budget Training, Gender and ICT, and Leadership Skills Training.

Kazanka Comfort is the general secretary of the Fantsuam Foundation. The organization facilitates access to microfinance, ICT and volunteering as tools for the alleviation of poverty among rural women in Nigeria. She works closely with the programme director to monitor and provide professional and logistical support for the various programmes. She teaches basic computer skills to girls and women at the Bayanloco Community Learning Centre, as well as integrating ICTs into the various programmes at Fantsuam. One of her initiatives was awarded the first Hafkin Africa Prize (www.apc.org/english/hafkin/2001/2001/).

John Dada has been a volunteer with the Fantsuam Foundation since its inception in 1996. He has responsibility for the development of programmes that complement the gender- and youth-focused ICT initiatives, rural connectivity and microfinance services of the organization. Some of the programmes of the Fantsuam Foundation have been featured in the Nigerian press, *Le Monde*, CNN and the BBC World Service and have been selected as finalists for the Stockholm Challenge 2008 award for ICT for Development projects and for the World Bank's Development Marketplace for African Diaspora in Europe competition for funding for entrepreneurial projects.

Polly Gaster is head of ICTs for Development at the Eduardo Mondlane University Informatics Centre (CIUEM). She was a member of the Mozambican team that pioneered telecentres in rural districts in 1999, and more recently she coordinated the Community Multimedia Centre Scale-Up Initiative in Mozambique for UNESCO. Her interest in local development, communications and community media has led her towards a combination of practical work and research activities around ICT for Development issues, and she acted as adviser to the Mozambique GRACE researchers.

Lucia Ginger is a lecturer in information systems technology at the University of St Thomas in Mozambique. Her research interests include computer networking, geographical information systems and open source solutions. She participated in the data collection and analysis for the Mozambique GRACE Project.

Leila Hassanin has a PhD in Public Administration and twenty years' experience in socio-economic development and institutional capacity-building. Dr Hassanin served as information officer for UNDP's Sustainable Development Networking Programme (SDNP) in New York and has been a national officer for UNICEF and WHO in Egypt. Hassanin is founder of ArabDev, which since 1999 has focused on ICT for development and has spearheaded grassroots ICT initiatives in Egypt in close cooperation with the Ministry of Education, local and regional NGOs and the Ministry of Communication and Information Technology.

Grace Bantebya Kyomuhendo holds a PhD in Sociology and Social Anthropology and a MPhil in Social Anthropology. Grace is currently a professor in the Department of Women and Gender Studies of Makerere University, Kampala. She is a distinguished social anthropologist and an experienced trainer/lecturer, researcher and advocate for gender equality and social transformation.

Grace has done extensive research in reproductive health, in particular maternal health, and in HIV/AIDS in conflict situations. She has also researched women and ICTs. She has published widely, most recently completing a book entitled *Women, Work and Domestic Virtue in Uganda*, which received an award from the African Studies Association in 2007.

Esselina Macome is assistant professor in Information Systems (IS) at Eduardo Mondlane University, where she is teaching part time, and a member of the board and executive director at Mozambique's Central Bank. Her research interests include ICT for development, e-government, gender, and the development and management of IS in organizations. She has led a number of studies following the progress of telecentres in Mozambique and has acted as adviser to the Mozambique GRACE researchers.

Gertrudes Macueve is a lecturer in computer sciences at Eduardo Mondlane University in Mozambique. She is currently doing her doctoral studies in the field of Information Systems. Her research interests include ICTs for development in general, and e-government and gender in particular. She has been involved in telecentre research activities since 2000 and was lead author for the Mozambique study.

Judite Mandlate is a lecturer at the Math and Informatics Department of the Science Faculty at Eduardo Mondlane University in Mozambique. Her main research interest is in data communications and networking and open source solutions. She was a member of the Mozambique GRACE research team, working in particular on data collection and analysis.

Buhle Mbambo-Thata is the executive director of Library Services at the University of South Africa. At the time of the research in 2006/07, she was university librarian at the University of Zimbabwe in Harare. She has extensive knowledge of the ICT environment in Africa through her involvement with African libraries. Her research interests are in information literacy and women and ICT. She holds a DPhil in Information Science.

Ruth Meena is a feminist activist and educator who taught for thirty-five years at various levels, including secondary school, teachers' colleges and university. She has won several awards, including a Senior Fulbright Fellowship at the University of Stanford in the USA, Ford Foundation and IDRC research competitions, as well as being a visiting scholar at several universities in the USA and Canada. She has a passion for working with young people, as they are a potential transformative force against oppressive systems, including patriarchy. She is now running a multidisciplinary learning centre whose mission is to support young people to 'Be the Best They Can Be'. Of her publications the one she treasures most is 'A conversation with Bibi Titi' in Marjori Mbilinyi and Mary Rusimbi (2003), *Activist Voices: Feminist Struggles for an Alternative World*. She is the current chairperson of the Tanzania Gender Networking Programme.

Elizabeth Mlambo is currently the deputy librarian at the University of Zimbabwe. She is the coordinator of the Information Literacy Skills programme, a course designed for undergraduates and postgraduates. Previously she was the Head Librarian of the Institute of Development Studies. She sits on various committees at the University of Zimbabwe and is the current vice-chairperson of the Women's Action Group (WAG) Board, a non-governmental organization responsible for the outright promotion and advancement of women's human rights.

Jocelyn Muller is working towards completing her MPhil in Development Studies at the University of Cape Town. She works as a research officer at the Energy Research Centre at UCT. Her current research interests include the adaptive capacity of emerging winegrowers and the communities living on farms in the wine industry, and poverty alleviation in low-income urban households through improving access and use of energy services in the community. Her particular interest is in gender and development issues, specifically centred on developing, designing and introducing participatory methods as a capacity-building tool so that women are able to articulate their development needs to policy-makers.

Precious Mwatsiya is the Faculty of Arts librarian at the University of Zimbabwe. She is responsible for liaising with the faculty for purchases of library material and coordinating and teaching Information Literacy Skills, a course that equips students with skills needed to access electronic resources. She is currently studying for her master's in Library and Information Science. Her research interests lie in ICTs and their usage in learning, information literacy and digital libraries.

Angela Nakafeero is a Ugandan gender activist. She spearheaded the formation of the NGO Development Alternatives (DELTA) and the Uganda Women's Caucus on ICTs (UWCI). She is currently the executive director of DELTA, a member of Women of Uganda Network (WOUGNET) and of the Forum for Women in Democracy (FOWODE). Angela is a trainer in gender analysis, gender budgeting, policy advocacy and strategic planning. She has extensive experience in gender audits/assessments, policy analysis/research and advocacy. She has undertaken several gender mainstreaming initiatives for the African Union and for national organizations.

Dorothy Okello is coordinator of Women of Uganda Network (WOUGNET), whose mission is to promote and support the use of information and communication technologies by women and women's organizations in Uganda. She has been active in getting more women, small-scale enterprises and rural communities engaged in the information society for development via gender and ICT policy advocacy and via programme implementation, monitoring and evaluation. Dr Okello is a member of the Strategy Council for the Global Alliance for Information and Communications Technology and Development (GAID), hosted by the United Nations Department of Economic and Social Affairs.

Salome Awuor Omamo holds a Master of Studies in Non-governmental Organizations and Management and is a consultant in research and sociology. She is currently a research associate with Own and Associates Centre for Research and Development and a community development manager with Plumbers without Frontiers, both of which are NGOs based in Nairobi, Kenya. She works with gender analysis and mainstreaming, research and policy analysis in the social sector, conducting both qualitative and quantitative research, lobbying and advocacy, and capacity-building in the fields of water and sanitation, community mobilization, HIV/AIDS and participatory rural appraisal (PRA). She also undertakes organizing and facilitation of workshops/seminars. She has trained and worked with several organizations, including ILO-INDIA, World Vision India, USAID-APAC Programme India, and Ministry of Education-UNICEF, Kenya.

Mary Rusimbi is a founding member and was the executive director of the Tanzania Gender Networking Programme (TGNP) for ten years until March 2007. As a founder and board member of several organizations, she has been playing key leadership roles in the women's movement for many years, promoting gender equality, equity and social transformation in the country, the region and the world. She previously worked as a gender programme officer for the Royal Netherlands Embassy and the Canadian High Commission in Tanzania. Mary is currently working as a gender and development specialist in gender and policy analysis, gender budgeting, participatory training and facilitation, research and organizational development of civil society organizations. She has published numerous articles and book chapters on gender and development issues.

Ibou Sane is a researcher and lecturer at the departments of sociology at Dakar Sheikh Anta Diop University and Gaston Berger de Saint Louis

University, Senegal, and holds a PhD in sociology from the University of Lumière (Lyon 2), France. He teaches urban sociology, political sociology, development sociology, informal sector sociology, sociology of the associations' movement, social science research methods, assessment projects methods and sociological theories. His work focuses on the Senegalese commercial informal sector, on development and historical demography, and presently he is looking into gender, ICT and development.

Olive Sifuna holds a bachelor's degree in Communication and Community Development from Daystar University, Nairobi, Kenya. She is a research associate at the RESEARCHWEB Centre. Currently, she is working at Jomo Kenyatta University of Agriculture and Technology as an administrator. She is also pursuing her master's degree in Business Administration.

Amina Tafnout graduated from the Information Sciences School in Rabat, Morocco, with a master's in Information Sciences. She has worked in the National Documentation Centre of the Ministry of Planning and is currently a project manager with the Social Development Agency. She is a member of the Association Démocratique des Femmes du Maroc (ADFM) and is responsible for communications within the Réseau Africain des Centres et Cliniques Juridiques des Femmes dans l'Espace Francophone.

Amina has been head and director of the Nejma Centre for Information and Legal Assistance for Women Survivors of Violence, the national coordinator of the National Network of Legal Centres for Women Survivors of Violence (ANARUZ), the project coordinator of Mashreq Maghreb Gender Linking Information Project (Mac-Mag GLIP), and was a member of the Preparatory and Organizing Committee of the African NGOs Forum for the assessment of the implementation of Beijing platform 2004/05.

Elise Tchinda holds a master's degree in Management Sciences and is now undertaking a PhD in Entrepreneurship at Strasbourg Louis Pasteur University, France. She is teaching at Douala University Institute of Technology (Cameroon). Elise is in charge of studies at Douala's Association for the Support of Women Entrepreneurs (ASAFE). She has conducted several studies for ASAFE, both internally and with the public authorities of Cameroon.

Aatifa Timjerdine, a sociology major, taught philosophy at a secondary school in Rabat before joining the Committee on Human Rights and

Citizenship within the Ministry of National Education. She is a member of the women's association l'Association Démocratique des Femmes du Maroc (ADFM) and coordinator of the National Network of Women Victims of Violence (Anarouz). She was also a member of the bureau of the Moroccan Association of Teachers of Philosophy from 1993 to 1997. She has participated in many national and international activities dealing with issues related to gender-based violence, gender equality, human rights and leadership.

Mamadou Balla Traore is a researcher-lecturer at the Gaston Berger de Saint-Louis University (Senegal). His present work focuses on the socio-anthropology of development and social change. He is an editor of the *Cahiers* of the Interdisciplinary Research Group for Support to Regional Planning and Local Development (GIRARDEL) and chief editor of the magazine *Afrique, Sociétés, Recherche*.

Alice Wanjira Munyua is the co-founder and convener of the Kenya ICT Action Network (KICTANet) and acts as its national coordinator. She is a commissioner with the Communications Commission of Kenya (CCK) and a board member of the Kenya Information Network (KENIC), Kenya's country code top-level domain (ccTLD) organization. Her interests are information communication policy and regulation.

Gisele Yitamben, an economist by training, is a senior international expert consultant well known on questions of entrepreneurship development, ICT and gender. She is the founder and president of the Association for the Support of Women Entrepreneurs (ASAFE), a non-profit enterprise. She was also the vice-president of the board of Diaspora Digital Initiative (UNIFEM).

She is an ardent defender of the rights of underprivileged persons, notably women and youths, and her actions have always been targeted on ameliorating the welfare of those around her through searching for access to productive resources and technical services (alternative finance, training and high-added-value jobs, etc.). She initiated street football in Cameroon in 2004. Her team ranked sixth out of forty-eight countries represented at the 2006 Homeless World Cup in Cape Town, South Africa.

Index